The Price of Success

THE PRICE OF SUCCESS

The Authorized Biography of
Ryan Price

PETER BROMLEY

Hutchinson/Stanley Paul
London Melbourne Sydney Auckland Johannesburg

Hutchinson/Stanley Paul & Co. Ltd
An imprint of the Hutchinson Publishing Group
17–21 Conway Street, London W1P 6JD

Hutchinson Group (Australia) Pty Ltd
30–32 Cremorne Street, Richmond South, Victoria 3121
PO Box 151, Broadway, New South Wales 2007

Hutchinson Group (NZ) Ltd
32–34 View Road, PO Box 40–086, Glenfield, Auckland 10

Hutchinson Group (SA) Pty Ltd
PO Box 337, Bergvlei 2012, South Africa

First published 1982
© Peter Bromley 1982
Reprinted 1983

Set in Linotron Sabon by Computape (Pickering) Ltd

Printed in Great Britain by The Anchor Press Ltd,
and bound by Wm Brendon & Son Ltd,
both of Tiptree, Essex

British Library Cataloguing in Publication Data
Bromley, Peter
The price of success.
1. Price, Ryan   2. Horse trainers –
Great Britain – Biography
I. Title
636.1'2'0924   SF336.M/

ISBN 0 09 149880 5

To Dorothy, Joe, Anne and Penry

Contents

	Foreword	1
	Acknowledgements	7
1	The Day the Winners Stopped	11
2	The Child is Father of the Man	15
3	Point-to-Pointing	25
4	Wartime	36
5	The Commandos	40
6	Civilian Life	56
7	Early Days at Lavant	60
8	Downs House	70
9	The Golden Days of Findon	77
10	The Rosyth Case	97
11	Suspension	116
12	The Hill House Case	121
13	The Lure of the Flat	156
14	Ginevra	162
15	Sandford Lad	169
16	Giacometti	177
17	Enter the Sheik	181
18	Bruni	184
19	The Last Straight	190
20	The Finish	198
	D-Day Bibliography	201
	Index	203

'Unremitting attention to business is
the price of success'
CHARLES DUDLEY WARNER

Foreword
by Lord Lovat

Peter Bromley has done a first-class job in recording the racing exploits of an old friend in this biography which will appeal to all those associated with the turf: I refer particularly to the good sportsmen, owners, trainers and jockeys who struggle against bad weather conditions to make a precarious living under National Hunt Rules.

This, in short, is the success story of a trainer who came out on top, the story of a man I have known for forty years, both as a soldier and as a civilian, who never spared himself and whose restless energy and forceful expressions kept him continually on the boil since straddling his first pony.

After skipping lightly through the formative years of a boy whose country life, shared with the rest of the family, centred on the riding, schooling, and making and breaking of horses for the show ring or the hunting field, we discover, in Ryan, a most promising pupil. Old Man Price was a disciplinarian, and the watchword 'Die rather than cry' gave his children strength in the saddle. Ryan was a rough rider before he finished winning pony class events. He had a sister who rode better than himself, and from the autocratic father, who provided the difficult animals to gentle, he inherited the greatest of all gifts – a good eye for a sound horse, judged in all shapes and sizes. Point-to-point racing came next, and after some winning rides, Ryan developed growing self-assurance verging on intolerance, even contempt, for competitors less gifted than himself.

When I came down from Oxford in 1932 and joined the Scots Guards on the same day as Bobby Petre (who went on to win the Grand National), there was no doubt that at meetings in the Home

Counties, and particularly those south of London, Ryan Price was the hardest man to beat in the open races. It was diagnosed that he also suffered from a swollen head! In retrospect, this rough and tumble period, with little money and many hard knocks, gave a brash young man the iron physique and immense determination, along with total disregard for convention, that helped turn Ryan into a first-class officer later in the war.

Peter Bromley has not managed to persuade Ryan to divulge enough personal details on his years of active service, and if there is a special point in my writing this introduction, it is that perhaps I can chip in to praise Ryan's Commando soldiering.

For reasons already suggested, he did not start the war on the right leg, and the first posting to a tented camp on Hurst Park race course in the role of a latrine orderly understandably failed to charm. The phoney war of 1939 was hard for everyone to bear: for some unknown reason Ryan, disguised as a gunner (instead of joining a Cavalry Regiment), next found himself serving with an anti-aircraft battery outside Newbury. From there he applied for a commission – this time to the Infantry. He was accepted and passed through OCTU with good marks to join the 7th Battalion of the North Staffordshire Regiment, 'where nobody talked to me for six months'. Ryan had run up against the stereotyped Commanding Officer of the kind we had to put up with before the shooting really started. A jaundiced view on life in the army was not improved by a move to Northern Ireland, where the threat of invasion once lay heavy on the land. Then came a posting to the bleak Shetland Islands with no earthly chance of a day's hunting or the sight of a decent horse. It was about this time that the Prime Minister wrote what has become a famous memorandum to Chiefs of Staff and the War Cabinet, which ran as follows:

> I feel that the Germans have been right in both world wars in what use they have made of storm troops. The defeat of France was accomplished by a small number of highly equipped and brilliantly led spearheads. There will be many opportunities for surprise landings by nimble forces accustomed to work like packs of hounds instead of being moved about in the ponderous manner which is appropriate for regular formations: we must develop the storm troop or Commando idea. I have asked for 5,000 of these 'Bands of Brothers' capable of lightning action.

FOREWORD

Today the Commando role requires no explanation. Sufficient to say all ranks were then volunteers who stepped forward from many regiments. There is an old saying that one good volunteer is worth ten pressed men, and this proved to be the case, despite a sticky start and much opposition from regular formations. Commando soldiers were in no way supermen, but they were superbly trained, and they had good officers to lead them. In a new spirit of respect for the individual, a hardy independence and undragooned discipline, these early enthusiasts were to bring a fresh approach to established concepts in the profession of arms.

After the Dieppe and Sainte Nazaire raids, where a whole Commando went down, killed or captured after destroying the German base, I was given a Brigade to prepare for D-Day. This meant recalling two units of seasoned veterans from Italy and North Africa, where officers had suffered severe casualties in difficult campaigns. One of my first tasks was to find suitable replacements, and particularly the class of officer capable of breaking a way through Hitler's Atlantic Wall at first light in the Normandy landings. Talent scouts reported a rather wild young subaltern seen picking off a cock grouse with a service revolver at extreme range in the Shetland Islands. Ryan himself may have been unaware of the existence of the Commandos, but by strange coincidence his father had already approached me on the subject. My own parent had a good Irish chaser in training with Bob Gore at Findon back in the early thirties, and I must have met Old Man Price going round the stables on a visit. That small contact proved a lucky break for all concerned. The grim realities of boating in the Shetlands perhaps helped his aquatics, for I do not think Ryan was born a sailor, but he took to the amphibious life of Combined Operations like a duck to water. Trained for D-Day by the legendary Irish Guardsman, Derek Mills-Roberts, CBE, DSO, MC, who commanded No. 6 Commando, and was chosen to lead the advance inland after breaching the Wall to join hands with airborne forces dropped overnight six miles inland, Ryan's landing craft suffered a direct hit on the run in to the beach. It is a disconcerting sight to see a boatload of forty good men keeping station in line abreast, each craft the length of a cricket pitch apart, suddenly blown up and sunk in deep water. Half the troop was killed, and all lost their weapons and came close to drowning, but by sheer force of example, Ryan got the survivors ashore, re-equipped them with weapons discarded by a demoralized formation lying on the sand, and caught up with the advance. The Brigade, after eighty-three days in the fight without being rested, came out of the Normandy battle with the loss of seventy-seven officers and 897 men. Quick to make a name for himself, Ryan was singled out to protect General Montgomery's Advanced Operational Headquarters in the field. Later he was sent to deal mercifully with the carnage inflicted by the RAF on the enemy's horse-drawn vehicles in the Falaise Gap – two notable achievements for a junior officer.

Ryan was subsequently promoted, and became Adjutant of No. 6 Commando. 'The Captain', as he has been known ever since, had proved himself a man. Under Mills-Roberts, this great Brigade led the way through France, Holland and Germany, keeping up a shock-troop role, which included hard-won assault crossings of the five great rivers, the Maas, Rhine, Weser, Aller and the Elbe. Ryan and men like him sustained the indomitable spirit and resourcefulness of that 'Band of Brothers' who never turned their heads in hand-to-hand fighting, generally against the odds.

The post-war years did not prove easy: there was no fairy tale beginning for a young man without a house, a horse, a stable, gallops, or an owner to help him launch into the career of a National Hunt trainer, for Captain Price had grown too heavy to become a jump jockey. It was in November 1945 that Ryan, now weighing upwards of 14 stone, travelled to Guildford to collect his army gratuity and the suit of civilian clothes that was thrown in with the demobilization papers. That first winter he sent two runners to Windsor Races – Leafy and Money Glass. One horse got round, the other fell. Both animals were beautifully turned out and caught the eye in the paddock, an important first step and a tribute to the early days with his ponies in the show ring. Ryan had made a start.

In February he had another fallen horse at Cheltenham and in March he married Dorothy Dale, who rode out with the small string of horses from stables leased near Wisborough Green. At first they lived in the local hotel. Besides proving to be a wonderful wife, Mrs Price took on all the paperwork at a time when economies were essential. It was not until May 1946 that Ryan, still on the bread line, saddled his first winner, Broken Tackle, in a selling handicap at Plumpton. I think he was the only horse to win for the stable that season in a yard that could only boast half a dozen very moderate animals. Ryan obviously needed better nags.

That summer, without the cash to pay for them, he went to

Ireland, and bought a couple of chasers that were on the market. Later in the year he moved to another rented yard at Manor Farm in Lavant village, making his home in a caravan. It was to be the start of several years of very hard living. The severity of the 1946-47 winter almost broke his heart – as well as his bank account. Looking back over recent decades of spectacular success, it seems hard to believe that, in a desperate struggle for survival, Ryan wound up that very lean season by winning seven races worth a total of £862, having only succeeded in catching the judge's eye at humble local meetings like Folkstone, Plumpton and Fontwell Park. Clearly something had to be done and done quickly in order to survive.

Ryan never knew the meaning of the word 'surrender'. That summer he found a wealthy patron, Gerry Judd, who raised the cash to buy a better class of horse in France. Then Gerry Judd and his brother Bill started to win races. Ryan's enthusiasm knew no bounds. Now he got into another kind of trouble. The optimism of an extrovert had strengthened with the war years. Always a man of strong character, fast becoming a personality in a wider field, he now enjoyed handing out plenty of free copy to the press, never hesitating when the need arose to call a spade a bloody shovel! It has been suggested that he was becoming arrogant, and also outspoken to officials, in days when small trainers were expected to show a deferential respect for the authorities.

Ryan got into trouble at Cheltenham (March 1949) when his French purchase, Priorit, became the object of a successful gamble in the Blagrave Memorial Chase. Ryan had not been involved in the betting: his part had been the preparation of a horse that had improved physically since arriving from the Continent; he left the gambling to the gamblers. But Ryan was sent for by the stewards, and asked to explain the improvement in his horse, which had reversed the placings with another runner, Hypernod, which had won impressively three weeks before at Lingfield.

In view of the heavy betting and some irresponsible talk, Ryan's answer that the going had changed and Priorit had not been sufficiently acclimatized was not considered an acceptable story. The stewards then heard evidence from Bryan Marshall and Martin Molony, the greatest steeplechase jockeys of the day, who had ridden Priorit in the two different races. Ryan was recalled – I imagine in a none too friendly mood – and cautioned by the stewards as to the future running of his horses.

The rest is hearsay, but there must certainly have been a clash of personalities. The moral to this tale is that stewards do not like gambling stables or gambling owners. But the damage was done, casting a long shadow, which was to stay with a brilliant trainer for the rest of his life.

Peter Bromley goes on to describe in detail the victories subsequently achieved under both Rules after moving to Findon. So the seasons ticked away always on a mounting scale, climbing steadily to the top of the tree. Ryan could now take on the best horses at the big meetings. In 1962 he achieved a lifetime ambition, winning the Grand National with Kilmore, a small horse picked up in a snowbound field in County Tipperary, and ridden to victory two years later by the stable jockey, Fred Winter, at odds of 50 to 1.

I have said enough – with one last paragraph to add, stressing the loyalty and skills of the back-up team (with many interesting names), whose tireless efforts, inspired by the man in charge, have contributed so much to lasting success on a race course.

Acknowledgements

Many people have helped me during the preparation of this book. First, I must record my gratitude to Dorothy Price and to Ryan's sisters Lynkie Price and Sheila Benson, who have given me tremendous encouragement. Penry, Ryan's brother, read the final draft before his sad death; and Bill Scrimgeour, Ryan's long-time secretary, gave me much assistance, as did 'Tighe' and Tom Nickalls.

I gleaned much valuable intelligence from Ryan's famous former jockeys, Fred Winter, Josh Gifford and Bryan Marshall, from Ryan's old assistants Bob McCreery and Guy Harwood, and also from Sid Dale, Ryan's old head lad. Tony Murrary very kindly flew over from Ireland especially to talk to me about his days with Ryan.

For information about various phases of Ryan's career I should like to thank the following: Mr and Mrs George Coles and Michael Williams on Ryan's point-to-pointing days; Captain Peter Cruden, late of No. 6 Commando and Major Beadle of the North Staffordshire Regiment on Ryan's Second World War service; John Locke on the time at Lavant; Joe Sullivan on Beaver II; Tim Nelligan on the golden days of Findon; Peter Richards for background information on Ginevra and Bruni; and Charles and Robin Olley on Sandford Lad.

Ryan's owners proved to be a most valuable source of stories. Nat Cohen not only gave me much valuable information about his time as an owner with Ryan, but also spoke freely about the part played by his friends 'Pinky' Taylor, Ben Rosenfield and Stuart Levy. I am indebted to him for all his help and kindness. I am also grateful to Sheik Essa Al-khalifa for giving me his time.

I must also express my thanks to Ryan's staff at Soldier's Field, to his assistant Con Hogan, to his head lad Geoffrey Potts, and to Tommy Winters and Norman Freeman; also to Ryan's physician, Dr John Chard, who has been such a constant source of encouragement.

Shirley Robinson typed the manuscripts, while John Haslam of the BBC read and corrected my English. The whole text was hammered into shape by Roddy Bloomfield of Hutchinson.

I am extremely grateful to them all for the part that they have played in the production of my first book.

Photographic acknowledgements

The publishers and the author wish to thank the following for permission to use copyright photographs: Aumente; P. Betrand Chantilly; Central Press Photos Ltd; Cheltenham Newspapers Ltd; Rex Coleman; *Daily Mirror; Evening News*; J. Findlay Davidson; *News of the World*; David Nicholls; *Sun*.

1
The Day the Winners Stopped

The long snout of the Mercedes roadster cleaved through the heavy commuter traffic as it made its weary way out of London and down the Brighton Road. The driver's face was taut and his knuckles showed white as his hands fiercely clenched the wheel. His eyes, lit up by the glare of the oncoming headlamps, were cold and hard. Captain Ryan Price was in no mood to be trifled with.

The most successful trainer of jumpers since the war was returning home, but not on this occasion in triumph. Beside him, silent, sat his stable jockey, Josh Gifford, who stared ahead through the windscreen, oblivious of their speed or the close proximity of the traffic flashing by only a few inches away as the Captain roared past a tightly bunched lane of cars. So many times the two had driven home after the races with a warm glow of success inside; the smug feeling of a treble or a big race landed. Tonight everything was different. There was the sour taste of disgrace and ignominy. On this dark grey February night in 1964 they were driving home to what? Both would have longed to know the answer to the question.

The inquiry into the running of the hurdler Rosyth, trained by Ryan Price, had been convened that day at the Jockey Club headquarters at Cavendish Square, just two weeks after Rosyth had won the Schweppes Gold Trophy for the second year running. The unsaddling enclosure had been a merry place until the stewards' secretary had tapped Ryan on the shoulder and said, 'Captain Price, the stewards would like to see you.'

Half an hour later Ryan had elbowed his way through the clamouring group of pressmen with a look of thunder. 'They have referred the case to the National Hunt Committee,' was all he said.

Tonight, Ryan could hardly believe the stewards' decision. He had thought that there was really no case to answer; he had spent no time preparing his defence; now, in the eyes of the racing world he was condemned for cheating. He knew in his own mind that there had been no cheating; on that score his conscience was clear. He was innocent of the charge. Under the laws of the turf, however, he was 'off', disqualified for an unknown period. So, after the wonderful years of winners sent out from his Downs House stable at Findon, his career as a trainer was over.

Josh broke the silence. 'I think they never listened to us. I think they had made up their minds what they were going to do before we got there.'

As the car roared on, Ryan began to wonder what would become of him, his family, his jockey, his lads, and his horses. He was now in familiar country, passing fields over which he had hunted as a small boy. His whole life had revolved round horses. Take his racehorses away, and what was there left? Farming, breeding steeplechasers, perhaps even having the time to enjoy hunting again. He thought again of those eighty horses, among them several potential champions in the making. Suddenly he felt sick and weary, and thankful to be home.

The car swept up the drive to Downs House, which nestles by the side of Findon Downs. Ryan strode through the yard, took the steps four at a time, and rushed into the house without speaking to any of the dozen lads who were busy attending to the horses.

Dorothy Price, his tall, slim, blonde wife, was in the kitchen when Ryan burst in. 'They have disqualified me for life; I'll never train another horse.' Dorothy was visibly shaken. The colour drained from her face as the full implication of Ryan's words hit her. As Ryan went into the sitting room to break the news to his lifelong friend and stable secretary, Bill Scrimgeour, Dorothy broke down. Josh, a silent witness to this private family drama, went to comfort her.

'It will kill him,' she cried. 'What the hell is he going to do?' For a moment she wept, held against Josh's shoulder. Then, as she struggled to regain her composure, she begged, 'Please, Josh, don't let him see me like this.'

Within five minutes, the four were able to discuss the stewards' sentence more rationally. Ryan was now jaunty and confident, he seemed to have taken the whole thing in his stride. 'We can go round the world, Dorothy.' But his bravado hardly pierced the gloom.

Bill Scrimgeour wanted to know what the stewards had actually said about the horses and the stables, but Ryan couldn't remember. It soon became apparent that neither Ryan nor Josh could remember the details of the sentence. Josh had been given a six-week suspension, but it was not until Bill Scrimgeour telephoned Major Derek Wigan, a member of the National Hunt Committee, that the full intention of the stewards was clarified. It was that Downs House must effectively cease to be a training stable. All horses in training must leave the yard within forty-eight hours. Any horses that remained could be at livery only. The length of sentence was not specified. The efforts of a lifetime were to be taken apart in just forty-eight hours. That effectively killed any possibility that Fred Winter, who was about to retire from riding, could move in and take over. Fred had no wish to train anyway; he was hoping to become a stewards' secretary, or a starter. (Fortunately, he had second thoughts!)

While they had supper, Bill Scrimgeour was on the phone, making arrangements for moving the horses. When he joined them, he up-dated Ryan on what had been worked out. Some horses were to go to Sid Dale – Ryan's old head lad – who now trained at Epsom. Rosyth, the cause of all their anxiety, was to go to Tom Masson at Lewes.

Josh left soon after supper and drove himself home, unhappy at the thought of missing the National Hunt meeting at Cheltenham and the next six weeks' racing. His feelings were with his 'Guv'nor', wondering how he would survive. Indeed, most of Ryan's friends were wondering how this incredibly active man would take to a life of imposed inactivity.

Back at Downs House, the telephone now abandoned by Bill Scrimgeour, the household went to a troubled sleep.

In the morning Ryan was up at the usual time. He assembled the lads in the yard and told them that from now on Downs House was no longer a training establishment; that all the horses in training would be dispersed to new stables; and that the lads would, if possible, stay with their horses. For the first time since Ryan Price moved to Findon, the yard was quiet; the noise, bustle and clamour of a successful stable was silenced as the lads pensively went about their work.

Later a deputation assembled. The lads wished to remain with the Captain, without pay, until he got his licence back. It was a moving demonstration of faith and loyalty, especially as Ryan had, on so many occasions, given them all a taste of the fearsome lash of his tongue.

Then the horseboxes started arriving, and the first contingent of horses was on its way. Ryan had to choke back his emotion as the ramps swung home and his favourite horses were lost from sight.

'Ryan would rather die than cry,' his brother Penry used to say, talking about their childhood in Sussex. 'He was tremendously brave and tough for his age as a child. No one could get the better of him.'

It was all too much for the man who had fought with the Commandos through the European campaign. He walked out of the yard, across the gallops, and onto his beloved Sussex Downs. He had to come to terms with the greatest personal crisis since the Normandy landing and the war.

On Chanctonbury Ring, he looked down at his stables far below, and, with only the wheeling seagulls as witness, out of the sight of his fellow men, the tears rolled uncontrollably down his cheeks. His brother had been wrong. This was the day that the winners had stopped. The day they had taken the horses away.

2
The Child is Father of the Man

There are few successful adults who were not first successful children
ALEXANDER CHASE

The small boy stood by his window looking out at the stables, choking back his tears. Henry Ryan Price was ten and desperately unhappy. He was going back to school tomorrow, to the dreaded lessons and strict discipline of a Victorian preparatory school.

The young Ryan was a sturdy, strong boy, with a mind of his own, afraid of nothing and no one save his father. He did not like school, but that was not the principal cause of his present unhappiness. He enjoyed sport and could run as fast as anyone in his own age group. He could stand up for himself when bullied. What brought tears to his eyes was the thought of having to leave his pony behind. There would be no more riding until the Christmas holidays.

He could just see his pony looking out above the stable door. Putting on his dressing gown and slippers, he left the sleeping household and crept quietly down the stairs, out through the back kitchen and across to the stables. He often went to talk to his pony when things became awkward in the house, and tonight he let himself into the stable and poured out his troubles to the wise and friendly partner of many horse-show victories.

Riding was Ryan Price's great joy. It was just as well because he was born into a household that lived, talked and slept horses. Encouraged by his father, and with his eldest sister, Kitty, already established as an international show rider, Ryan took to the saddle early. He was a natural, never showing the slightest fear. He developed a flair for competition and, as he grew older, he became a formidable member of the Price family riding équipe.

His father, George Penry Price, was a man of powerful build, sporting a large walrus moustache. He had a military bearing and was a martinet in his own home. His family originated in Llandovery, 'the Church in the waters', in Carmarthenshire. The Prices were a famous Welsh sporting family; George Penry's father was a judge who enjoyed hunting, and it was his old silver hunting horn that Ryan carried with him in action with the Commandos in 1944.

Though his brother became a lawyer, and thus followed in the family tradition, George Penry was too much of a man of action for a career at the Bar. At the age of twenty he sailed with a party of what would now be called mercenaries to Greece, where there had been disturbances between the Greeks and the Turks. The party had purchased their own rifles and ammunition before they left. They went to the aid of the Greeks, but the young adventurer was disappointed to find, when he arrived at the front line, that the Greek forces had surrendered. In disgust he left Athens and went to Egypt where he enlisted in the Welch Regiment.

It was while he was serving in Egypt that he met his future wife, Catherine Ryan, who was acting as a companion to a wealthy family who were wintering in Cairo. The couple met while on a visit to the pyramids and discovered that they shared a love of horses and riding. Catherine was a dazzling figure, very Irish; she was born in Ahascragh near Ballinsloe, County Galway.

On George's retirement from the army he and Catherine set up home in Hindhead in Surrey. There George lived the life of a gentleman farmer, though he does not appear to have spent much time actually farming. The farm was really an excuse for having horses, and it was to the horses that he devoted most of his life.

For not only was George Penry Price a consummate horseman, he was a horsemaster supreme. Painstaking and a perfectionist, he achieved remarkable results with hunters and show horses. From his home at Pitfold Farm, Hindhead, he proceeded to build up an enviable reputation in buying and making young horses. He possessed an uncanny eye for a horse, and would often acquire for a few pounds off a farmer an animal which eventually became a champion.

He also sired a remarkable family. Ryan's mother, Catherine, was fairly tall, with dark hair which she wore in a bun. She possessed a radiant personality, charmed everyone she met, and over a span of twenty years produced a family of five sons and three daughters. The first three, John Rhys Lymington (Jack), George Percy (Pat), Mary Catherine Irene (Kitty), all arrived within a few years. Then there was a gap of six years until the fourth child, Penry Williams, was born in

1909. Three years later Henry Ryan was born on 16 August 1912. Catherine Price always said that she had two families. She had apparently settled for three children, and then much to everyone's surprise produced five more. There was a twenty-year gap between the eldest son and the youngest daughter.

When Ryan was born his two elder brothers were already well-established riders; so too was his eldest sister, Kitty, who developed into an outstanding horsewoman, and rode in the big shows in Britain and Ireland. She inherited a natural side-saddle seat from her mother, and was much in demand to partner the best-known hacks and hunters in the country. Ryan, therefore, had a standard to emulate and perhaps it was Kitty more than anyone who helped him to reach such heights as a boy rider.

Ryan's father was, however, a severe task master. He was never satisfied with anything other than the absolute best. His unerring eye did not miss a thing in or out of the stable. Ryan and his brothers and sisters soon learned that you could not get away with anything. If you attempted to cut corners, you were inevitably found out and then the world descended upon your head. Their father was a formidable man, and all his children were absolutely terrified of him. In later life, however, they came to realize that his bark was far worse than his bite. He actually had a very soft centre if challenged, though, as children, none of them dared do that.

In spite of this regimentation as far as the horse activity was concerned, the Prices were a happy family, and a close-knit one. Amidst all the hubbub, at work and play, Catherine would serenely minister to any needs. With their father aloof and unapproachable, it was to their mother that the children brought all their troubles. Though George Price set the standard of discipline and behaviour in the strictest possible way, it was Catherine Price who instilled the qualities of grace, manners and character into her extravert family. She knew everyone; the Price house was always open and there were frequent guests. Visitors were expected to hunt whether they could ride or not! Friends would arrive for the weekend without warning, and it was never certain how many there would be for breakfast. Aided by the family cook, 'Cookie', Catherine ran the household with uncanny efficiency. There was never any money except for horses; yet on quarter days the tradesmen called, presented their bills, were paid, given beer and cake on the lawn, and departed satisfied.

In later years the children were to wonder how this slim, attractive woman was able to maintain such an establishment. Even allowing for the fact that in 1914 the pound went a good deal further than today, the source of the Price family income remains a mystery. True, George Penry Price bought and sold farms; he also bought and sold horses and ponies. However, he was not in even the remotest sense a dealer. If he had been, the family fortunes would undoubtedly have been healthier, but often, after the children had outgrown their ponies, these perfectly schooled animals were given away to a good home.

The commercial side of their riding activities was not exploited at all. The children were expected to succeed simply for reasons of pride and prestige. Money never entered into it. They were a family who lived for riding, and because there was really nothing else to do, the family merely changed their riding activities according to the season. They all had one common bond – horses. They rode harder, tried harder, and probably fell harder and more often than any of their contemporaries in Sussex. Father Price had little sympathy for his children if they fell while out hunting or schooling. Indeed, he could hardly understand how it was possible to be unseated. To a small boy who had just been 'buried' after jumping an enormous open ditch in the hunting field, the sound of his father bellowing out, 'What on earth are you doing down there, Ryan? Get up at once and follow me,' had a dramatic effect. You did not lie on the ground for long with old man Price anywhere near. You quickly clambered back on board, and bit your lip to quench the pain. To lie on the ground and to pretend that you were hurt was a sign of weakness, something that children from other families did. Under no circumstances were the Price family allowed to walk away from a fall. They remounted immediately.

While Kitty was without question the outstanding rider in the family, Ryan soon developed into the best of the boys, a fact which did not go unnoticed by his father. Ryan's brothers were aware that Ryan was the apple of their father's eye, and treated him to a rough-and-ready time. Penry, in particular, was far from being a proficient rider. He wanted to engage in other sports such as football and cricket, and had absolutely no intention of devoting his entire life to foxhunting.

Both Ryan and Penry had been born at the farm in Hindhead, but in 1914, at the outbreak of war, a detachment of Canadian soldiers from nearby Bramshott Camp had created such havoc locally with drunken and riotous behaviour that George Price moved to Sussex, to Wisborough Park, in the village of Wisborough Green. The village was the centre of the family's sporting life. All the boys played cricket and football, and became active participants in the day-to-day life. Wisborough Green was a very sporting village, and prided itself on its cricket and football teams. Though the Price children were frequently up to assorted pranks, the villagers never let them down by reporting them to their father. The local police constable, PC Chissel, was remarkably tolerant, considering the provocation to which he was put!

Such was the reputation of George Price that horses and ponies would arrive from other riding families, to be 'sorted out'. Horses that refused were made to jump. Runaways were tamed. Lively ponies that were too hot for their well-heeled owners were quietly restrained, became perfect rides, were returned to their original owners, and after due passage of time came back again as unmanageable. Thus the Price children eventually became the owners of some of the best and 'hottest' ponies in Sussex.

The work behind the scenes to 'make' a pony was unremitting, but all the time the old man was there on the ground to give advice and to suggest a course of action with a difficult horse. He was steeped in horse lore, and his patience and tremendous understanding of the horse resulted in some dramatic successes. The standard of stable help available at that time was of a very high order. It was, of course, the age of the horse. Everyone had horses, and in those days there was no shortage of expert grooms. That is hard to understand, living as we do now in a mechanical age. The respected trades in the village were those connected with the horse – the vet, the farrier, the stable lads and grooms and nagsmen.

The head groom was the centre of the stable routine. He usually knew all the answers, after a lifetime's experience of dealing with a stable of hunters and show horses. All the old-fashioned remedies were at his disposal, and he would have been mortally offended if the vet had been called into the yard. The vet was summoned only in a dire emergency.

In 1922, when Ryan was ten, the family left the big rambling house at Wisborough Green and moved to The Ridge, Fittleworth, situated between Arundel and Petworth, but only a six-mile point from Wisborough Green. Ryan remembers the move for the practical reason that it was a shorter hack to the meets at Petworth Park. The Ridge stood in its own grounds and overlooked the woods of Flexham Park. The glorious, unspoiled countryside was ideal for riding. There were grassy rides between the woods which provided naturally springy turf and the occasional fallen tree became a ready-made schooling fence.

The Ridge was a delightful family house, but after four years the family moved again, this time to a large, three-storeyed house three miles north at Beechfields on the Petworth–Wisborough Green road. So Ryan's entire youth was spent in a triangle bounded by Wisborough Green, Fittleworth and Petworth.

The Sussex countryside was mainly grass, the fences solid timber, 'cut and laids', or iron railings and gates. However, the Price family could never be bothered to open gates – they were there to be jumped. Often when hacking to a meet the children would have a mini hunt. Frequently they arrived with coats plastered in mud. On one occasion, while jumping a huge open ditch, Ryan's sister Sheila fell and landed in a stream. She arrived at the meet soaking wet and spent the rest of the day in that sodden condition.

Ryan used to organize mounted games like Cowboys and Indians round the woods and tracks near the house. His younger sisters, Lynkie and Sheila, fell under his spell, and he found them willing participants – the girls having to withstand full-blooded ambushes by the most athletic cowboy in Sussex. Small wonder that Ryan was reluctant to return to school.

The short journey was a nightmare for everyone. Ryan complained about everything, while his father's driving was 'alfresco', to say the very least: his route to school usually took him straight down the centre of the road. Everyone they met had to get out of the way, and he was apt to say 'Whoa' when he wished to stop instead of applying the brakes! On occasions like this it was Catherine Price who smoothed things over.

At school Ryan saw out time. He excelled at sport, playing football with an almost suicidal determination which enabled him to blast his way through bigger boys in order to score the winning goal. He hated losing and always wanted to be on the winning side. Sport made school palatable and the competition brought out the best in him. But the last days before the end of term were almost unbearable.

Then home for Christmas. This was his favourite holiday for it meant hunting. Lord Leconfield, who owned Home Park, Petworth,

3
Point-to-Pointing

A gentleman rider – well, I'm an outsider,
But if he's a gent who the mischief's a jock?
You swells mostly blunder,
Dick rides for the plunder,
He rides, too, like thunder – he sits like a rock.

ADAM LINDSEY GORDON

Time went quickly, but the summers seemed to hang fire. Ryan was impatient for the hunting season to start and the beginning of training the point-to-pointers. Everything else was blotted out of his mind. He raised his leathers by six holes, and also the standard of his riding. To watch him was a revelation. He went the shortest way, giving the inside to no one. He walked every course, picked out the best going and, instead of simply going hell for leather as most other riders did at the time, introduced the element of tactics into his race riding.

No matter how hard he tried or how vigorously he rode, Ryan did not win all the races he competed in, and he wondered why. He realized that many of the horses that he rode simply were not fit enough. Having hunted them all season, their owners believed that they were fit enough to win a point-to-point. They went for two miles, but Ryan found that in the last mile they wobbled and staggered, and it required all his strength to keep them off the floor.

Ryan suggested to his father that they should take the best racers into their own stables, and Ryan would supervise their preparation for the point-to-points. He would feed, train and ride them. He would arrange their gallops and schooling and charge owners accordingly. His father agreed, and so, at the age of sixteen, Ryan collected the best of his season's rides soon after Christmas, and started to work them up to point-to-point fitness. He charged the owners £3 a week, and even made a small profit. The Fred Darling of Sussex was in business.

At no stage in his life was he happier than during those days. With his father behind him, Ryan's confidence grew every day. His father encouraged this independent attitude and only expected to be called in the last resort.

As the 1928 point-to-point season approached, Ryan could scarcely contain his excitement, and with ill-concealed pride he soon entered the winner's enclosure on a horse than he had ridden and trained himself. Returning home in the cattle truck with Jack Yeatman – the box driver who helped him at the races – Ryan could not believe his luck. To come home with a winner in the box and to receive the acclaim of the stables when the hero of the day was led down the ramp gave him the maximum amount of pleasure. Quite suddenly he realized that riding horses he had trained was what he wanted to do, and he determined to become the best in the country.

So far, most of his teenage life had been happily devoted to horses. Even at seventeen he had not felt constricted by the Victorian attitude that his father applied to his children's upbringing. The house was locked at 10 p.m. and even the older children had to ask their father's permission to remain out later. Though now a young man of seventeen, Ryan had not yet visited London. His horizon stretched as far as the Sussex boundary and no farther, and he found a totally contented life in the confines of his own closely knit family and their sporting friends.

Then, in 1929, an event occurred which shattered the peace and happiness of the Price family. Ryan's mother died after a short illness. She had unselfishly ministered to the individual needs of every single member of her family, and the sense of loss to all the children was grievous. None of the girls was domestically minded; their entire training had been in the saddle. They could not cook, knit or sew, or even begin to run a household. In this hour of need Cookie came to the rescue of the family she loved. She immediately took over the running of the house, and became a mother to Sheila, who was a wet-eyed ten-year-old.

The death of his wife, the lynchpin of the family, made George Price even more aloof than usual. As Ryan grew in stature and confidence, tensions between the two men became more apparent. Ryan had been a rather sickly youth, but now his restless energy and the constant outdoor life had made him physically strong. He now found his father's Victorian attitudes constricting and stifling. His mother's death had removed a soothing influence and he was more often in conflict with his father.

Ryan at twenty was 'a handsome young devil', recalls one of his girlfriends. He had dashing good looks and brown flashing eyes. The young ladies of Sussex were smitten in unison. Ryan turned no party invitation down, and parties now went on much later than before. Though the house was still locked up at ten o'clock, Ryan knew the way down the drainpipe and the way up in the early hours. The storm came sooner rather than later. One night his father was disturbed from his sleep by Ryan, more than a little the worse for wear, returning to Beechfields from a party. In that state he muffed the drainpipe procedure and there was an unholy row. The solution was simple. Ryan moved out of the rambling old house and into the summer house, where his nocturnal absences would cause no disturbance to the rest of the household.

The new-found freedom had an unfortunate result. One day Ryan did not appear for breakfast. No one thought anything of that. He was not seen around during the day, but, again, this caused little concern. When he did not appear for breakfast on the second morning, however, a search was made. Ryan was discovered in bed, a ghastly yellow colour, literally dying of peritonitis. He was rushed to hospital and operated on in the nick of time.

On his recovery, Ryan's riding life continued with little change. He had still not visited London, spending his life amidst his family and his friends. However, his younger sister, Sheila, now detected a growing dissatisfaction in him. She saw that he desperately wanted to be somebody, to break out and to do something important and to be well known.

He admired Kitty, now a famous and much respected figure in the show world. The outfitters Bernard Wetherall provided all her riding clothes free of charge and, mounted side-saddle, she was a living advertisement for style and perfection. She was in constant demand to ride the very best show hacks and hunters at all the international horse shows.

Ryan now believed that his own particular path to fame lay in point-to-pointing, and his arrival on the scene was a shattering experience for his competitors. It was his riding of a brilliant point-to-pointer, Goldfish III, owned by Sir John Leigh of Witley Park near Godalming, that first placed young Ryan in the spotlight. He had come in for the ride through George Coles, a friend of the Price family and now Sir John's agent. Ryan had already enjoyed a string of successes in farmers' races on horses like Arun Lad, Swan River, Hardham Gate, Harkaway I, and Mrs E. A. S. Murray's Rufus

III. George Coles had always had a profound respect for Ryan's horsemanship, and it was Ryan's handling of Harkaway I, a particularly difficult horse, on whom he won several point-to-points, that convinced George Coles that he was the right man for the potentially brilliant Goldfish III.

Michael Williams in his history of hunt racing, *The Continuing Story of Point-to-Point Racing*, records that, in his opinion, Ryan Price was the outstanding rider in the south in the thirties. He goes on to say:

> Ryan could have won on a cart horse, and he had a personality to match his ability, presenting a handsome, debonair figure as he rode around the paddock before each race smoking the inevitable cigarette.

At one hunt meeting Ryan rode five winners, but according to Michael Williams, the two best horses that he rode were Sir John Leigh's pair Goldfish III and Thistle Blue.

George Coles invited Ryan to Witley Park to give Goldfish III a workout. His first visit to that amazing place made a vivid impression on him – as well it might – for Sir John Leigh's life style belonged to a bygone age. There were six entrance lodges, stables, garages for six Rolls-Royces, beautifully tended gardens, shrubs and trees; there were 130 miles of roads and fences. There were no less than thirty gardeners employed on the estate. Each year they had to bed out 80,000 bedding plants, 40,000 tulips and, according to Sir John's agent, 'half a mile of dahlias'!

Sir John Leigh had made his fortune in the First World War through munitions and cotton waste. He was a rough diamond with an abrupt way, but he became the very epitome of a country squire. He had bought Witley Park from Lord Pirrie, and had made his successful bid for the property by offering 'One hundred and twenty-five thousand pounds for it as it stands – and leave the sheets on the beds.'

At one time the house had been the home of the financier, Whitaker Wright, who had entertained lavishly and had been responsible for building the ballroom under the lake, the bed of which was illuminated so that the dancers on the ballroom floor could see the fish swimming above their heads.

Whitaker Wright, described as a plausible rogue with a glib tongue, was born in the north of England in 1845. At the age of twenty-one he went to the USA where, with the help of his qualifications in engineering and chemistry, he rapidly acquired a fortune through mining. He returned to England in 1889 and began promoting mining shares. He must have been adept at persuading people to part with their money, for he quickly made another fortune. In 1903 his luck ran out and a warrant was issued for his arrest on the grounds that he had issued false prospectuses and balance sheets on several companies. He left the country in a hurry but returned voluntarily to face trial. In 1904 he was sentenced to seven years' imprisonment, but while awaiting transport to prison, committed suicide by swallowing potassium cyanide.

On his death Witley Park was sold to Lord Pirrie, Chairman of Harland and Wolff, the Belfast shipbuilders who, in future years, were to be responsible for building many ocean-going liners, including the ill-fated *Titanic*. All the wrought-iron work for the gates at Witley Park were fashioned by the craftsmen of Harland and Wolff, every gate opening silently on oiled hinges.

George Coles presided over this estate run to the very highest standards, and though the size of his task was enormous, he still managed to find time to prepare the point-to-pointers. Following his trial ride on Goldfish III, Ryan expressed his delight with the horse and agreed to ride him in all his point-to-points.

In 1936 they became a formidable pair, winning nomination races at the Surrey Union, the Chiddingfold and the Crawley and Horsham. Sir John Leigh, who did not start riding until he was over forty, thoroughly enjoyed his success as an owner.

George Coles now set his sights even higher, and suggested to Sir John that he should try to acquire a horse that was good enough to win a hunter chase. Sir John reacted in his usual way: 'Get me a horse that will win the big hunter chase at Lingfield,' he demanded.

George Coles then approached the well-known horsedealer, Oliver Dixon, who recommended a small quality mare called Thistle Blue. Sir John paid £200 for her, with a contingency of a further £100 if she won the Lingfield race.

In 1937 Ryan Price was to be the stable jockey again, and in their first workout at Witley Park, trainer and jockey were convinced that they had something special. In her first race Ryan put her to the test by making all the running to win the open race at the Surrey Union, and in that season they won every open race they competed in. Though Thistle Blue was temperamental, smaller than Goldfish III and more difficult to ride – she used to take some fearful chances with her fences – Michael Williams asserts that she was the better of the two.

The climax to a highly successful season was the Gone-Away Hunters Chase at Lingfield, when the opposition consisted of the best hunter chasers in the country, ridden by the best of amateur riders. When George Coles arrived at the weighing room with the colours, Ryan met him with a glum face and some bad news. 'I'm sorry George, I've just seen the racecard, Thistle Blue only has to carry 10 stone 9 pounds, and I cannot do the weight.' Fortunately Bobby Petre was available; this fine amateur later won the Grand National on Lovely Cottage. In the parade ring George Coles' orders were brief: 'Go to the front and stay there.'

With Ryan watching from the stands – seething with frustration – Bobby Petre carried out his orders to perfection and won by three lengths. The prize money paid Oliver Dixon's contingency with £2 over. The runner-up was a tremendous horse called March Brown IV, trained at Hambleton in Yorkshire by no less a person than Noel Murless.

If Ryan was disappointed not to be on board during Thistle Blue's finest hour, at least to George Coles the satisfaction was complete; he had bought the horse to win that particular race and trained it as well. Sir John Leigh might have won the Grand National.

Later that year George Coles was instructed to organize a dinner for all the local farmers. It was to be held at Witley Parish Hall, and the menu card had a photograph of Thistle Blue with Mr Ryan Price up on the cover. All the cups and trophies won during the season were on display. There was an eight-course meal, cigars for everyone, two bands and a cabaret. It was while two nubile young ladies were performing their dance that George Sadler, a well-known local follower of the hunt, was heard to remark: 'I wish I were forty years younger, I wouldn't half have whopped it into one of they.'

'Curiously,' George Coles recalls, 'no one thought of ever giving Ryan a present for all the success that he had brought to the Witley Park stable. Nor did Ryan ever ask for one. We were wrong not to record his skill and loyalty in some tangible way.'

Ryan's success on Goldfish and Thistle Blue made him a celebrity, at least in Sussex and Surrey where point-to-pointing was then the major sporting interest at the close of the foxhunting season. Whenever there was a difficult point-to-point ride, Ryan was called in. He teamed up with a character horse called Arun Lad, a hunter with a lot of ability but with definite ideas of his own. Ryan was walking the course with his innumerable girlfriends – he always had a great many enthusiastic followers – prior to riding Arun Lad at the Leconfield meeting. To his alarm he came upon a fence with a sharp turn by the stables. He was sure that Arun Lad would run out at that point. The followers were briefed, and all stood with their shooting sticks by the side of this fence. Arun Lad came galloping towards them with the bit out of the corner of his mouth and, in unison, they all waved their shooting sticks. Although he had every intention of running out, Arun Lad changed his mind, jumped the fence and won. The rider of the runner-up was far from happy, but Ryan had forestalled any protest by reporting himself that a rowdy bunch at one of the fences had almost caused him trouble.

In 1937, at the end of the point-to-point season, the already taut relationship with his father came under even more strain when, returning home late one night after a party, Ryan crashed his motorbike into a ditch. The resulting explosion was dramatic and the consequences severe. His father finally decided that Ryan had grown too big for home, and that it was high time that he got away from the riotous young blades of Sussex. It was time, in fact, that Ryan earned a living of his own.

George Price not only knew horses, he knew everyone of importance connected with them. He at once arranged for Ryan to go to a friend of his, Arthur Thompson, who ran a hunting livery stable at Market Harborough in Leicestershire, deep in the heart of the Pytchley country. In the thirties, hunting in Leicestershire was very much the vogue. The smart moneyed set bought hunting lodges in the middle of the fashionable hunts. They rode fabulous Irish-bred hunters and they went hard by day and by night. A bold, well-schooled hunter fetched a premium, and Arthur Thompson mounted the gentry of the Pytchley and the surrounding hunts, at a price.

The engine room of this remarkably successful enterprise was the schooling area where his nagsmen jumped the horses over every type of obstacle that a horse was likely to meet out hunting. The nagsman would then take the horse in the field, at pains to show just how each horse coped with difficult places, knowing who the likely customers were and always hoping to be able to give them a lead over a nasty fence.

There would probably be 250 followers out with the Pytchley on a Saturday. Most were well mounted and triers. A large proportion of the field would jump everything. At least fifty riders wanted to be first at every fence, and there were always a couple of dozen who seemed to have only one thought in their head: immediate suicide!

Ryan threw himself into his new job which was tailor-made for his exceptional skill at making horses jump fences. There is no finer feeling in the world for a true horseman than a fast thirty-minute hunt over the grass of Leicestershire. He hunted three horses a day, six days a week, and there was hardly a fence in the county that he did not know.

Ryan met the swells in silk top hats and mahogany topped boots. The standard of turnout was breathtaking. He also discovered an even more exotic collection of girlfriends. One such young lady was the daughter of a baker from Kettering, a dashing figure on horseback, always superbly mounted. She drove to the meets in a 'Green Label' Bentley. Ryan fell heavily. At the weekends she would drive Ryan back home to Sussex for him to ride in the point-to-points. A kindred spirit to Ryan, she was tremendous fun and extremely rich, but, as Ryan discovered to his cost, already married!

In high Leicestershire, one of Arthur Thompson's best customers was Lord Nunburnholme. He was a tall, lean, amateur rider, usually with a permanent drip on the end of his nose. Known as 'Mad Jack', he was a Squire Mytton character, who lived for hunting, racing and gambling. At his home at Arthingworth Manor, he had fifty hunters in his yard, any one of which, according to Ryan, could have won a three-mile steeplechase today.

One day, out hunting, Lord Nunburnholme asked Ryan if he would like to train some jumpers for him. He had bought some young potential steeplechasers and was looking for someone to bring them on and eventually race them. This was just the opportunity that Ryan had been waiting for, and he accepted immediately.

Lord Nunburnholme already had a flat-race trainer, Hubert Hartigan, who trained at East Hendred. He had, however, also sent horses to Noel Murless to train at Hambleton near Thirsk in Yorkshire. The previous year as an amateur rider, Lord Nunburnholme had won a race at the Bibury Club meeting at Salisbury on a 'jady' five-year-old called Bishop's Move. This horse was then transferred from Hubert Hartigan to Noel Murless, who did not have much success with him, and when Ryan moved up to Hambleton, he took over Bishop's Move and a grey named Duncan's Bay.

Hubert Hartigan had pulled a clever stroke with Bishop's Move when he won at Salisbury. The start of the race was immediately in front of the grandstand. When the runners were at the start, Hubert walked out of the stands and across to Lord Nunburnholme. Carefully and deliberately, with the entire crowd watching him, he removed the spurs from Lord Nunburnholme's boots and walked back to the enclosure. The whisper went round that Bishop's Move was not 'busy', and his price drifted in the market. At this point Hubert Hartigan backed the horse. Hartigan was shrewd enough to realize that the tall gangling peer could not use the spurs effectively anyway. In a driving finish Lord Nunburnholme won by a head from two of the most experienced amateurs riding, Mr John Hislop and Mr Ronnie Strutt, now Lord Belper.

Ryan moved to Yorkshire and took up residence in a caravan in the back yard of the local pub, the Hambleton Arms, Hambleton. Nearby, Noel Murless was installed in Hambleton Lodge, but he rented a number of boxes in the pub yard. A few of these he leased to Ryan, who now got to work with some of the most unpromising material any trainer ever had to deal with. Two moderate flat racers and a dozen raw, green jumpers. Not only that, the winter of 1937–38 was particularly severe, and Sutton Bank was no place for the chicken-hearted when the wind blew and the snow came.

Working for Murless as schooling jockey and horsebox driver was Bryan Marshall, later to become one of the greatest steeplechase jockeys of all time. Ryan and Bryan used to escape from the monotony and boredom of Hambleton in an old Armstrong Siddeley, driving over the windswept wolds to Scarborough and the flesh pots therein! The car, never a particularly good runner, had a permanently leaking radiator, and on the way home would overheat. The solution assisted them to overcome the 'calls of nature', though extreme caution had to be exercised when topping up a piping hot radiator!

In the summer of 1938, Ryan decided that he could not endure another winter at Sutton Bank with the disappointing string of which he had charge. Lord Nunburnholme, eccentric and erratic, was steadily running through his fortune. One day, in order to satisfy certain creditors, he sold his entire string of hunters, including some of his wife's most treasured and priceless horses.

Ryan gave up the job and moved south to the more temperate climate of his beloved Sussex. In those days a whole host of trainers had strings in the Sussex villages nestling in the folds below the South

Downs, where the gallops were among the best in England. Bob Gore trained at Findon, so did Alex Law at Netfor Lodge, once a magnificent stables, now a housing estate. Victor Gilpin was at Michel Grove.

Back among friendly farmers, Ryan began to get a string together. An old friend, Irene Mann-Thompson, sent him Hardy Annual, an ex-point-to-pointer, and both Archie Neal and Jack Ash sent him horses. He started the 1938–39 National Hunt season with a dozen chasers, no money behind him, but a grim determination to succeed this time.

It was training on the bread line, and the prize money for the local tracks at Plumpton and Fontwell and Wye was woefully small. His best horse turned out to be Hardy Annual II, but at Liverpool this game horse was beaten a head by O'Dell in the Foxhunters'. O'Dell was the greatest hunter chaser of the day. He had won the Foxhunters' the previous year, and in 1939 he finished second. He was ridden on each occasion by Major (later General) Prior-Palmer, the father of Lucinda, the famous event rider.

Even as early as 1938, Ryan's efforts to ride and train winners were sometimes misunderstood by the racing public. After two near misses with a gelding called Cyclamen, Ryan saddled the seven-year-old to win a selling chase at Towcester with Bobby Petre in the saddle. Starting at 8 to 1, Cyclamen had been retained at the subsequent auction for 75 guineas. Later in the month Ryan rode the horse himself in a similar race at nearby Fontwell Park. Disaster struck at the second fence when Ryan's stirrup leather broke and he hit the ground with a bone-shattering crash.

The following day at Fontwell Ryan saddled Cyclamen again in another seller; this time Bobby Petre rode him. A well-backed favourite at 13 to 8, Cyclamen won easily by three lengths. There was weighing room talk of a substantial coup landed, and there was some spirited bidding at the auction, Ryan eventually losing the horse at 260 guineas to Lady Lindsay, who had her horses trained privately. There was no coup, just Ryan's owner trying, as it turned out, successfully, to get the money back that he had lost the previous day. However, some people accused Ryan of engineering his fall at Fontwell Park in order to effect a more favourable return the following day.

Before the 1938–39 point-to-point season, Ryan learned through the Sussex grapevine that the secretary of the Leconfield Hunt was alleging that Ryan was being paid to ride in hunt races. The secretary let it be known that when Ryan presented himself to ride at the next Leconfield meeting, he would be objected to on the grounds that he had ridden for hire. Though Ryan had never taken payment for rides, he did not give the secretary that pleasure; he had already decided that it was time to turn professional and he was granted a licence to ride under National Hunt rules. His point-to-point days were over and he retired, having ridden over a hundred winners. His outmanoeuvred opponents must surely have welcomed his departure from the ranks of the amateurs.

By this time Ryan's natural weight was 11 stone. He realized that, as a professional, he would have weight problems, but at this stage he was more concerned with the schooling and the training of his jumpers at home than about his race-riding career.

In the summer Ryan was looking forward to the new season, with a string of thirty-two, but just as the season was getting under way, war was declared on Germany and, on 3 September 1939, his training career, which had started so inauspiciously at Sutton Bank, now came to a swift and tragic end. Not being breeding stock, all but two of his string were slaughtered within twenty-four hours. Hardy Annual II had been rescued by his owner to work on the farm, and Ryan managed to get April Day II away to Epsom to the stable of Peter Thrale.

With the smell of death in the now silent stable yard, Ryan was broken-hearted. In despair and anger he now took stock. He had tried – how he had tried – to break into the close world of training, but the war had intervened just at the moment when he was about to make a name for himself. He was twenty-seven, virtually unknown outside Sussex. He had not a penny in the bank, and goodness knows how many years of war lay ahead before he could try again.

The next day he went to Farnham and enlisted in the Royal Artillery.

4
Wartime

Ryan's first posting was to the tented camp on Hurst Park racecourse; his first military job, latrine orderly!

During the phoney war of 1939, life at the camp was unreal. After only a few days in uniform, Ryan formed up to his commanding officer and asked for a day pass in order to attend Windsor Races.

'Why do you want to go racing?' asked the Colonel, bristling fiercely.

'I own a horse which is running.'

'A gunner owning a racehorse,' blasted the Colonel. 'Has it got a chance?'

'Yes,' replied Ryan, 'it'll win.'

'Meet me outside the orderly room at twelve o'clock and I'll take you myself.'

Ryan and his Colonel arrived at Windsor in style in the staff car and Ryan organized badges and lunch tickets. Then he sought out Peter Thrale who had charge of the chaser that Ryan had slipped out of the back door and saved before his string had been destroyed. This was April Day II. The horse was well schooled and fit enough to win. He reported his findings to the Colonel.

'How much are you going to have on?' he asked Ryan.

'Twenty pounds each way.'

'Put a fiver each way on for me.'

In spite of considerable vocal assistance from the Colonel and the Gunner from the stands, April Day II could only finish third in the last race, but with the odds at 100 to 8 they drew the place money.

Earlier Matt Feakes had saved the day by riding the winner of the

1.30 race at 20 to 1, which Ryan had told the Colonel to back. They returned to barracks with pocketfuls of white £5 notes. One could say that Ryan's inside information was a great help to his military career. Following further successful visits to Windsor, Gatwick and Newbury, Ryan was very soon appointed Battery Sergeant Major.

His next posting was to a newly formed RA battery armed with anti-aircraft guns near Newbury. As BSM, and knowing very little about these big 20-cwt, 3-in naval guns, he organized gun drill. Unfortunately there were no practice rounds, only live shells. One day one of the teams succeeded in getting a live round stuck up the breech. Nothing would shift it, and in the absence of even a manual on the wretched gun, Ryan decided to fire off the round. He pulled the lanyard and the noise woke all Newbury.

'It was the loudest explosion that I heard during the whole war,' remembered Ryan, 'and I heard a few! I thought that I had solved the problem rather well until to my astonishment I was put under close arrest.'

The next day Ryan was marched in front of the Brigadier.

'You have made a fine mess of this, Price. It's a good job that I know your father. You have two alternatives: either you face a court martial here or else you go to the infantry.'

Outside the Brigadier's office Ryan had the good fortune to meet an old friend of his, Derek (now Lord) Wernher. A brief discussion took place and Wernher's advice was to settle for the infantry. So Battery Sergeant Major Price – the man who pulled the lanyard – caught the train from Newbury en route for Shorncliffe. His new posting turned out to be an infantry OCTU (Officer Cadet Training Unit). Ryan had hardly been there ten minutes when the Colonel sent for him. 'Now, Price, you've been sent to us under the most peculiar circumstances. I wish to warn you that anyone has to be bloody good to pass out of here, and you yourself will have to be better than anyone else to get your commission.' So, for the next two months Ryan buckled to and worked like a Trojan. It seemed to make little impression for he was then marched in and told that he was not pulling his weight. Unless he improved he would be returned to his unit.

After that smack in the eye, Ryan knew that there was no justice in 'this man's army'. Fortunately for him, one of his fellow cadets was the son of the vicar from Petworth. They had known each other for years. Whenever Ryan was in danger of making a mistake, his friend usually helped him out. The net result was that the parson's son passed out first and Ryan was second.

In April 1941, Second Lieutenant H. R. Price was posted to the 7th Battalion the North Staffordshire Regiment, pausing briefly in London to be photographed in his new uniform and badges of rank. The 7th was a Territorial battalion consisting of officers drawn from the local county set. Ryan was the first outsider to be posted to them It was rather like joining a club: they treated him as if he were a very new member – and ignored him. 'No one talked to me for six months.' Ryan was eventually given command of the carrier platoon – a job that caused him the greatest delight. He set out to make 'mechanized racehorses' of them.

Later that year the battalion was posted to Northern Ireland and Ryan found himself billeted on Downpatrick racecourse. The war was a long way away and Ryan was able to hunt three days a week with the County Down pack. It was a great relaxation from army life and he met many friends, including the legendary point-to-point rider, Willie Rooney – amateur rider, trainer and horsecoper extraordinary – whom he had known in Sussex. Suddenly the regiment was on the move again, this time to the Shetland Isles, bleak, isolated and bitterly cold. Making the best of this lonely station, Ryan devoted his spare time to duck shooting and deep-sea fishing. Whatever may have been happening in Crete and Greece and the North African theatre of war, at least Ryan was finding that army life was living up to the prewar recruiting-poster image of a sporting life in khaki.

Leave in London provided a welcome relief from the exigencies of service in the Shetlands. At a cocktail party Ryan met Lord Lovat, who confided to him that he knew his father. What senior army officer did not? wondered Ryan. Lord Lovat wanted to know what Ryan was doing. Hearing the catalogue of sporting activities, he asked, 'Would you like to do something really exciting for a change and make a real contribution to the course of the war?'

'Yes, sir.'

'Then give me your name, rank and number and the address of your unit, and I will have you transferred to the Commandos before you return from leave.'

After his leave, Ryan was marched in to his CO. 'What is all this about? Telegrams about you have been arriving from the War Office all week. Just when I begin to see some result in the efforts that I have been making to train you into a useful soldier, behind my back you get yourself transferred to a lot of Boy Scouts.' That particular Colonel – in company with many others – was reacting to the loss of some of his best regimental soldiers to Special Service Units.

In 1943 Ryan joined the Special Services – later to become the Commandos. At the time he believed that he would get into the war more quickly and that his new aggressive role would be more exciting and certainly more dangerous than that of a platoon officer in an infantry regiment of the line. How wrong he was proved to be: the 7th Battalion the North Staffordshire Regiment were to suffer heavy casualties in Northern Europe.

5
The Commandos

Ryan travelled down by train from the Shetlands to the Commando depot at Wrexham in North Wales. After a few weeks he was then posted to No. 6 Commando, part of No. 1 Special Service Brigade, under the command of Brigadier Lord Lovat. No. 6 Commando was at that time stationed at Hove; so it was back to Sussex by the sea. The Commandos all lived out in civilian billets, mostly in the Portslade area, catching local buses or cycling to parades.

Ryan thus donned the green beret of the Commandos, a volunteer force drawn from all walks of life and from many different regiments. They were tough and resolute troops, and many had already fought with the Commandos in Norway and in the raids on Dieppe and St Nazaire. Their commanding officer was Lieutenant Colonel Derek Mills-Roberts of the Irish Guards, and under him the training was demanding and rigorous. Ryan was athletic and very fit, but the tempo of training was far higher than he had been used to in an infantry unit. There was virtually no petty crime; few soldiers were marched in front of the CO for trivial offences. The threat of being returned to one's unit hung over everyone's head if they did not measure up to the standard set and demanded by the colonel.

In the spring of 1944, the war-weary civilian population of Britain had but one topic of conversation whenever the war was mentioned: The Second Front – the invasion of Europe by the Allies, the first scene in the final act of the war – when would it happen and where? Final victory against the Germans could only be achieved by a colossal onslaught against the Atlantic Wall, the coastal defence system that had been added to and strengthened ever since Hitler had realized that an Allied invasion of Europe was inevitable. No one in

No. 6 Commando was under any doubt that they were to play a vital role in that assault, for now, in the spring of 1944, their training took on a new intensity. With monotonous regularity they spent days being loaded into landing craft at Shoreham docks, and then being landed on the beaches at Middleton-on-Sea and Littlehampton. They also performed regular night exercises.

Great Britain was fast becoming a store house for war material. American and British troops in endless convoys of tanks, trucks and amphibious vehicles streamed through our towns and villages towards the south coast. To those waiting impatiently for the end of the war, the delay seemed unnecessary, but for the planners of operation Overlord, the code name for the invasion of Europe, every additional day was a bonus in extra men and equipment.

Every soldier and sailor in training for the great offensive was under no illusion as to the dangers and difficulties of a sea assault from landing craft against a heavily defended shore. For most of those who took part in the Normandy landings at H-Hour on D-Day, it was to be the most shattering, bewildering and frightening experience of their lives.

The Commandos' stock-in-trade was stealth and surprise and every landing they had performed on the enemy shore had brought more priceless knowledge and expertise. On this occasion they realized that, by the time they hit the beach, the enemy would be alerted and it would be like stepping into a hornets' nest. The recurring nightmare that every soldier with but an ounce of imagination kept on having was the vision of a long stretch of beach exposed to a well-sighted machine gun – a killing ground which many of the troops crossed in their dreams and nightmares a thousand times before the actual day came. They certainly crossed beaches at Shoreham and Middleton many times in practice.

One of the problems in the D-Day planning was the acute shortage of landing craft. The build-up of subsequent reinforcements depended on the same craft returning after having beached its original load. How the troops hated these slow, slab-sided boats. Fully loaded, they were unwieldy and ponderous, a sitting duck for German U-boats and E-boats. During a practice invasion at Slapton Sands in April, a force of German E-boats had run amok among some landing ship tanks (LSTs) and had sunk two with appalling loss of life – 638 men, two thirds of them soldiers, had been drowned. The Commandos were festooned with weapons and ammunition. They each carried a special rucksack weighing no less than 60 pounds and anyone who was unlucky enough to be swept into a heavy sea would almost certainly be drowned.

Apart from the decision to land on the Normandy beaches rather than on the Pas de Calais, the most significant problem was the time of the landing: dawn or dusk, day or night, high tide or low tide – what was the ideal combination? A great deal of thought was put into this vital question. The Army assault troops favoured a dawn attack; the Navy preferred daylight, influenced by the prospect of an armada of 7000 ships carrying 130,000 men milling around in the dark. A daylight landing would make the bombardment of coastal defences more effective. In the event, the decision was pre-empted when reconnaissance discovered the presence of underwater obstacles. These could only be rendered harmless in daylight and at low tide. These beach obstacles had only begun to appear in February and had been increasing all the time.

Bernard Fergusson in *The Watery Maze* records:

> The Germans had begun placing the obstacles at highwater mark and were working to seaward; by the beginning of June the obstacles had spread to the half-tide mark. If the assault were to take place at high water, the landing craft would be touching down among the obstacles and the losses would certainly exceed General Morgan's estimated ten per cent. If it took place at low water the infantry would be faced with an advance of several hundred yards across open beach wholly exposed to the enemy's fire.
>
> Montgomery's decision was to assault at a little before half flood, so that the landing craft would touch down just short of the obstacles and give the LCOCUs time to deal with them. The DD tanks would go in first, Hobart's specialized armour to deal with the mine fields next and then the first wave of the infantry.
>
> The ideal combination of time, tide and moon would occur on only three consecutive days in any given month. In June 1944, those days were the 5th, 6th and 7th. For time and tide there would be another possible three days a fortnight later; but the moon would be wrong, to the detriment of the Airborne landings. There remained in any case the horribly incalculable factor of the weather.

So, on 4 June 1944, the Supreme Commander, General Eisenhower, met with the Chiefs of Staff in the library at Southwick House, near Portsmouth. Some D-Day convoys had already sailed, working on a schedule for 5 June; many encountered rough seas and were forced to turn back. There was a forecast of dreadful weather: strong winds and rough seas – no weather for a landing. Eisenhower postponed the invasion for twenty-four hours.

Ryan's troop, in their tented bivouac near Bishops Waltham, were in a high state of readiness as the prospect of the invasion approached. At this stage no one at Ryan's level knew where they were bound for, or their time of landing. The news of the twenty-four hour postponement was an anticlimax; so everyone cleaned their pistols, rifles and machine guns for the hundredth time. Not wishing to appear conspicuous to an enemy sniper, Ryan carried a Garand rifle in addition to his .38 revolver. The troop stood down and everyone sat around in their tents, smoking and talking; some just sat quietly thinking, others scribbled what was to be for many a last letter home.

Back in Southwick House, Eisenhower called another conference at 4 a.m. the following day, and although the weather had performed exactly as the senior meteorological officer had predicted, there was promise of an improvement for 6 June. This gave a glimmer of hope. The prospect of cancellation until the next favourable period was too awful to contemplate! The morale of the troops would be harmed and the secrecy of the entire operation could be compromised by further delay. Eisenhower decided to invade, and the signals were sent out. It was a courageous decision.

The Commandos moved by trucks to their loading-up area at Warsash at the entrance to the Hamble River, where the landing craft were drawn up alongside the hard. They steamed out of Spithead in the evening dusk with Lord Lovat's personal piper playing in the bows of the leading craft. It was an emotional moment for everyone. In the lee of the Isle of Wight the motion of the craft was tolerable, but once they felt the full brunt of the dying Channel gales the journey was unbearable. Their immediate objective was now the rendezvous point south of the Isle of Wight known as Area Z.

As soon as the armada was afloat, maps were produced and, with the aid of aerial photos the final briefing took place. For the first time the troops knew where they were going. In the case of the 1st Brigade it was to be beaches at Ouistreham at the entrance to the River Orne. This was on the extreme left flank of the invasion front. Their D-Day objectives were the bridges across the Caen Canal and the River Orne, which should have been captured by the 6th Airborne during the previous night in a daring assault by gliders and by parachute

THE SEA PASSAGE

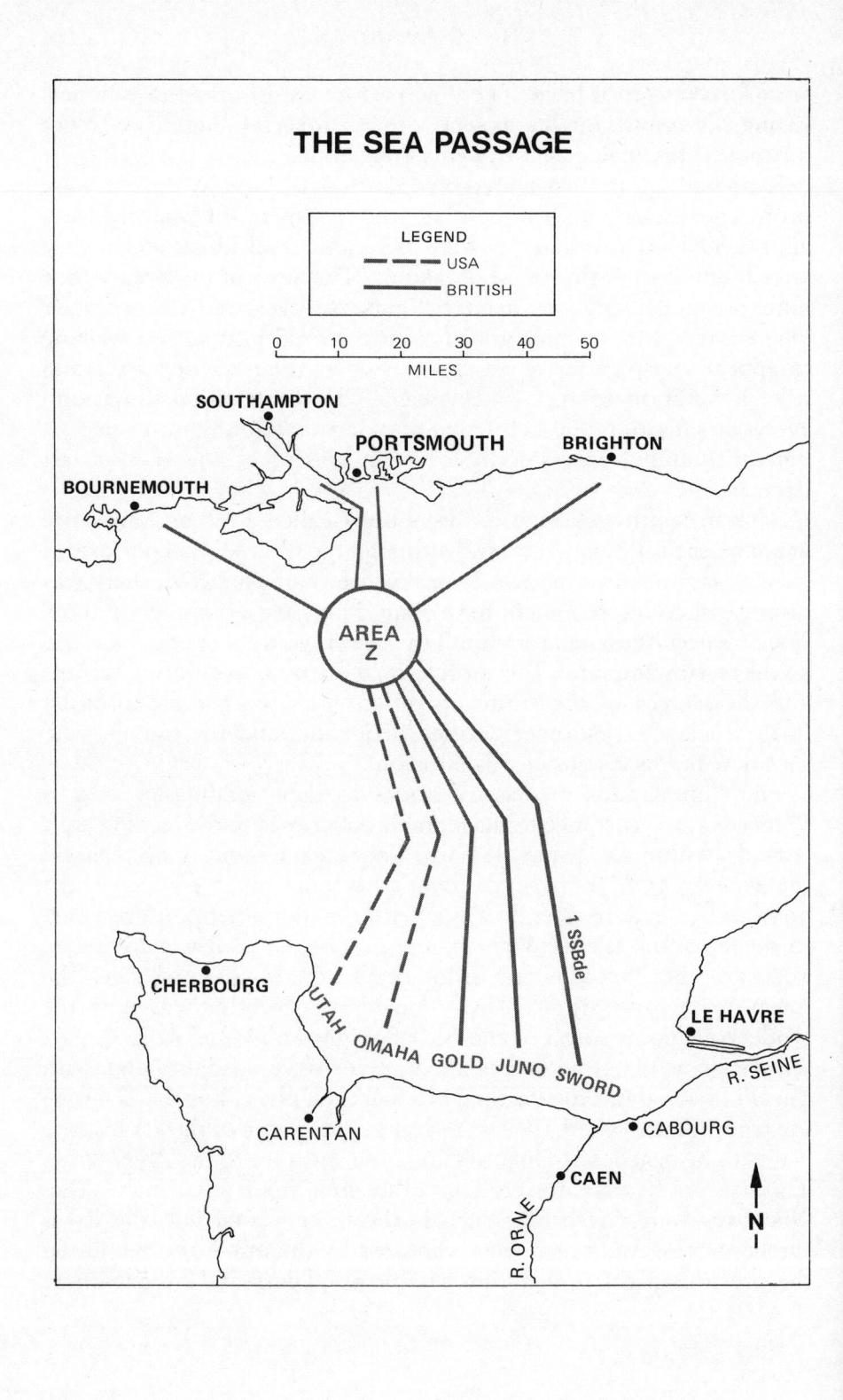

troops, and held until the Commandos broke through to support them.

Studying the maps with his fellow officers, Ryan now realized why they had been rehearsing the invasion at Littlehampton, for the terrain there closely resembled the mouth of the River Orne. He recalled countless assaults up to the bridge over the River Arun.

During the passage there was still a heavy sea running in the Channel with waves of about 5 or 6 feet high and a 15-knot wind. The LSIs' speed was only 5 knots and they wallowed and yawed their way to the rendezvous in the dark. All Ryan's troop – without exception – were sick and soon the steel gangways were awash with the remains of human wretchedness. No troops ever sailed to a battle better trained, more prepared, or with a more complete plan, yet by midnight, less than six hours before the assault, on board the heaving decks of the landing craft, there was hardly a man fit enough to fight.

By first light the convoy of LSIs was near the coastline and the Commandos could see the full extent of the invasion armada. They were terribly vulnerable to attack by E-boats, but there was a massive naval presence, and as the first assault waves went ashore it was apparent that they had achieved complete tactical surprise.

On its final run ashore, Ryan's LSI missed the beach obstacles and grounded on a shallow sand bar. The two ramps came crashing down and Ryan was the first man down. It was 0840. Instead of landing on sand, Ryan disappeared from view; the water was well over his head and, with a 60-pound pack, he was perilously close to drowning. He pulled the quick release of his pack and slowly came spluttering to the surface. To the bottom went all his ammunition, twenty-four hours' rations and grenades.

As he fought to clear his lungs of salt water, there was an earth-shattering explosion above him. His landing craft had taken a direct hit: the cramped steel decks were twisted open, buckled and smoking, revealing terrible carnage amongst Ryan's troop inside. Half of the men died instantly when the shell struck. Had the Germans been using high explosive and not armour-piercing shells, the casualties would have been 100 per cent.

Soaking wet, half drowned, still suffering from the effects of sea sickness, Ryan now felt a new sensation – one of blind and uncivilized anger at the destruction of so many good men. He staggered farther up the beach; there was still sporadic firing coming from one corner of the sand dunes. For all his training he felt weak as a sparrow and very frightened.

The survivors limped quietly ashore and Ryan organized them into a fighting group. Many had lost their personal weapons and ammunition when the LSI had gone up. They scavenged around on the beach, removing rifles and bandoliers of small-arms ammunition from the bodies of troops of the East Yorkshire Regiment who had been killed in the first assault. The first priority was to get the hell off the beach, and Ryan and his depleted troop pushed on over the dunes, leaving the town of Ouistreham on their left.

In this next phase No. 6 Commando was in the lead; they had to effect a link-up with the airborne forces at the canal bridge. There followed a series of short, sharp and extremely bloody actions. Away from the houses the ground was open and exposed. The Germans were in well concealed and heavily defended positions in depth. The fire was accurate and Ryan's troop leader was killed.

Pressing forward, Ryan passed what he thought was the dead body of his close friend, Lieutenant Peter Cruden, lying motionless in a pool of blood in a hedgerow. Ryan made a mental note to tell Peter's girlfriend when he returned to England. However, Peter Cruden saw her first; he was wounded in the chest and was unable to move owing to the weight of his pack. At 11.30 the Battle of Normandy had ended for him. He recovered from his wounds and later rejoined No. 6 Commando in October at Petworth.

There was a tremendous noise of firing from the town of Ouistreham, which was being cleared by the Free French Commandos. Lord Lovat had learned, at the time of landing, that the bridges over the Orne had been captured intact by the Airborne troops and he now urged the Commandos on to effect a link-up. Though No. 6 Commando tried to infiltrate between the known enemy strong points, they still had to assault four pillboxes and a four-gun artillery battery which had been shelling the beaches. The pillboxes had to be attacked without artillery support. The six and a half miles between the beach and the bridges was covered in three and a half hours. Lord Lovat made contact with the Airborne commander and apologized for being two and a half minutes late.

Ryan and his troop crossed the bridge with bullets and mortar shell wanging-off the steel girders; miraculously only one man was hit. Then, with the support of the 6th Airborne, they captured the village of Le Plein and dug in on the high ground to await the inevitable German counter-attack. Ryan became troop leader.

At 1400 hours on 6 June, Lord Lovat and the remainder of his brigade crossed the bridge with Lord Lovat's personal piper at their head playing a cheerful tune. Hilary St George Saunders in *The Green Beret* captures the moment marvellously well:

> So the Green Berets mingled with the Red. Men of formations which had sustained the valour of British arms in the cold, clear fjords of Norway, in the dank jungles of Madagascar, in the stinging sands and stony hills of Africa, in the streets of Vasterival, in the tracer-lit docks of St Nazaire, met with the men who were performing a like office in the green fields of Normandy.

The brigade was now holding a line from Merville in the north to Bréville in the south. Little did Ryan realize that they would be clinging desperately to that vital piece of Normandy against repeated German attempts to dislodge them for the next two months.

The troop now dug in on the high ground beyond Le Plein. The Germans were entrenched in the next village, Bréville, half a mile up the road, and another troop was detailed to take it. They met heavy resistance and suffered casualties; the troop leader, Alan Pyman, was killed. Bréville had to be evacuated. Derek Mills-Roberts took a jeep into the village and, as dusk lengthened into night, ran the gauntlet through enemy fire to bring out the wounded. This now left Ryan's troop holding the extreme left flank of the entire British bridgehead.

Derek Mills-Roberts had already given his orders for the defence of the vital position at Le Plein. Ignoring the obvious positions on the ridge's forward slope, he sited his troops on the reverse slopes. This meant that although their own field of view was limited, the enemy could not see the defensive positions until they had crossed the ridge and by then they would be in the Commandos' fire trap or 'killing ground'. Ryan sensed an impending attack and urged his batman, a Staffordshire miner, to dig his slit trench deep. The camouflage of the area had to be maintained and the spoil from the weapon pits carefully hidden.

During the night of D-Day plus one, enemy snipers infiltrated through to the area of the ridge, and, at first light, opened fire. Ryan's troop had orders not to return the fire and thus give their positions away. Sure enough, when the German batteries began their dawn bombardment, they 'stonked' the ridge heavily. When the German infantry followed up this bombardment with an assault on the ridge, they were surprised to find it deserted. They were even more surprised when the Commandos opened up on their leading troops from point-blank range and broke up the attack.

It was now apparent that the Germans were using Bréville wood to bombard the Commandos' positions, so Derek Mills-Roberts decided to mount an attack on the wood. Ryan's commander describes the battle in a chapter in Lord Lovat's book, *March Past*:

> ### THE BATTLE OF THE ORCHARD
> I chose John Thompson's and Ryan Price's troops and arranged a quick-fire plan. The medium battery would give Bréville a good beat-up, our three-inch mortars trimming the forward edge of the wood; the assault was to attack from the right to capture the battery. It was a great success. The troops went through the wood – after the medium battery had clobbered it – like men possessed and captured four field guns in record time. The only casualty on our side was one man killed. Apart from the guns the raid took fifteen prisoners; we hauled the guns back into our own position by means of two jeeps.
>
> As Ryan came up the road I heard him say to his batman, 'Why the hell did you fire up into a tree when we were going through the wood?'
>
> 'There was a sniper there,' replied his henchman and then in an injured voice, 'He was just going to shoot you sir, when I picked him off.'

On the morning of 7 June the troops ate the first meal that they had had since leaving Southampton. Hardly had they finished, than the Germans attacked. For the next five days they probed the Commando line, hoping to feed their troops through at a weak spot.

On 12 June No. 6 Commando attacked and took the village of Bréville, but suffered heavy casualties in the process from enemy counter artillery fire. Among those wounded was the brigade commander, Lord Lovat. Lieutenant Colonel Derek Mills-Roberts took over and commanded the Brigade until the end of the war, Lieutenant Colonel Tony Lewis taking command of No. 6 Commando. The relief promised after forty-eight hours never came, and so the Commandos and the Airborne slogged away, keeping the vital left flank of the invasion secure.

The Brigade then turned its attention northwards and secured the east bank of the River Orne by capturing Franceville-Plage. Attempts to move along the coastline to Cabourg were held up by strong enemy defence.

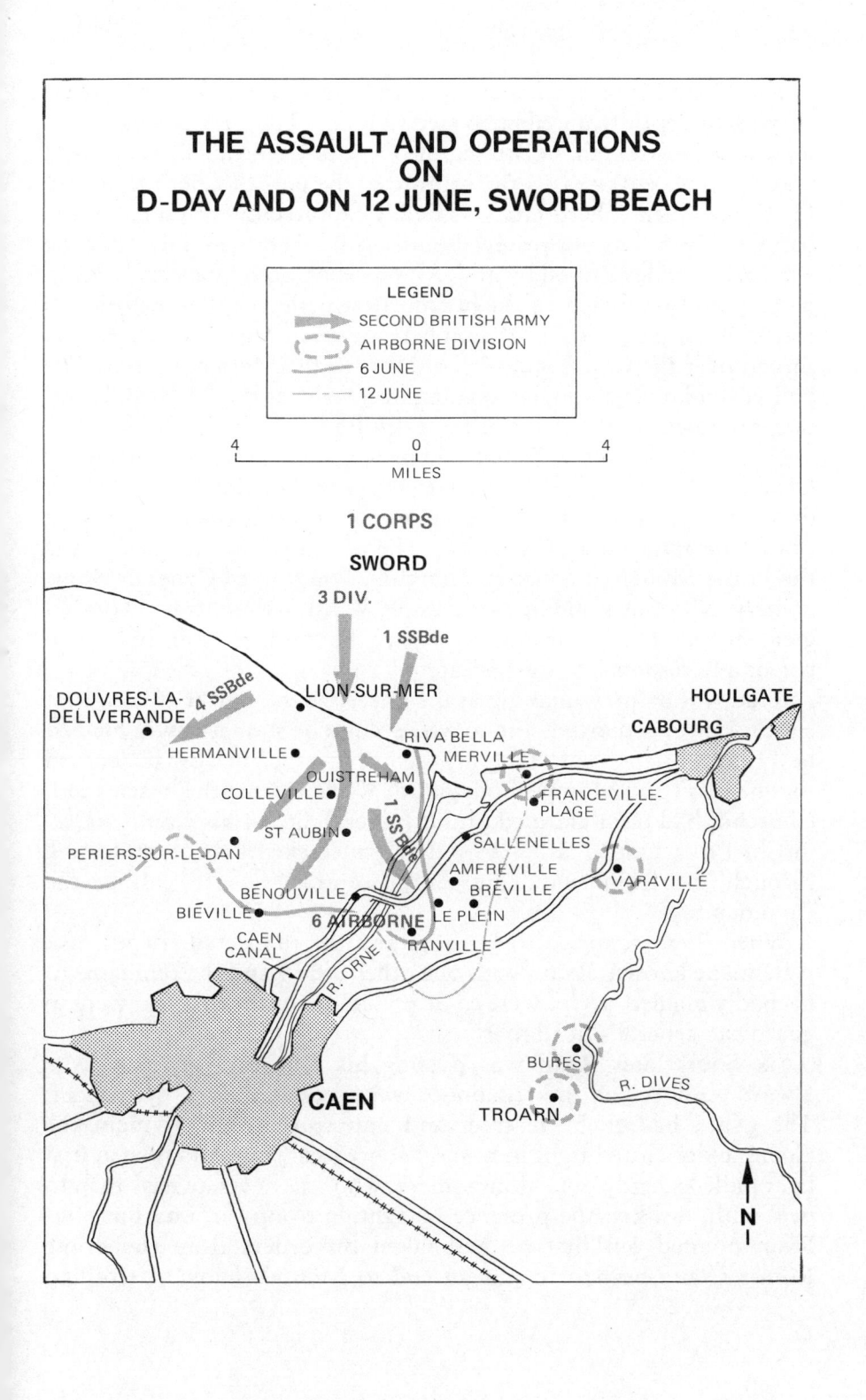

THE ASSAULT AND OPERATIONS ON D-DAY AND ON 12 JUNE, SWORD BEACH

The Allied bridgehead was now firmly linked in a fifty-mile front varying in depth from eight to twelve miles. The 51st Division was increasing in strength, bolstering the Orne bridgehead. The emphasis was now concentrated on the capture of the port of Cherbourg, and the city of Caen. Cherbourg was finally captured on 25 June, but the battle of Caen was not resolved until 9 July, and then only after the city had been devastated by an RAF precision bombing attack. Ryan had a grandstand view of the horrific destruction of that historic old town. Wave after wave of bombers came in from the coast and turned over the Commandos' positions for their bombing runs. The pall of smoke, dust and debris hung over Caen as the RAF 'took out' this key town on the flank of the front line.

On 21 July Ryan was dispatched by jeep on a mysterious errand to General Montgomery's headquarters. After waiting for an hour, during which his morale sank to a low ebb, he was ushered by a staff officer into the general's office. There, seated at the desk, was the Prime Minister, Winston Churchill. Pointing to General Montgomery, who was standing on one side, Winston thundered, 'This is a great man.' Then, turning to Ryan, he said, 'I will hold you personally responsible for his safety.'

Ryan was by now quaking at the knees; he thought that he was at least for a court martial, and maybe even to be shot at dawn. He had never been briefed as to the purpose of his visit, but now he learned that he was to be Monty's bodyguard. While visiting the beach head, Churchill had been alarmed at the vulnerability of his Commander-in-Chief to a sudden attack by a determined enemy force infiltrating through the front line. Churchill's solution was to call in the Commandos.

When Ryan returned to his adjutant, the full details of his task were made known. Ryan, with one other officer and the remnants of his badly mauled troop, were to be pulled out of the line and were to guard the general's headquarters.

Six hours later Ryan was posting his sentries. Ten men were always on duty and the remainder were dressed and ready to fight. The guard had to be discreet and unobtrusive, but at night the Commandos closed right in round Monty's caravan, and then at first light pulled silently out. Montgomery, who was never an easy man to deal with, disliked the presence of fighting troops around him, but Ryan pointed out that he had taken his orders from the Prime Minister, and he had to put an end to Monty's habit of strolling round the countryside on his own. Ryan came to know all the Corps and Divisional Commanders who visited the caravan, frequently passing on such vital intelligence as to whether the Guv'nor was in a good mood today or not!

Just when it seemed that a total stalemate had arrived, on 18 August the order to advance was given. The German armies in France were trapped in a pincer movement which closed at the Falaise Gap. The Commandos now began to speed the departing guest. First, though, there was a set-piece attack on enemy strong points at Dives and at Dozulé. The enemy was defending these areas in some strength, and the only way that the Commandos could get to the heart of the defences was to attack at night. 1st Brigade went for Dives; they started at midnight and, following a difficult route marked by white tape, they infiltrated through the outer defences and achieved complete tactical surprise. The Brigade then had to endure no less than four savage counter-attacks by the Germans, in one of which Captain Johnnie Clapton of No. 6 Commando distinguished himself by charging at the head of his troop straight at a group of Germans who were preparing to assault.

Hilary St George Saunders in *The Green Beret* illustrated just how superior the Commando troops were. He wrote:

> Their fire discipline was so good at this time that units such as No. 3 and No. 6 Commandos would wait until the Germans were within a few yards, then open up and kill the lot. No troops however good – and the Germans were most skilled – will continue to make attacks from which no one returns. That evening under cover of a heavy smoke screen some forty Commando wounded were taken back by jeeps. At the cost of one officer and eleven other ranks killed, one officer and forty-two other ranks wounded, the brigade had captured and held a position which the enemy might with justice have regarded as impregnable.

In five days the Brigade had covered forty miles, fighting by day and night in the face of fierce German defence. By 26 August, the enemy was retreating across the River Seine. The Brigade had been fighting for a total of eighty-three days without being rested. Of the 146 officers and 2252 other ranks who landed on D-Day, 77 officers and 890 other ranks had become casualties.

This was to be No. 6 Commandos' last major action in France. At the end of August, No. 1 Special Service Brigade was at last pulled out, and left Normandy to return to Britain to refit and reform in preparation for operations in the Far East. Leaving General Montgomery alive and well, Ryan and his troop returned once again to Petworth Park where, as a child, he had ridden so often; here the seasoned warriors licked their wounds.

Throughout the late autumn of 1944, No. 6 Commando continued to reorganize in Petworth and to absorb replacements for the Normandy casualties; they then returned to Hove. No. 4 Brigade was still in operations to open up the port of Antwerp and to capture Walcheren. Training now took place on the Sussex Downs prior to the departure of No. 1 Brigade to the Far East.

The Battle of the Bulge changed all that. Ryan was promoted to Captain and became Adjutant of No. 6 Commando. Just as he was organizing Christmas leave he received a signal from the brigade headquarters: ALL LEAVE CANCELLED STOP 6 COMMANDO ON 24 HOUR STANDBY. At a time when everyone thought that the Germans were finished, Hitler unleashed one last madman's stroke. During appalling weather, when low-level air reconnaissance was impossible, the Boche launched a savage attack in the Ardennes, splitting the British and American forces. Tactical surprise was complete as eight Panzer divisions smashed through the Americans towards Bastogne.

By Christmas Eve the advance units had crashed their way as far as Dinant, and the direction of this thrust was clearly the port of Antwerp. For a time utter confusion reigned amongst the American troops caught up in a steam-roller offensive that few had thought, at this stage in the war, the enemy was capable of mounting. Eisenhower was forced to call in his reserves, and the British and American Airborne divisions were recalled. General Montgomery then took overall command of the northern sector, and as the steam went out of the enemy's desperate thrust, and the advance Panzer units ran out of fuel, order was gradually restored and the bulge contained.

The result was that No. 1 Special Service Brigade was diverted from its original destination – the Far East – and on 17 January sailed back into the European conflict, landing at Antwerp and then moving to Asten near the River Maas. It was going to be a case of finishing off the Boche first.

On 21 January Ryan's unit crossed the ice on the Juliana Canal and occupied Maastricht. 'Suddenly we were in the river-crossing business.'

The next set-piece battle was to be the crossing of the Rhine. The brigade's objective was the heavily defended town of Wesel. The plan was to cross the river in assault boats by night, and to infiltrate through the enemy's defences following a heavy raid on the town by the RAF. Crossing the Rhine in soft-skinned boats was no picnic, and several of Ryan's friends were lost, many drowning in the fast-flowing river in the dark. In spite of the difficulties, No. 6 Commando led the attack, working stealthily through the outposts laying white tape for the following troops. There was a full moon and they succeeded in reaching the centre of the town and surprised the German garrison who were only just recovering from the shattering effects of the air raid. By the evening of 25 March, Wesel was taken. The Brigade had captured over 850 prisoners, and many hundreds of German dead lay in the ruins of the town, at a cost of two officers and nine other ranks killed, seventeen missing believed drowned, and six officers and sixty-two other ranks wounded. The technique that had been used so successfully at Dives in Normandy had worked again and was to be used again and again in the river assaults at which the Commandos had now become specialists.

The Maas and the Rhine were behind them, but now the Brigade was confronted with the River Weser, deep and fast-flowing. There was, however, a bridgehead already established at Leese, and so once again No. 6 Commando crossed at midnight and marched in the now approved Commando fashion – in single file along a white tape – in order to outflank Leese and the defences positioned for a head-on assault across the river. Once again No. 6 Commando achieved complete surprise, and Captain Peter Cruden and his troop rushed a gun emplacement and captured four 20-mm guns intact.

Now No. 6 Commando teamed up with the 11th Armoured Division and succeeded in forcing a crossing over yet another river, the Aller. After finding the road bridge was heavily defended, they worked downstream and crossed by the railway bridge, only to discover on the far bank that the enemy were dug in and well entrenched in the woods which ran alongside the river. At any moment the road bridge might be blown, which would further delay the advance. The woods were defended by German marine fusiliers. They had, it seems, never faced Commandos before. There was only one thing to do; No. 6 Commando fixed bayonets and charged through the wood. The air was filled with blood-curdling yells and the silver notes of Ryan's hunting horn maintaining the direction of the attack. Finally, the tank crews waiting by the roadside heard Ryan's triumphant 'gone away' which was the signal that the bridge was intact and secure. The cavalry rolled and in no time the advance squadrons were pushing on through the village.

The incident was written up by war correspondent George McCarthy:

> COMMANDOS CHARGED TO THE SOUND OF THE HORN
> A Commando bayonet charge in daylight through a thick wood pitted with enemy entrenchments cleared a bridgehead through which the 11th Armoured Division crashed their way beyond the River Aller. They had dug themselves in under heavy enemy fire and in the morning No. 6 Commando were given the order to clear the wood. They fixed bayonets and went at full speed, as high above the din of battle ranged the notes of a hunting horn. It was the call to charge. The Commandos shouted as they ran, some Germans stayed to be bayoneted, but most waited until the charging troops ran to within twenty yards and then they broke and ran with the British in full pursuit. Five minutes after the charge began, the hunting horn was sounding a 'view hallo', a call that announced that the road bridge beyond the wood was safely in our hands.
>
> The brigadier told the story – it was the adjutant, Captain Ryan Price, a racehorse trainer, who carried the hunting horn, and he certainly never blew it at a better moment.

Once again it was the sheer pace of the Commandos' attack that won the day, taking a heavily defended wood in just five minutes. The most bewildered and demoralized troops at the Aller were the German marines, now they had experienced being 'bounced' by the Commandos. Whether at night by stealth, or with dash and devil in daylight, the Commandos were greatly to be feared in battle.

By now the enemy was in full flight and the end of the war was in sight; the Brigade reached Luneburg and was attached to the 15th Scottish Division for the crossing of yet another river, the Elbe. Again a night assault was planned over the 300-yard wide river. Bad visibility prevented a similar RAF operation to Wesel. On the night of 29 April, the Commandos crossed in Buffalos – armoured amphibious tracked vehicles – and Captain Johnnie Clapton and Captain Peter Cruden took their troops up the steep cliff in the face of German fire. Though the enemy had the jump on them, the Commandos quickly outflanked the defences which were then attacked from the rear.

The final climax to what was, even for the Commandos, a daring and brilliantly successful operation, was the seizure intact of the main bridge over the Elbe–Trave canal – and the capture of the demolition party who were just about to blow it up.

By the end of April all opposition in the area had been overcome, and the Brigade pushed on to the Baltic, arriving at Neustadt in the first weeks of May. On 4 May Field-Marshal Montgomery accepted the surrender of the German Armies on Luneburg Heath. On 7 May the war in Europe was over.

Amongst No. 6 Commando there was much jubilation and endless celebration. Ryan missed out on most of this; suddenly he felt very tired and old and cold. He crept away to bed where he slept for a week.

6
Civilian life

On his return from Germany, Ryan, now weighing 14 stone, was posted to take command of Pycombe rifle ranges on the downs near Brighton. This suited his purpose admirably for he was able to lease the stables which he had used before the war at Hawkhurst Court near Wisborough Green. He gathered together a string of half a dozen horses which he trained in the early morning before his not too arduous duties at the ranges began.

Then, in November 1945, Ryan made the transition from Commando captain to racehorse trainer. He travelled to Guildford to collect his gratuity and his demob suit. The following month he saddled his first postwar runners at Windsor. Hours were spent preparing the two horses for public view – the standard of turnout was probably more in keeping with Olympia than the racecourse. Leafy and Money Glass were groomed, plaited and polished until they shone. Money Glass was the first to run and fell in the novice chase. Leafy fared a little better but finished tailed off in the novice hurdle. He subsequently received the accolade of *Chaseform*'s expert paddock judge: 'Looked well.'

It was a start, and Ryan reasoned that if his horses continued to be noticed in the paddock sooner or later someone would send him their horses to train. Impeccable turnout has always been the hallmark of the Captain and in later years awards to lads for turnout were won with embarrassing regularity.

In December Ryan took his eight-year-old chaser Blue Steel to Fontwell but, to his acute disappointment, the gelding fell at the second fence. However Blue Steel ran second at Fontwell in February and later in the month finished third at Windsor. Ryan's friend Tony

Ryan on the Downs. He rode out every day of his life

Dorothy Price, a calming influence on a tempestuous character

Ryan with his old campaigners, Le Vermontois (left) and Persian Lancer

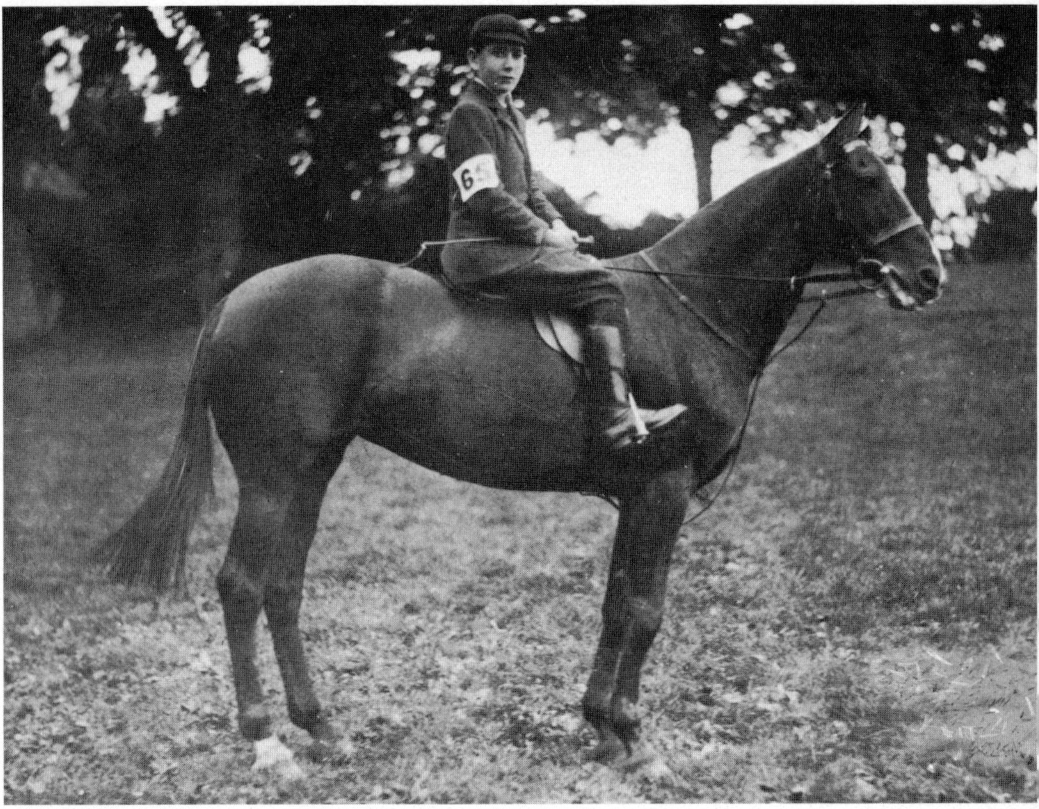

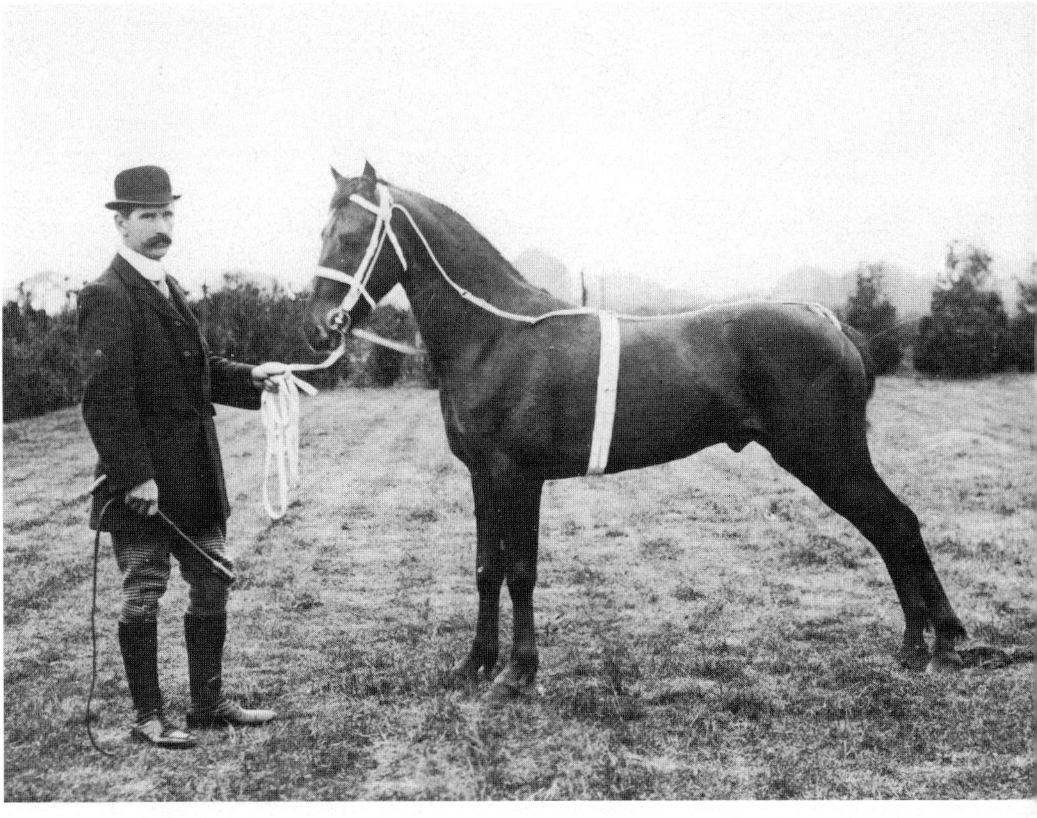

Opposite page above Ryan, aged thirteen, on a pony called Bunty

Opposite page below Ryan's father, George Penry Price, with a Hackney

Left Ryan in Commando uniform

Below Ryan, seated on Field-Marshal Montgomery's right, with his Commando troop at Monty's headquarters in Normandy

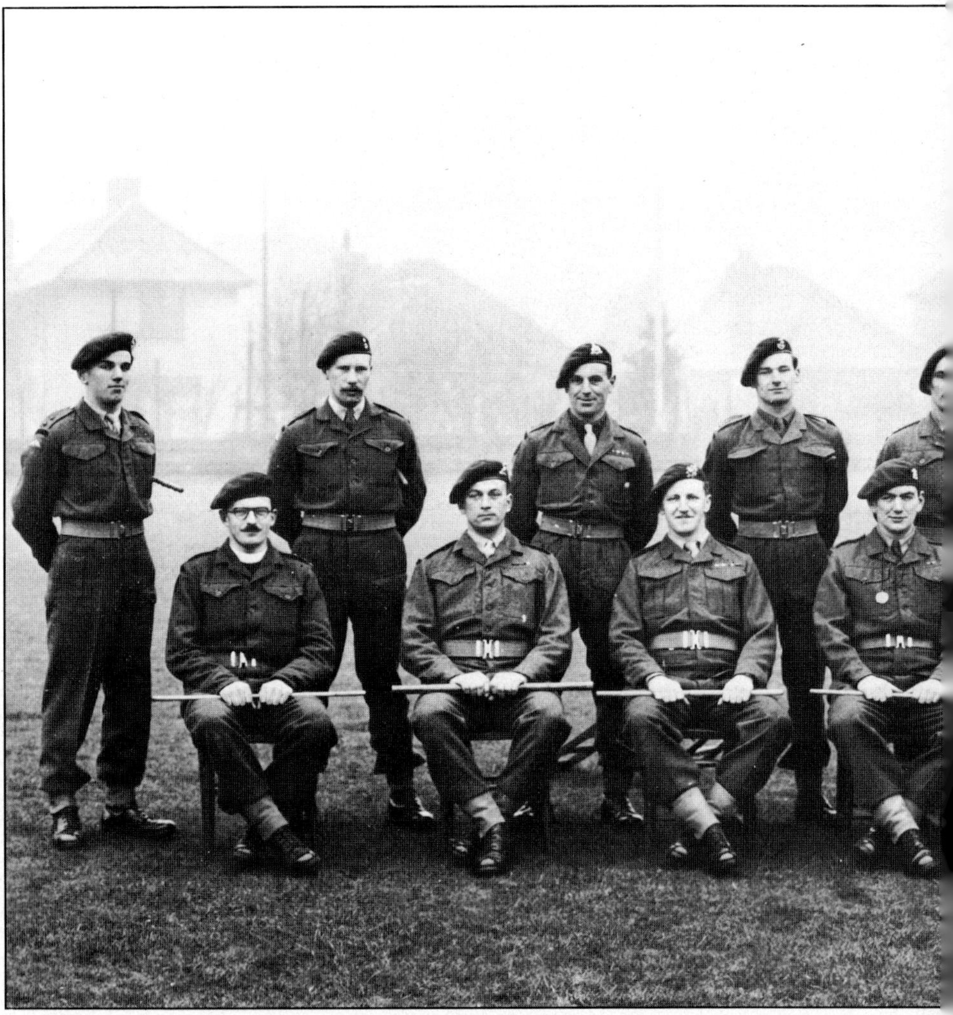

The Officers of No. 6 Commando at Shoreham in January 1945. Ryan, the Adjutant, is seated on the CO's left. Peter Cruden is standing second from left

Wedding day at sister Sheila's house at Wisborough Green. The Chiddingfold and Leconfield hounds came for the reception and the huntsman blew 'gone away'

The Downs and stables from the air. The bungalow that Ryan and Dorothy built is in the near foreground triangle

Ryan riding Wicklow Granite

The Price family well mounted. Anne on the left with Joe, flanked by Dorothy and Ryan

Above In bad weather Ryan took his jumpers to the seaside. Clair Soleil (left), ridden by Tommy Winters, leads a stablemate ridden by Ron James

Opposite page above Gerry Judd leads Clair Soleil through a crowded gangway after winning the Champion Hurdle at Cheltenham

Opposite page below Clair Soleil leading the Irish hurdler Stroller at the last flight before winning the Champion Hurdle. Ryan Price versus Vincent O'Brien with Ryan coming out on top on this occasion

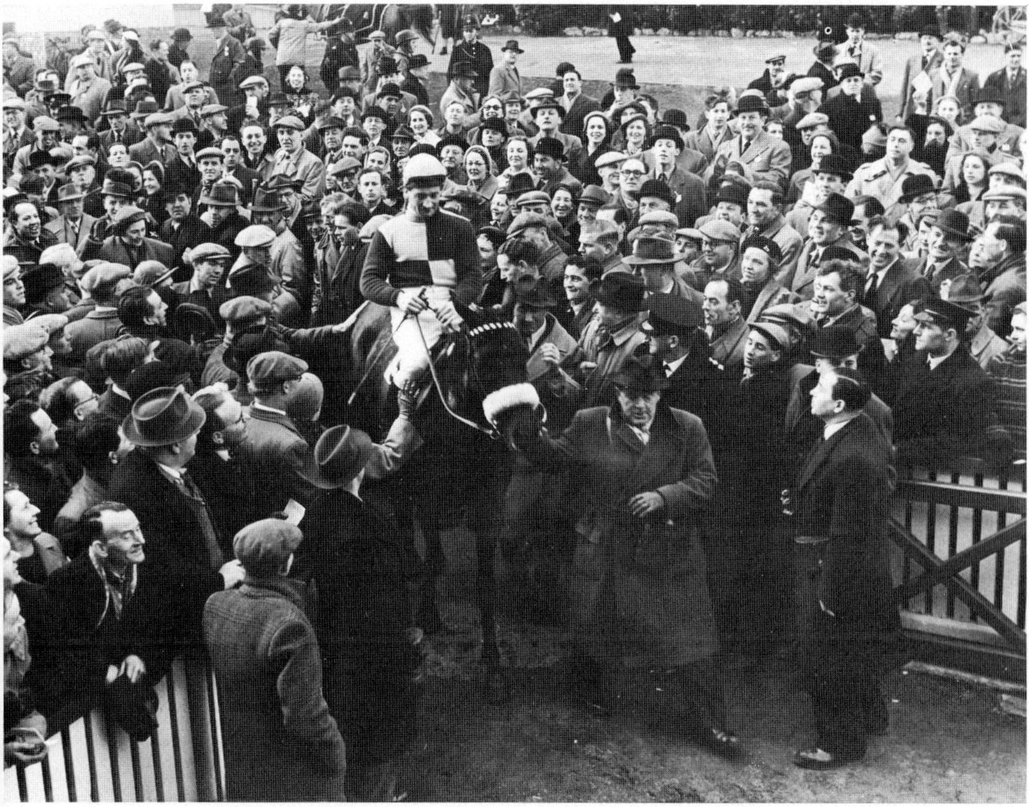

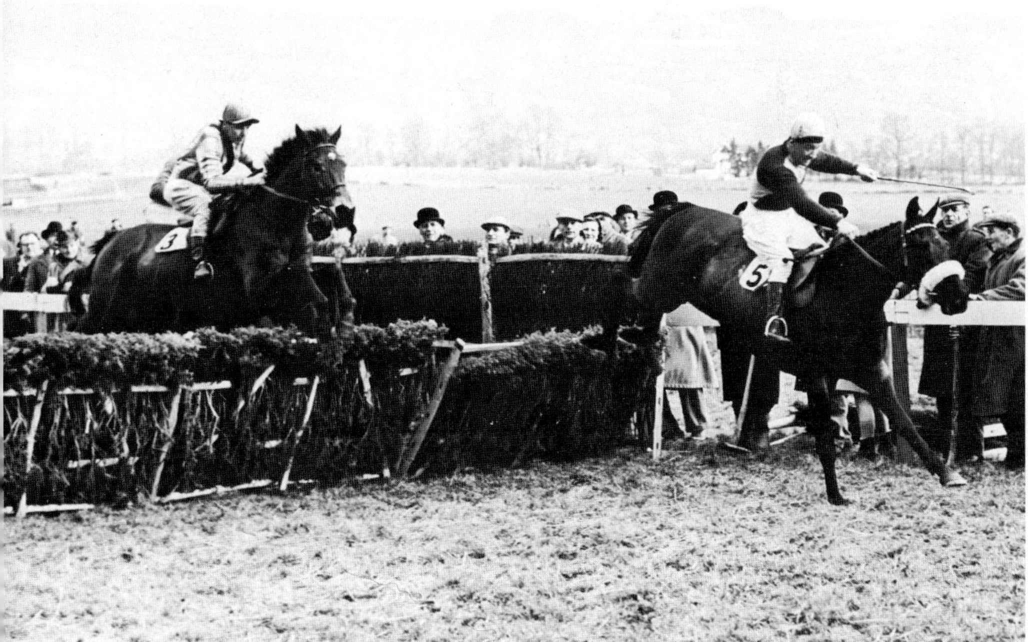
3
5

Left Frederick Thomas Winter with H.R.P. – a successful sixteen-year partnership

Opposite page above Ryan's second Champion Hurdle winner, Dr B. N. Pajgar's Eborneezer, taking the last flight

Opposite page below Kilmore after winning the Grand National. Fred Winter with Ryan at the horse's head, Snowy Davis (behind camera), Tim Fitzgeorge-Parker (centre)

Below Kilmore is paraded through Findon village after winning the Grand National. Iris Bull, his devoted 'lad', is leading Kilmore

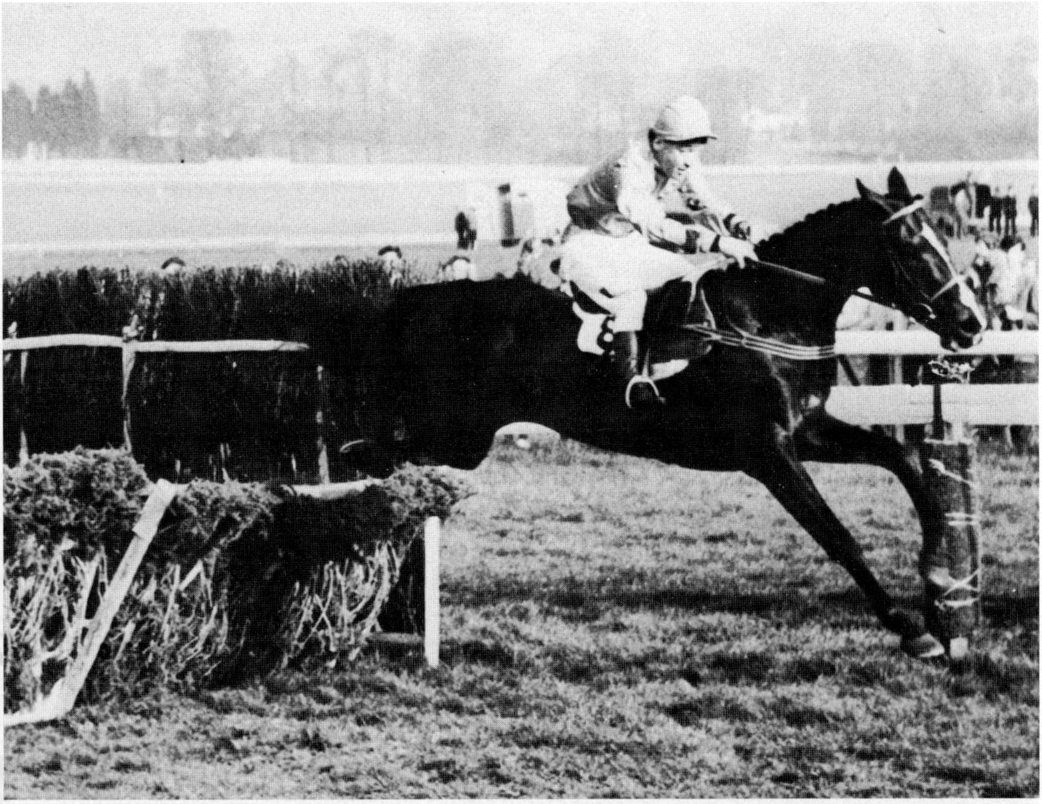

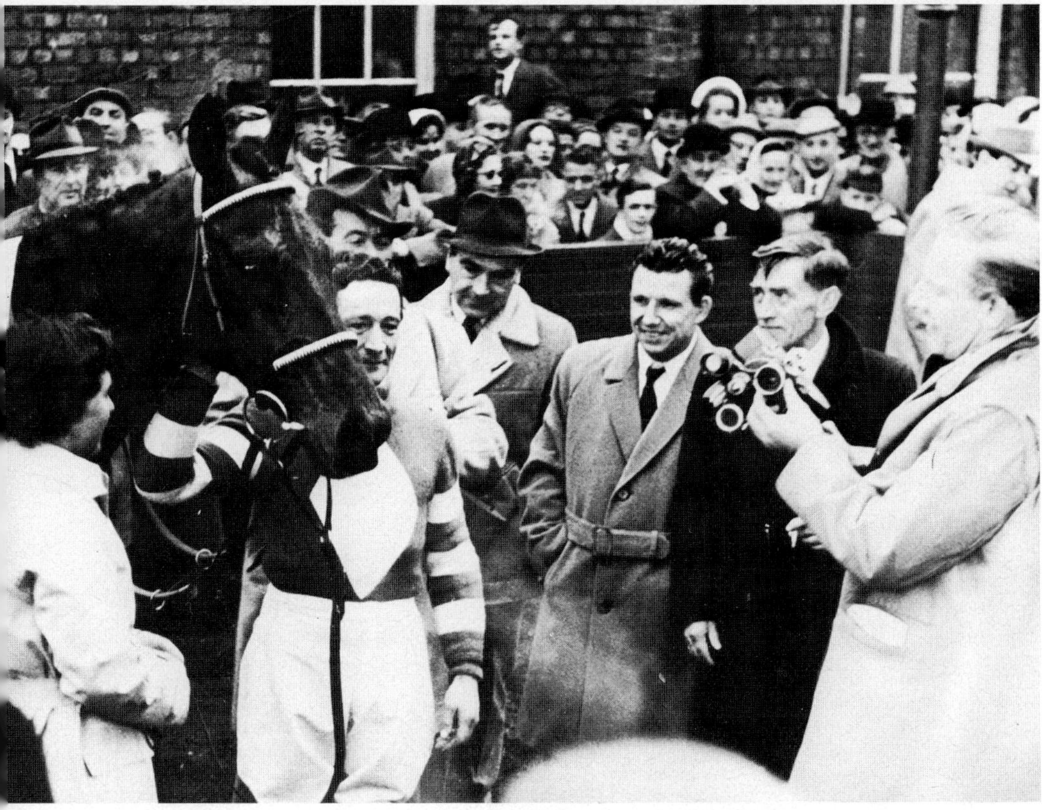

H.R.P. with Josh Gifford

One of the best-selling platers, Sir d'Orient, winning at Newbury with Réné Emery up

Grantham rode the horse in the National Hunt Steeplechase at the Cheltenham Festival Meeting but although they were up with the leaders for a circuit, Blue Steel fell at halfway. Once again Ryan's runner was magnificently turned out, but his first winner was proving elusive.

One day in March Ryan was driving his noisy sports car down the main street of Midhurst when he spotted a tall, slim girl wearing jodhpurs. He screeched to a halt and said hello. Ryan did not recognize the girl whom he had already met before the war when she had been at school with his sisters Lynkie and Sheila in Chichester. Her name was Dorothy Dale and she now experienced a bad case of heart flutter on seeing Ryan again, for she had been smitten as a seventeen-year-old the first time she had been introduced to him. She had served in the WAAF during the war but was now living with her parents in Midhurst.

Ryan whisked her away to have tea with his sister Sheila and in no time at all he announced that he was going to marry Dorothy. Sheila had her reservations: Dorothy was undoubtedly devastatingly attractive, but knowing Ryan as she does Sheila admits that she never thought that the attraction would last.

Events now moved rapidly. Ryan obtained a special licence at Chichester and he and Dorothy were married at Midhurst on 25 March 1946. It had been a whirlwind courtship but the honeymoon was hardly glamorous. Ryan was living in the hotel at Petworth and the morning after the wedding the couple rose at 6 a.m.; at 6.30 Dorothy was riding out with the string from Hawkhurst Court.

Dorothy found Ryan's paper work in complete chaos. She spent the next few weeks attempting to sort out owners' bills from race entries and all the other letters. Thereafter she became the acting and unpaid secretary. Ryan rarely wrote letters, preferring to conduct his business by long, involved telephone calls after which neither party could ever remember what had been decided! When he went to the West Country with a string of horses and was away from the stables for a week, he did however write one letter consisting of one page. That, as far as Dorothy can remember, was the only time that he ever committed anything to paper.

Shortly after their marriage, Ryan took Dorothy over to meet an old friend of his, Bill Scrimgeour, who on leaving the army had gone to live by the sea at Selsey. When Ryan's car drew up Bill was trimming his hedge.

'Bill, I want you to meet my wife,' said Ryan. Bill Scrimgeour, who in later years in his efforts to protect Ryan from difficult owners, inquisitive press and punters, majored in the fine art of being calculatingly rude, now showed his unrevealed talent. Bill thought that Ryan was pulling his leg and was now showing off another girlfriend. He hardly bothered to say hello and carried on trimming the hedge muttering, 'Wife, my foot.' Dorothy inquired of Ryan if all his friends were as rude as that man. Ryan was acutely embarrassed.

Later in the day, when Bill had checked that Ryan was indeed married, he went round to see the couple in order to apologize. Since then Bill has more than made up for that lapse in manners for it was entirely through his business sense that Ryan became financially independent and he helped to make a highly successful venture out of Ryan's undoubted skill with horses.

In April 1946 Ryan was very disappointed with his own progress. It seemed unlikely that he would have a single winner. He had just one horse that might possibly land a modest seller – Broken Tackle, now a ten-year-old with very bad tendons. Up to April he had run six times without gaining a place, but Ryan had now managed to get him fit enough to win.

The target was the seller at Wye and so Ryan borrowed £300 to back the horse. Tony Grantham was to ride for the gamble. On Monday, 6 May, the horsebox duly set off for Wye races. Ryan and Dorothy followed in the car but on the way it broke down and by the time Ryan had organized a lift the deadline for the declaration of the horse to run had passed. It turned out to be a kindly act of fate, though Ryan did not think so at the time. The Tonbridge Selling Chase, with Broken Tackle a non-runner, was easily won by the odds-on favourite Santac, trained by John Goldsmith and heavily backed by his connections. Ryan felt that Broken Tackle would have stood no chance of beating Santac, so he saved his money.

The next opportunity for Broken Tackle was a selling handicap chase at Plumpton on 18 May. This time Ryan arrived on the course early and, with Tony Grantham riding, Broken Tackle won by six lengths at 3–1. At the subsequent auction Ryan was able to buy the gelding in for 150 guineas. It was certainly training on the bread line for the prize money amounted to just £137. The important thing was that Ryan had broken the postwar ice. Not only was Broken Tackle his first winner of the season, he was his *only* winner. He wondered what might have happened if the horse had failed to win;

it would certainly have been a hard struggle to get through the summer.

Ryan needed fresh horses and he flew to Ireland to look over some chasers that were on the market. He bought two: the nine-year-old Lexamine and Flying Wind. When he arrived back at Lavant he admitted to Dorothy that he did not have an owner in mind, or the cash to pay for them. It was a situation in which Ryan was frequently to find himself during the next thirty years. Then quite by chance Ryan was introduced to Gerry Judd, a wealthy company director who lived in Sussex and was very keen on racing. Within a few minutes he had succeeded in selling both his Irish purchases to Judd, who eventually became his most important owner.

In August Ryan saddled Roman Flight to win at Buckfastleigh and the following month Lexamine won for his new owner at nearby Fontwell Park.

Ryan had been looking around for another stables and the opportunity came when the owner of Manor Farm at Lavant agreed to lease him the stables, yard and barn. Ryan accepted, but this was to be the start of hard living.

7
Early Days at Lavant

The very first winner that Ryan sent out from Lavant was Mr Jack Puttick's mare Slender, bought from Tom Grantham and ridden on this occasion by Tom's son Tony. Slender was a flighty mare and very few people could ride her although she did accept Dorothy who rode her out with the string every day. Slender ran fifty-five times over six seasons, won eleven races and was placed on twenty-two occasions.

By now Ryan and Dorothy had left the hotel at Petworth and moved to a caravan parked in the stable yard at Lavant. Here Dorothy not only rode work in the morning, fed the lads and did the secretarial work, but she also drove the horsebox.

The winter of 1946–47 was no time to be living in a caravan; once the snow came towards the end of January the freeze-up was total and there was no racing until March. Ryan used to take the horses in the horsebox generously given as a wedding present by Dorothy's father, to work on the sands at West Wittering and so managed to keep the string reasonably fit.

It is a well-known fact that the residents of the south coast enjoy an extremely mild climate. Often the area basks in sunshine while the rest of the country is enveloped in cloud. The winters are milder and this gave Ryan a considerable advantage training for National Hunt racing on the South Downs, first at Lavant and later at Findon. Even so, when racing did resume, there were only two more winners to add to the five races won before the big freeze-up. Ryan ended the season winning seven races worth £862. It was difficult to win even at the more humble local courses such as Wye, Folkestone, Plumpton and Fontwell. In those days there was not nearly so much National

Hunt racing as there is now, which meant that the big stables could almost totally dominate the small tracks; it was extremely hard for the trainer of moderate horses.

After two seasons, Ryan's tally of eight winners did not seem the kind of start he had in mind when he left the army. He was still unknown and his entry into the ranks of trainers hardly caused a stir amongst the giants of the game who were, at that time, Fulke Walwyn, George Beeby, Reg Hobbs, Tom Rimell, Gerry Wilson, Peter Cazalet and Vic Smyth.

In the summer of 1947 Bill Scrimgeour became involved as an owner: he bought the ex-point-to-pointer Tasman from Mrs Withers. Bill had intended to go to live in South Africa, but he had become bitten by the racing bug and now, with a horse in the stable, he bought a caravan and moved in among the 'wigwams' in the yard at Lavant. He immediately placed the stable on a businesslike footing. His presence relieved Dorothy of a good deal of the secretarial work and his business acumen seemed to have a miraculous effect on the slow payers of training fees. Furthermore, he had some excellent contacts and brought in several new owners.

In September the circus went to the West Country and Ryan ran a plater called Bennett's Hill in the seller. Just as the field came under starter's orders, Ryan casually informed Bill that he had backed the horse for him and that Bill had £100 on the nose. Bill was horror-struck; he had never had more than a tenner on a horse in his life. With a great deal of vocal encouragement, the horse duly obliged, and Ryan retained him at the subsequent auction for 225 guineas. Later Ryan handed Bill £350 in crinkly white fivers and said, 'Well done, Bill. Bennett's Hill now belongs to you.'

Life among the wigwams was hectic, strenuous, but never dull. In the 1947 edition of *Horses in Training*, Ryan was listed as having sixteen horses and one two-year-old in his care. They were only platers – moderate horses – but they were afforded the kind of attention more usually given to Classic three-year-olds in a fashionable yard. Ryan put his heart and soul into training them and gradually his efforts began to be noticed. His staff was small but enthusiastic. Sid Dale was head lad, and Syd Woodman, who lived in Lavant, was full-time horsebox driver (he now holds a trainer's licence of his own).

In the autumn of 1947 Ryan decided to strike early. In the West Country, a little four-year-old mare called Nobby's Pet gave him a tremendous start; owned by the brothers Bob and Percy Clark, fruit farmers from Horsham, and ridden by Peter Woods, the mare won five races in three weeks. Later in the season, she won a handicap at Fontwell and was returned at 25 to 1.

Ryan once again went shopping in Ireland. He came back with the eight-year-old Offaly Prince, which he bought on behalf of Gerry Judd. In November the horse ran extremely well at Wincanton to finish fourth, and Ryan now laid the gelding out for a coup on Boxing Day. Offaly Prince won a handicap chase at Wincanton, starting at 3 to 1. The following day Tasman won the novice chase at 5 to 4 favourite. Both were ridden by the amateur rider, Mr 'Tubby' Parker. It was the first time that Ryan had laid out horses for specific races and all his owners profited from the double.

In March 1948 Ryan took three of his string up to Liverpool to run in the Grand National. Serpentine, ridden by Cyril Mitchell, got no farther than the first fence, and the ex-Irish gelding Bora's Cottage, ridden by Ted Vinall, fell at the fourth. Offaly Prince completed the course but was unplaced.

Bora's Cottage was owned by Mrs F. L. Vickerman. She and her husband had horses in training with Vincent O'Brien who won the Cheltenham Gold Cup for them with Cottage Rake on three occasions. Mrs Vickerman sent Bora's Cottage to Ryan on the recommendation of an Irish-born bookmaker, Paddy Kelly.

Ryan next took Bora's Cottage and Tasman to Newport races where the Welsh Grand National was the target. During the night Tasman became cast in his box and Ryan only decided at the last minute to run him. There was very nearly a grand slam, for Tasman came to the final fence lying third, only to fall. Bora's Cottage ridden by Eddie Reavey won at 100 to 8, beating a good horse, Royal Mount, who finished third in the Grand National the following year. The Welsh Grand National was Ryan's most important win so far. It brought £1030 in prize money, more than he had won for his owners in two entire seasons. It was also some compensation for Eddie Reavey, for he had lost a winning chance in the Grand National on Zahia by taking the wrong course.

At the end of the season Ryan had won seventeen races with nine horses, and a total of £3116 in stakes. Success in the Welsh Grand National had put him on the map and through Mrs Vickerman he acquired another valuable owner, Mrs E. J. Lewis, who became one of his staunchest patrons.

In the summer of 1948 Bill Scrimgeour heard through a friend, Cecil Drabble, that a nailing good chaser called Priorit was for sale in France. Ryan flew to Chantilly, liked the horse and bought him on the spot for £4000 on behalf of Bill and Gerry Judd. The cost was an absolute fortune for a chaser in those days, but Priorit had class, and it was hoped he would turn out to be up to Gold Cup standard. It was the most significant purchase of the season.

The first race in England for Priorit was the King George VI Chase at Kempton Park on Boxing Day. He raced effortlessly with the leaders for two miles but dropped back at the fourteenth fence; out of contention his jockey, Vince Mooney, pulled him up before the straight. The race was won by Mr F. L. Vickerman's Cottage Rake, trained by Vincent O'Brien. Ryan was bitterly disappointed with the horse's running, but Mooney reported that Priorit had failed to stay – he was simply a two-miler.

For Priorit's next races Ryan engaged one of the greatest jockeys ever, his old friend from Yorkshire days, Bryan Marshall. With orders to hold the horse up Bryan rode him at Lingfield where for a moment it seemed that they might win, but Priorit faded over the last two fences. In March 1949 Priorit returned to Lingfield and, again ridden by Bryan, he ran a good deal better to finish third.

Priorit's next race was the Gratwick Blagrave Memorial Chase at Cheltenham. Once again Bryan was approached to ride, but he was claimed by his stable as jockey for the promising Oliver Twist for Miss Dorothy Paget. He warned Ryan, 'You can't possibly beat me. Don't take on Oliver Twist.'

However, Ryan was not to be deterred. He felt that Priorit had now become acclimatized and had improved physically since his Lingfield races. He therefore engaged another brilliant Irish jockey, Martin Molony. On 11 April, Priorit – a springer in the market, he was backed from 5 to 1 down to 7 to 2 – won by a length from Unconditional Surrender with Oliver Twist two lengths away third. The prize money amounted to a mere £342, but both Gerry Judd and Bill Scrimgeour had gone for a good touch which helped to pay for their expensive purchase.

Priorit was Ryan's first winner at Cheltenham and this achievement against top-class two-milers vindicated his judgement in paying such a steep price for the French chaser. In those days there were very few outlets for two-mile chasers other than the run-of-the-mill handicaps; sponsorship had not yet arrived and the only hope that an owner had of recouping the cost of an expensive horse was through gambling.

After the race Ryan was in his element; he loved winning and enjoyed this particular moment because he knew that the connections had both backed the horse – Bill had a monkey on and Gerry Judd considerably more. Ryan had got his owners out; they now had a free horse. Ryan himself was not involved in the betting; his part was the preparation of the horse – he left the gambling to the gamblers.

The press surrounded Judd like flies round a honey pot. Judd, always indiscreet, was telling the journalists what a killing he had made. Suddenly the mood outside the weighing room changed. The stewards' secretary told Ryan that the stewards wished to see him. Ryan felt the cold atmosphere the moment that he was ushered into their presence. The official handicapper, Mr Dan Sheppard, was thumbing through his form book. The stewards – Mr Clive, Mr Fred Withington, Mr Stanley Howard and Colonel Gresson – asked Ryan to explain the improvement shown by Priorit between his failure at Lingfield and his win in the Gratwick Blagrave.

At Cheltenham Priorit had beaten two of the horses that had finished in front of him at Lingfield. At Lingfield Hypernod had given Priorit an 11-pound beating. At Cheltenham Priorit, on 10 pounds better terms, had reversed the form with Hypernod and had now beaten him by thirteen lengths. This was a turnaround of 20 pounds and accounted for the presence of the handicapper.

Ryan explained that the horse had taken a long time to acclimatize since coming from France but that the colt had improved physically since his Lingfield race in March. He had run his race out gamely enough at Lingfield but his jockey that day had reported that the horse was all at sea on the very holding going. Here, on good going, the horse had been able to use his superb action. The stewards then heard evidence from Bryan Marshall and Martin Molony who had ridden in both races. Ryan was recalled and the stewards informed him that they did not accept his explanation and cautioned him as to the future running of his horses.

On his way to the car Ryan noted ruefully that in the previous race there had been another reversal of form. In the Holman Cup a horse called Inverlochy, ridden by Martin Molony, had beaten Jack Tatters, the favourite, by a neck, yet only twenty-four days before the two horses had run against each other at Sandown with a very different result. On that occasion Jack Tatters had won, with Inverlochy unplaced, fifteen lengths behind the winner. At Cheltenham on only 3 pounds better terms Inverlochy had now beaten Jack Tatters. The going was the same for both races. Ryan felt that there was probably a perfectly innocent explanation in this particular case, but Inverlochy's trainer was not called to answer for it.

It was clear that Ryan was being watched. He suddenly realized that he was under the stewards' closest scrutiny. It was through a combination of circumstances. First, there was a clash of personalities: Ryan's whole attitude challenged the autocratic control of the stewards. Ryan was a character, fast becoming a personality, who could be guaranteed to give the press plenty of copy. He was outspoken and arrogant to the officials. Trainers were supposed to be subservient and respectful; they were, after all, paid servants of the owners, but this one seemed to be running the show.

The stewards did not like gambling stables or gambling owners and Gerry Judd's indiscretions had done little to help Ryan's cause. Ryan had now been warned that his horses were being noticed; however, he left Cheltenham with a perfectly clear conscience. He had broken no rules of racing, he had landed the goods for his owners and now he had another commission from Judd to go to France to buy another Priorit.

Ryan had another tilt at the Grand National that season but it was an ill-starred venture. Bora's Cottage fell at the eleventh fence and was killed, and Ryan's other runner, Offaly Prince, came down at Valentine's Brook. The loss of Bora's Cottage was a bitter pill to swallow and it affected everyone at Lavant.

Ryan started the 1949–50 season with seventeen horses, but Priorit was the only star. It was decided to try to win first time out with him at Doncaster in November, but Priorit, ridden by Martin Molony, was beaten into second place and on the way home Ryan's car broke down. When he reached Findon late that night he learned that Slender had finished first at Wincanton but had been disqualified for failing to draw the weight. Not a day that Ryan remembers with any affection!

He took it philosophically, however, having the extraordinary ability to put both success and failure behind him. In Kipling's words: 'If you can meet with Triumph and Disaster And treat those two imposters just the same.' This exactly sums up Ryan's attitude to the day-to-day rough and tumble of racing's fortunes.

Priorit was launched on a recovery mission at Lingfield in December. Bryan Marshall was the jockey and on the strength of his good race at Doncaster Priorit was a hot favourite to win a modest two-mile handicap. This proved to be a disastrous gamble and had unpleasant repercussions. Bryan found that the horse had no energy and he toiled in fifth, some thirty-five lengths behind the winner, having never given his connections the slightest hope that he would ever take a hand in the finish. When Bryan Marshall reported to Ryan that he had ridden a 'dead' horse, Gerry Judd was furious and charged Bryan with stopping Priorit. Judd stormed off and voiced his opinion to the stewards. Lord Mildmay, who conducted the inquiry, pressed Judd to state exactly what his complaint was. Judd now backed down and admitted that he was disappointed with the way that his horse had run and he had no criticism of the way in which the horse had been ridden.

The Lingfield drama brought home to Ryan the fact that he did not have a retained jockey of his own; now he had more horses of the calibre of Priorit he badly needed one. It was at this most fortunate of moments that Fred Winter entered Ryan's life. Ryan had been friends of the Winter family since before the war and greatly admired Fred Winter senior who was private trainer for Mr James Bartholomew at Southfleet, near Gravesend in Kent. Fred junior was attempting to carve out a career as a National Hunt jockey following his retirement from the army. He had served in the Parachute Regiment and had ridden a few winners, mostly for his father, when he suffered a setback which would have daunted a lesser man. He took a crashing fall at Wye in September 1948 and broke his back. He was out of the saddle for a year but now, with the help of Newmarket trainer George Archibald, he was trying to get going again. It was not easy. Ryan, on the spur of the moment, engaged Fred to ride a moderate horse of his at Taunton on 3 November. Dorothy drove him down but in spite of Fred's considerable efforts the horse, Smoke Piece, was beaten by a neck.

Returning to the unsaddling enclosure, Fred thought that was the last time that he would ride a horse for Ryan's outfit, but Dorothy came home full of praise at the way that Fred had ridden and urged Ryan to use him again whenever possible. A few days later Ryan had her high opinion of Fred confirmed when he won a race at Plumpton on Dick the Gee. Ryan saw all he wanted to see and the following month he offered Fred a retainer to ride for the stable for the rest of the season.

Fred was delighted and he found Ryan efficient and ambitious. 'We both had the same outlook, we both liked winning and we were both at the breakthrough point in our careers. We helped each other along.' So began a partnership that was to last for sixteen years and which was destined to become one of the great jockey–trainer relationships of National Hunt racing.

Fred was able to ride work for his father in Kent and did not have to visit Lavant. He discovered that once he had ridden a horse Ryan rarely gave him orders and this implicit trust gave Fred self-confidence from the start. In the car on the way home from meetings Fred would blame himself for narrow defeats, but Ryan would refuse to discuss such events, saying, 'That was yesterday, forget it.' There were no post mortems and there was no time to celebrate big winners. Ryan's attitude to winning and losing gave Fred a sense of proportion which carried him through sixteen eventful years, during which time he won every important race in the calendar and over 500 winners for the stable. According to Ryan, these included 100 wins that no other jockey would ever have achieved.

There was no written contract and the retainer was renewed by word of mouth each year. Only twice did Ryan express himself dissatisfied with Fred's riding: once when he won the Champion Hurdle on Clair Soleil, and once at Aintree when Fred went to sleep in a hurdle race and finished third. Ryan accused him of riding like an apprentice. One hour later Fred won the Grand National on Sundew. So Fred had the last laugh, but Ryan was the first to congratulate him after the race.

Over the years Ryan kept producing superbly schooled horses for Fred to ride and in this period he was champion jockey four times and Ryan was leading trainer five times. Paradoxically they were never champions in the same year.

At the start of the 1949–50 season Bill Scrimgeour had sold Tasman to George Varnavas, the proprietor of the Elysée Restaurant in Percy Street, a favourite haunt of owners and trainers. Tasman had won his last race in May and he started the new season where he left off and won three races off the reel in the West Country. George Varnavas proved to be an exceptionally lucky owner for Ryan. He later owned Canardeau who won over hurdles and then raced on the flat for nine seasons, winning nineteen races.

It was at this point that the Brighton bookmaker Morry Levy became involved at Lavant through his purchase of Sy Oui out of a seller at Fontwell. Levy asked Ryan to train the horse. The previous trainer, H. Gordon Bowsher, was presumably not too concerned at losing the French-bred colt, as Sy Oui had turned sour and savage. At Lavant Sy Oui responded to gentle treatment, though he did once chase Ryan round the yard. After winning two handicaps, Ryan put Sy Oui in a seller again and at the subsequent auction the colt was bought for 400 guineas by Baron Hatvany, a Hungarian emigré who made a habit of buying horses out of sellers at that time. The baron, a curious, melancholy figure to look at because of his sombre dress, was quite a character. He asked Ryan to keep the horse to train and in no time at all Ryan had charge of the Baron's string of extremely useful hurdlers and chasers, mostly French-bred, which had hitherto been trained by John Goldsmith at Aston Tirrold. In one season Ryan trained thirty winners for the baron, who one day turned up at the stables and presented the head lad with a ten shilling note, 'to share out among the lads who attended to his horses'.

The addition of the baron's horses had stretched Manor Farm stables to the limit. The barn had been adapted to house six more boxes, but Ryan was now having to turn horses away. There was no possibility of building any more boxes and so the only alternative was to find new quarters.

Yet new horses kept arriving from all directions. Sid Dale was one of many to admire Ryan's extraordinary judgement of a horse in the rough. On his travels Ryan would see a horse running wild and something undefinable would make him buy the horse on the spot. On many occasions when Ryan's Follies, as Sid sometimes called them, arrived at Lavant, Sid wondered just what Ryan could possibly have seen in the big wild gangling horses that came roaring out of the horsebox. On one occasion Sid was convinced that Ryan had bought a dud, but this particular gelding, Kantaka, won three races in the space of two months in 1953. And Ryan endured considerable banter when he arrived home with Lucky Dog whom he had rescued from the slaughterhouse. Lucky Dog said thank you by winning a handicap chase at Wye.

Ryan also possessed an uncanny wisdom in finding the key to difficult horses, often pursuing highly unconventional methods either to get the horse to feed, to settle or to work or perhaps simply to stop him eating the lads or the other horses. For instance, Bambi, who won five races, was fed on the lightest possible diet. A small bowl of corn three times a day and barely a strand of hay was all that this gelding received, and yet he thrived.

Sy Oui, though only a pony, was a terror in his box and was always tied up with two rack chains. He had disastrous thoroughpins which Sid Dale used to massage every night. Sy Oui won sixteen chases, more than repaying Sid's patience.

Sid recalls Dorothy's mare, Slender, as being virtually unridable. But Ryan quickly prescribed a cure. Dorothy was able to ride Slender round in a headcollar.

In April 1950 Ryan saddled his first National Hunt Festival winner when Slender dead-heated for the Mildmay of Flete Challenge Cup.

8
Downs House

During the summer break, Ryan went on expeditions along the South Downs to try to find suitable gallops and stables. He visited Michel Grove where P. P. Gilpin had trained. One day he went to the downs above Findon where Bob Gore had sent out Grand National winners Jerry M and Covertcoat in successive years before the First World War. The French ex-jockey Bobby Bates and Harry Davison now trained at Findon and Ryan liked the way the gallops were laid out. During his walk he met a man exercising his dogs. It proved to be a most fortunate meeting. The stranger was none other than Colonel Thynne who actually owned the downs and the gallops. Ryan explained his problem and after a brief discussion he obtained an option on the lease of the gallops.

The next logical step was to acquire the famous Downs House stables and the house which were then occupied by Bobby Bates, once described as the ugliest jockey who ever rode. Events now moved quickly, for Bobby Bates had to give up his licence and the stables became vacant. With help from Gerry Judd, Ryan purchased the stables and the fifty-four acres of paddocks around them. He could not get possession of the house as this was the subject of a legal wrangle, so he built a bungalow on a plot of land just by the stables. The stable buildings were in total disrepair and it took several weeks of working parties from Lavant to get them habitable.

Downs House and the stables had been built a century earlier by Henry Padwick, a local solicitor who had installed William Goater as his private trainer. Assisting Goater as secretary and head lad was no less than John Porter, then only seventeen years old. John Porter stayed ten years at Findon before setting up on his own as a trainer;

he later became one of the most successful of the Victorian trainers, saddling the winners of seven Derbys and sixteen other Classics, and travelled from Findon to Paris with The Ranger who won the first Grand Prix de Paris in 1863. The Derby winner Hermit had also been trained at Findon until just before the race. Fifty years later Bob Gore was to bring further glory to the village by winning the Grand National with Jerry M in 1912 and Covertcoat the following year. Gore remained at Findon until his death in 1941.

After the war Bobby Bates, later to be killed in a horse race in France, sent out a few winners from Downs House, but by this time this once proud establishment had fallen on hard times. The yard had become overgrown with weeds and the buildings were suffering from neglect. Ryan, with Sid Dale and an odd-job man, set to work. Sid recalled that Ryan's impatience to finish the job nearly finished *him*. After hours of back-breaking work, a lunch interval would be taken, but hardly had Sid unwrapped his sandwiches than Ryan would return urging him to start again. Together they laid concrete, paving stones and turf, repaired the broken-down stables, painted the doors of the boxes and removed barrowloads of rubbish. Ryan's energy and capacity for work amazed everyone who worked with him. He was like a demon who never seemed to get tired.

Sid Dale analysed Ryan's ability to get others to work for him: 'Ryan never asked anyone to do anything he could not do himself. He could perform every task, in the stable or out of it, quicker and better than any lad. If a job was not done to his satisfaction the air would be blue with invective and the unfortunate lad would be sent back with his horse until Ryan was satisfied.'

Sid Dale considers that Ryan ran his stable 90 per cent by fear and 10 per cent by example! Yet in spite or because of his refusal to accept anything but the very highest standard he always had staff of the highest calibre. Those that stayed were those who could take it; they stayed for the duration.

It was at this point that Tim Neligan joined the team. He arrived one day to ask permission to take photographs of the horses for a school project. Later, after abandoning a flying career, he was taken on as a pupil assistant trainer, just like John Porter a hundred years before. Tim Neligan witnessed from inside the yard the astonishing rise in the Captain's fortunes once he got to Findon.

After four years Tim left to join ICI and then the Guinness

organization but fifteen years later he returned to racing, first as general manager at Goodwood racecourse and then as chief executive of United Racecourses (Epsom, Kempton Park and Sandown Park). Though Tim Neligan's experience in industry was an enormous help in making him one of the most successful racecourse managers, he will always be grateful for the practical experience that he gained with Ryan. 'Never was so much learned so fast as at Findon in the early fifties.'

By November 1951 the stables were ready and the move from Lavant began. Though Ryan and Dorothy had been extremely happy at John Lock's farm, the living quarters in the caravan were cramped and now they were looking forward to a home of their own. To begin with they lived in the village pub, but at last the bungalow was ready and they moved into a home for the first time since they had been married.

Ryan's string had grown to forty-one and now at long last he had ideal conditions for training jumpers. He was right on the spot, he had paddocks and the famous Findon Downs gallops and schooling grounds, and more than enough loose boxes.

The locals were sceptical; Ryan was just a bit too flamboyant for their taste and he certainly did not measure up to Bob Gore who was a local folk hero. Ryan took off his coat and with that incredible restless energy drove his staff to the point of exhaustion. With Fred Winter as the stable jockey, they answered the locals in no small measure, for Ryan sent out fifty-nine winners in his first season at Downs House. The breakthrough that Ryan had been hoping and working for had at last arrived.

Some very good horses which were to be the foundation of his success at Findon came to the yard. In this period, Ryan reflects, he began to attract a different type of owner: the sort of person who did not gamble but owned horses for the sheer love of the sport. Owners like Mrs E. J. Lewis, who brought a chaser called Ur and also sent a mare called The Igloo which came from Gerald Balding's stable. The Igloo was a tearaway who when allowed to run free barely stayed a mile and a half. Ryan taught her to settle and with Fred Winter's riding skill the mare won three-mile chases.

Ryan's success brought his flamboyant personality out into the open. His trade mark was a white mackintosh and a battered trilby hat worn at a rakish angle. His swarthy features were now frequently seen in the winner's enclosure and the press found him a valuable asset. Ryan was now being noticed and he saw to it that people continued to notice both him and his horses. His habit of leading his horses out of the paddock and onto the course immediately aroused interest. One racegoer after closely observing this at one race meeting said, 'Ryan Price may not be crooked, I just don't know, but my goodness he *looks* crooked.' With a patch over one eye and a spotted handkerchief instead of the battered felt hat, he would have looked like a pirate about to plunder on the Spanish Main.

However, Ryan's plundering areas were still Fontwell, Plumpton Wye and Folkestone. He was never afraid to stoop to humble sellers and even allowing for the state of the pound in the 1950s he managed to buy in some of his selling plate winners for 'pennies'. He encouraged the belief that his horses had been the subject of hefty gambles, and although this brought a constant stream of new owners, it did make for trouble ahead with the stewards, who also began to take note of the flow of winners from Findon.

Many of Ryan's charges were French bred, a good number from John Goldsmith who had bought the Hatvany string in France, but some of his most successful hurdlers came from English stables and had been bought for a few hundred pounds. Ryan enjoyed a lifelong friendship with Doug Smith who was married to Fred Winter's sister, Pat. Following Doug's advice, Ryan bought Carrickbay for £350 from Dick Peacock. Another cheap purchase was Creek, which he bought from Arthur Budgett for £55. Creek went on to win sixteen races. Another top class hurdler, Campari, was bought privately from Sir William Cooke for £100.

One of the most successful money spinners was the selling plater Sir d'Orient. George Todd found out just how good he was when he took on Ryan's French-bred horse in a seller at Newbury. George, always patient, had engineered a tremendous gamble, but Sir d'Orient toyed with the Todd 'hot pot' even with 12 stone 7 pounds on his back and ran away from him.

Sir d'Orient was one of the greatest characters that Ryan ever trained; he was volatile and savage with other horses, he hated being near them and often tried to take lumps out of them. The other jockeys were terrified of him, not without reason, for if another runner came too close, Sir d'Orient would fasten his teeth on to the other horse's neck; he had actually jumped hurdles in that position. Réné Emery, who rode him so masterfully, exploited the situation and used to line up on the inside of the course. All the other runners would crowd over to the outside, leaving Réné and Sir d'Orient the track to themselves. Later Sir d'Orient ran his races in a muzzle.

The lad who had the unenviable task of looking after this wild horse was 'Ginger' Capelin – later to become Guy Harwood's travelling head lad. Ginger specialized in handling difficult horses for he also 'did' Sy Oui. Whenever he entered Sir d'Orient's box Ginger would throw a sack stuffed with straw on the floor. While Sir d'Orient was down on his knees savaging this sudden intruder, Ginger would catch him by the headcollar and chain him up.

Before he was saddled Sir d'Orient used to roar like a lion which helped to put off any likely purchasers at the subsequent auction. Usually he was led out without even a bid. At home he was an exciting ride. He would rear up on his hind legs and then proceed to walk the whole way across the paddock like a circus horse. Never once did he fall over backwards. Then, having made his point, he would go off with the string like an old hack. He needed lots of work and Ryan ran him frequently. Eventually he lost him in a seller, but, trained by Tom Gates, the old horse went on to win many more sellers. In a career that had begun on the flat in France, Sir d'Orient won $37\frac{1}{2}$ races. He even won a steeplechase.

It was through his contact in France, Colonel Bobinski, that Ryan heard of a high-class French hurdler which was for sale. This was Clair Soleil, who had won over hurdles in France and was due to contest the Triumph Hurdle at Hurst Park. Baron Hatvany had agreed to buy the four-year-old for £5000, but during Cheltenham week Ryan learned from France that the baron had not paid the money over. Dining with Gerry Judd at the Plough Hotel, Ryan expressed his concern that he was going to lose the horse, as the Triumph was due to be run on the Saturday. Judd agreed to buy the horse, so Ryan made arrangements to see Clair Soleil work at Hurst Park racecourse. He drove over in the early morning and watched this all-quality black horse, ridden by the French jockey. He was markedly impressed.

Ryan asked to see the horse school over a couple of flights of hurdles. Looking back on the incident Ryan recalled, 'They could not get the horse near the hurdle, let alone close enough to jump it.' It was a complete disaster, but he had been reassured by the horse's appearance that here was a high-class hurdler of enormous potential. Over breakfast Ryan made up his mind to have him and telephoned Judd to report that all was well. The cheque was sent and Fred

Winter was engaged to ride, though a special contingency of £500 pounds was agreed with the French jockey who was to have ridden him. Nothing was said about the attempt to school him.

Ryan ordered Fred to wait with the horse and to make his challenge from behind, one of the few occasions that Fred was ever given specific orders; Gerry Judd was ordered to have a monkey on at 10 to 1.

A high-class field turned out for the Triumph and the hot favourite was the French-bred Otari owned by Mr Maurice Kingsley, who also owned the Champion Hurdler Sir Ken, trained by Willie Stephenson. Riding Clair Soleil for the first time, Fred Winter was impressed with his action going to the post. However, at the start, while the runners were having their girths attended to, Clair Soleil suddenly took a dive at Otari and fastened his teeth onto Tim Molony's boot. Fred pulled his horse off but it was an unorthodox way of sorting out the opposition!

Hurst Park was a very sharp turning course, and going the shortest way, on the inside at the bend by the grandstand, Fred found he was being squeezed for room as the field bunched over towards the rails. Clair Soleil resented this and immediately began to savage the horse on his inside, burying his teeth in the other horse's neck. Again Fred managed to pull his horse off, wondering if they had ever fed this brute.

Now Fred Winter is a quiet, gentle man, the sort of person who loves children and is kind to old ladies. However, every once in a while, when he was riding, he had been known to 'lose his wool' and in such cases other jockeys kept out of the way, feeling a degree of sympathy for the horse under Fred. This was one of these occasions. Fred got really mad with Ryan's recent expensive purchase and he now sat down, gritted his teeth and, carefully keeping Clair Soleil away from the other horses, he proceeded to give him the hardest ride that he had ever given a horse. Out of the window went the orders to wait and Fred got Clair Soleil stoked up fully a mile from home.

'He wouldn't have won if I hadn't got at him,' said Fred years later. 'He was as tough as they come and he stayed for ever and every time that I asked for some more he gave it. He was a very brave horse and I eventually became very fond of him, but that day I hated him.'

As the leaders came to the last flight Tim Molony on Otari was in the lead and, with his nearest rival Clair Soleil still under the strongest pressure, Otari's owner and trainer thought that they had the race in the bag. Before anything had reached the post they both rushed down from the stand to greet their winner in the unsaddling enclosure. They really should have stayed in their seats, though it is doubtful if either would have enjoyed watching the finish as much as Ryan and Gerry Judd, for Fred Winter was enacting a scene that was to become a regular feature of the partnership. With his body and arms swinging in a rhythm that built up to a crescendo, Fred was extracting the last ounce from Clair Soleil. It was a combination of strength, fitness and sheer determination that forced Clair Soleil past Otari to win by threequarters of a length.

Willie Stephenson was all smiles in the winner's enclosure as the horses returned to scale, that is until Ryan appeared. 'Move over Willie, you belong in the second's place. We won the race.'

Willie Stephenson and Maurice Kingsley were absolutely shattered until Tim Molony confirmed that he had only finished second. Ryan thoroughly enjoyed this moment. He considers that Clair Soleil was the best hurdler that he has ever trained and Fred Winter confirms that opinion. Yet they both had considerable disagreements over the best way to ride the horse. One of the few rows that developed between them was over Clair Soleil, but after Fred's masterful ride in the Triumph no one could deny that he had ridden an epic race.

To Ryan's immense satisfaction Fred ended the 1952–53 season as champion National Hunt jockey with 121 winners, a record that was to stand for twenty-five years. Fred became the first jockey to ride a hundred winners since Fred Rees in 1924. Though the lion's share of his total was on Findon horses, Fred was much in demand with other stables.

For Ryan it had been a tremendously rewarding season: he saddled seventy-eight winners, netting £15,358, yet he was relegated into second place on the trainers' list by the quiet man from Tipperary, Vincent O'Brien. Vincent sent out only four winning horses over here, but they won five important races, Early Mist winning the Grand National and Knock Hard taking the Gold Cup. O'Brien beat Ryan's total in stakes by £157.

9
The Golden Days of Findon

Ryan saddled his first flat race winner, the ten-year-old Fala, at the Newbury meeting in April 1953. Owned by Mr Maurice Ostrer and ridden by Gordon Richards, Fala started favourite and won a two-mile seller.

On the same day Clair Soleil, ridden by Charlie Smirke, ran unplaced in the John Porter Stakes. Ryan also entered Clair Soleil for the Goodwood Cup. The horse ran disappointingly, but on the final day of the season Nuage Dore won at Lingfield.

The 1953–54 National Hunt season began with the customary raid on Newton Abbot in August. Ryan took down a string of six horses. Their turnout was exceptional and the Price early morning workout on the racecourse was well worth watching. Wearing his white mackintosh, Ryan controlled the exercise with military precision.

Yet the season started catastrophically for Fred Winter, who was riding Cent Francs, the favourite in the first race. This French-bred horse, which had been bought out of a seller at the end of the previous season, fell at the first fence. The race continued, but an uneasy hush settled over the grandstand as the racecourse ambulance made its way to where Fred lay motionless. Ryan beat the ambulance, but one look at the shape of Fred's leg in the boot told him everything. Fred had a compound fracture, and was whisked away to London for a grafting operation on the shattered bones. Complications set in, however, and the accident took a full year out of Fred's racing life. It was nine years before the leg was completely healed. Ryan was fortunate to be able to call on the services of the French-born jockey René Emery, who took Fred's place and rode with great dash and skill.

All in all, it was rather a disappointing season, during which Baron Hatvany removed his horses and sent them to be trained by Fred Rimell. Ryan took their departure philosophically, having always felt that the baron was too erratic to remain with him long.

As one owner left the stable, so another moved in. Nat Cohen, the film producer, had a horse called Alfarasio in training with John de Moraville at Childrey in Berkshire. Nat asked Ryan to take the horse to see if he was any good. So Alfarasio moved to Findon. His previous trainer had questioned the little gelding's courage, but the change of air seemed to suit him. At Folkestone, with Réné Emery riding, he won over fences, and thus began a long, prosperous and eventful association between Ryan and Nat Cohen and his partners in the motion picture business.

In the summer of 1954 Sid Dale, Ryan's head lad, left to start training on his own at Worthing. George Winders took his place.

Before the start of the new season, word spread round the yard that Fred Winter was back. He arrived, limping heavily, to ride work early one morning. He had spent the spring and early summer at his father's stables at Southfleet, desperately fighting a heroic battle to get fit enough to ride, and now, in the blazing July heat, on firm ground at Newton Abbot, he took up the reins again. Weighing out for the first race, he was riding the favourite, Fatum, conscious that many eyes were upon him and that many people were no doubt wondering if he had lost his nerve.

He wanted to win that first race and he nearly succeeded, but Fatum pecked on landing over the last flight and the pair went down by half a length. In the second race Réné Emery won the handicap chase on Alfarasio and then in the third race to everyone's delight Fred had his winner. He drove Triple A home to win the seller. Later in the afternoon he was beaten by a head into second place on Feerique. On his first day back after a year's absence he had ridden one winner and two seconds, a most satisfactory return to active service.

In September Fred teamed up with Alfarasio for the first time and in the space of three weeks they won three chases, which greatly helped Fred's morale. Fred was to win seven races on this little horse – no wonder that Alfarasio became one of his favourites.

An incident occurred in the autumn of 1954 that for a time disrupted the smooth owner–trainer–jockey relationship that had developed between Gerry Judd, Ryan and Fred Winter. Judd was now Ryan's most important owner with ten horses in the yard. At Fontwell on 14 September Fred rode the French gelding Nid d'Abeilles for Judd in a four-year-old hurdle. It was the gelding's first run of the season since arriving from France and though well schooled over hurdles the horse was not completely fit. Ryan informed Judd of this fact and in the paddock gave Fred orders that he was to give the horse an easy race. The favourite was Alto trained by Harry Thompson Jones and ridden by the ace hurdle race jockey Johnny Gilbert; Nid d'Abeilles was second favourite at 9 to 2, the bookmakers going 10 to 1 bar the two. Alto ran a shocking race, jumping atrociously, and eventually finished tailed off. Fred kept lobbing along and, without subjecting his horse to a hard race, won by three parts of a length.

In the unsaddling enclosure Judd, his face as black as thunder, blew his top. 'You will never ride for me again,' he snarled at Fred. Fred was astonished but not unduly disturbed as racing rows are usually of short duration and Judd was clearly 'talking through his pocket'. But the next day Ryan, acutely embarrassed, told Fred that Judd was sticking to his decision and that Réné Emery would ride the Judd horses in future. Fred Winter senior was incensed at this slur on his son. 'How can a jockey get the sack for winning?' he asked Ryan.

Fred junior made an appointment to see Judd at Plumpton races, but nothing came of it. Eventually, on 10 November, Ryan telephoned Fred to tell him that he could ride for Judd again and would he please partner Nid d'Abeilles at Cheltenham the following day. To Ryan's immense relief Fred accepted and in a driving, furious finish was beaten a neck by the 13 to 8 favourite Shottsford, ridden by Ken Mullins. However, Fred had been hampered in the uphill finish and Nid d'Abeilles, who started at 100 to 8, was awarded the race following an objection. Fred had made his point and for the rest of his career he continued to ride many winners for Gerry Judd. They never had another disagreement.

At this time Fred received a retainer to ride the Contessa di Sant Elia's smart chaser Halloween in all his races. This did not affect his arrangements for riding for the Price stable as Fred ruefully recollected that Ryan never had a Gold Cup horse all the time that he was riding for him.

However, Ryan had hurdlers in profusion and he carefully prepared his star, Clair Soleil, for the Champion Hurdle. The first race chosen was a conditions hurdle at Sandown in November which the horse won readily. Ryan then sent him north to the Rose of Lancaster Hurdle at Manchester in January, where his old rival Otari was favourite. Fred made plenty of use of Clair Soleil even though the going was exceptionally holding, and he won by ten lengths.

The going was soft for the Cheltenham National Hunt Festival and Ryan ordered Fred to wait with Clair Soleil. Considering the going, the pace set by the leader, Prince Charlemagne, was suicidal, but Fred gave no ground away and at halfway was well placed at the head of the pack. As the leader tired he made a disastrous mistake and dropped out of contention. This left Fred in front at least threequarters of a mile from home, far sooner than he or Ryan had intended. They were still in front coming down the hill, but the Irish challenger Stroller was closing fast and actually jumped into the lead at the second last flight where Fred was now applying maximum pressure just to stay in the race. Stroller swept round the final turn, with T. P. Burns exuding confidence in the saddle. The Irish roar could be heard in the Promenade, but no race with Fred Winter in it was over until the post was passed. Once again on this remarkably game horse Fred showed what exceptional strength he possessed. Somehow he conjured another run out of Clair Soleil and just when Stroller seemed home, Clair Soleil came again and snatched the race by a head. It was a superbly fought contest. It raised the crowd to fever pitch and aroused all the passions of the annual confrontation of the English and the Irish at Cheltenham.

In the unsaddling enclosure Fred and Ryan had their inevitable row over Clair Soleil. 'You made too much use of him; if you had have come from behind you would have won by ten lengths,' Ryan said. Fred replied with refreshing candour, 'This horse stays and stays for ever. I had to go on when I did. Anyway, I won the f—ing race, didn't I!'

The argument over the right way to ride this particular horse continued into the following seasons. Fred rather proved his point by winning the three-mile Spa Hurdle on Clair Soleil in 1959, making all the running in hock-deep going. Still Ryan remained unconvinced and perhaps only then did Fred realize that you could never, ever, win an argument with Ryan; he rarely attempted it again.

Fred ended the season by winning on another of Gerry Judd's high-class French-bred hurdlers, Vermillon. This was a superbly made horse of outstanding ability. However, Fred maintains that he was a moody customer who had to be 'kidded' in a race. Not only that, he was savage at home, very difficult in his box. Vermillon won his last four races, handicaps at Lingfield in March and at Cheltenham in April, and at Newton Abbot and Wye in May. It was a final flourish to a wonderful season and when Clontarf won the seller at Stratford at the end of May, Ryan shut up the shop for the summer, the leading National Hunt trainer.

He had saddled twenty-four individual winners of forty-seven races, and his £13,888 in stakes put him at the top of the list. This time Vincent O'Brien, although he had won the Grand National with Quare Times, was only runner-up. Tim Molony was champion jockey, only two winning rides ahead of Fred Winter, who would undoubtedly have been champion had he not been stood down for two months by Gerry Judd in the autumn. Judd was second on the owners' list, his six winners taking ten races and £6481.

By this time, Ryan had discovered a new interest, a novel way to pass the time during the summer months: flat racing. His first attempt to break into the closely knit world of the flat had misfired. While away with his jumpers in the West Country, he had wanted to run a horse on the flat at Brighton. He drove all the way from Newton Abbot, only to be informed by the Clerk of the Scales that the horse couldn't run as he had no flat trainer's licence. Once he was granted a licence, the flat horses did almost as well as the jumpers. In 1955 Ryan sent out nineteen winners of £5876.

He followed the same pattern with the flat as he had adopted with jumping: he employed the best jockeys available. Doug Smith, Scobie Breasley, Lester Piggott and Geoff Lewis all rode winners for him. Canardeau was the most prolific winner and Doug rode him to three of his six wins. Scobie was on Salute, who began the season as a selling plater but went on to win handicaps.

Ryan's arrival on the flat race scene created little attention although one or two paddock judges noted how well turned out his runners were.

By Findon standards the 1955–56 National Hunt season was relatively unsuccessful. Alfarasio won on the opening day, but curiously there were no winners from then until the end of October. Only one big race was won, the Coronation Hurdle at Liverpool, but Fred Winter regained his National Hunt jockeys' championship with seventy-four winners.

In January 1956, Ryan and Dorothy, who had worked flat out since the wigwam days of Lavant, were overjoyed at the arrival of a son. Ryan George Victor (Joe) was followed in 1957 by Catherine Anne. The children were scarcely out of their prams before they were mounted on the best first ponies in Sussex, and Ryan had Joe earmarked for an early gymkhana success.

The other important event of 1956 was the purchase of the brick and flint period house which adjoined the stables at Findon. It had suddenly become vacant and Ryan bought it with financial help from Gerry Judd. Gerry moved into a self-contained wing, and after repairs and alterations Ryan and Dorothy moved the few yards from their bungalow into Downs House in September. It was to be their home for twelve momentous years.

In 1956 Bob McCreery, an outstanding amateur rider, joined Ryan as his assistant. Having a man of Bob's calibre was a tremendous help, and he won many races for the stable.

The 1956–57 season was highly successful. Ryan turned out seventy-nine winners, the most he has ever saddled in a National Hunt season, but once again the trainers' championship eluded him, although he was leading the list right up to the closing weeks. By training the winner of the first new sponsored chase – the Whitbread Gold Cup, which was worth £4842 – in April, Neville Crump took the championship, with Ryan second.

Although the Cheltenham Festival meeting was disappointing, Ryan started off well at Liverpool by sending out Rattler in Gerry Judd's colours to win the Lancashire Hurdle. However, the big gamble of the Aintree meeting went astray on the Friday when Cortego, the 9 to 4 favourite, was beaten into third place by Pallissy. Ryan considered that Fred had ridden a really bad race and ought to have won, and told him so in no uncertain terms. He accused him of going to sleep, adding, 'I have apprentices at home who'd have won on Cortego.'

In later years Fred admitted that on that occasion he did give the leaders too much rope; perhaps his mind was on the Grand National, the next National Hunt race on the card, in which he was due to ride Sundew, trained by Frank Hudson at Henley-in-Arden. Still smarting from Ryan's outburst – it was only their second row since the partnership started – Fred was in a filthy temper as he changed into the colours for his National ride. As he rode out onto the course on the huge 17-hand gelding, Fred was still muttering to himself. The previous year they had fallen heavily at Bechers when Sundew had been leading the field, but this year the big horse safely negotiated

Bechers on both occasions and after making all the running won by eight lengths from Wyndburgh, with Tiberetta six lengths away third.

Ryan was the first to congratulate Fred who, with a huge grin, gave him the Boy Scout salute, only with less fingers. Champion jockey Fred Winter had registered his first Grand National winner. He wished it had been for Ryan. Sadly, Sundew broke his back the following year in a fall at the water jump at Haydock Park.

In 1957 Ryan had his best season so far with the flat horses, training twenty-three winners of £12,452, which was almost as much in stakes as he was to win with fifty-seven winners over the sticks in 1957–58. By now he was winning races with dual-purpose horses which could run on the flat and over hurdles. He rarely took a holiday, and the switch to the flat was exactly what he needed to soak up the excess energy which was going to waste during the close season for jumping.

Ryan's crowning achievement in 1957 was to train Chief Barker, the winner of the Manchester November Handicap, for Nat Cohen and his friends of the Variety Club. Ryan had bought the horse – then called Polar Lodge – from Arthur Budgett, who had trained him to win once as a two-year-old and once as a three-year-old. At four the horse had become unreliable and would swerve at the finish of his races, so Budgett weeded him out. Ryan immediately had Polar Lodge gelded and passed him over to Nat Cohen, who was serving a term as the Variety Club's Chief Barker, hence the horse's new name. By the autumn Ryan had managed to get him out over hurdles – he ran unplaced at Hurst Park with Fred Winter in the saddle – and now he entered Chief Barker for some of the big autumn flat races, favouring the Manchester race because it was usually run on soft ground which the horse appeared to enjoy.

Ryan had another intended runner for the Manchester Handicap: Gold Wire, owned by the Scottish bookmaker, Jimmy McLean junior, for whom the lightweight jockey 'Kipper' Lynch had already been engaged. Ryan rated Chief Barker at least 10 pounds in front of Gold Wire, and it was his intention to take out McLean's horse and switch the jockey onto Chief Barker.

A final gallop after racing at Lingfield confirmed his assessment of the two horses and he tried to contact McLean. But for some reason McLean would not take his telephone call and it was not until the Wednesday that Ryan was able to inform him of the plan. To Ryan's consternation, McLean insisted on Gold Wire running in the race. Ryan had to find another jockey quickly. He heard of a strong lightweight in France, but although Nat Cohen agreed to pay generous expenses, the arrangement came to nothing. On Thursday Chief Barker still had no jockey; with a list of forty probables for the last big handicap, all the well-known lightweight jockeys had already been engaged. In desperation Ryan telephoned Eddie Magner for help, and was given the name of Dennis Walker, who was apprenticed to the Dringhouses trainer, Harry Woodroffe. Ryan engaged Walker for Chief Barker.

Gold Wire made the running in the Manchester November Handicap but, two furlongs out, his stable companion, Chief Barker, took over. Spaceman, ridden by Peter Robinson, then started to challenge, and throughout the last furlong the two horses were locked together. Robinson was applying the maximum pressure on Spaceman, who was leaning in on Chief Barker. Walker was squeezed onto the rails – when he returned to scale, he found his boot was scraped with white paint – and Chief Barker for once had no room to swerve. Perhaps he resented the unwelcome attention of his rival but it spurred him on and in the very last stride he pushed his nose in front to win by a short head in a photo-finish.

Throughout the desperate struggle, which took place before the days of the camera patrol, Walker had kept his head and ridden with great determination in the face of severe provocation. He was so small – he only weighed 5 stone 6 pounds – that 'Boggy' Whelan, who had been in charge in Ryan's absence, had to lift the boy up to reach the girths.

Meanwhile, in London, at Nat Cohen's flat, the other partner in the horse, Ben Rosenfeld, and their friends, Stuart Levy and 'Pinky' Taylor were undergoing agonies. They were listening to Raymond Glendenning's radio commentary, and though they had heard the result of the photo-finish, when they contacted the Press Association for the starting price they were told that there might be an objection. Knowing Chief Barker's habit of swerving, they were concerned that he might have been the culprit. In due course the 'weighed in' was given, and the result stood. The friends had backed the horse at 50 to 1 and they had all profited; so had many members of the Variety Club.

Ryan was so impressed when he heard how Walker had ridden his horse that he bought Walker's indentures from Harry Woodroffe.

Later that year the tiny apprentice was the guest of honour at a Variety Club dinner when he was presented with a watch by Nat Cohen and Ben Rosenfeld.

Walker did not stay long at Findon and soon left racing altogether. Ryan telephoned Nat Cohen one day to tell him that Walker had left. 'Nat,' he said, 'you are the luckiest chap alive. How that jockey managed to win that race I shall never know; he falls off every horse I put him on.' Dennis Walker retired having won just two races – an apprentice seller at Edinburgh, and the Manchester November Handicap.

Ryan really enjoyed putting one over the flat race trainers, and his resurrection of Chief Barker gave him immense pleasure. He was living in an ideal world; cock of the walk in the National Hunt league and yet able to land the odd coup for his show-business owners on the flat.

At the end of the 1958–59 National Hunt season Ryan was once again the leading trainer. The total stakes won amounted to £26,550, a personal record, helped by Fare Time winning the Champion Hurdle and by the success of Done Up in the Whitbread Gold Cup.

Ryan does not rate Fare Time as one of the greatest Champion Hurdlers. He was never a fluent jumper but he was tough and a resolute stayer. Ryan selected the Oteley Hurdle at Sandown as a 'prep' race for the big Cheltenham event and Fare Time came through his test with flying colours. Fred Winter had won the opening race at the Festival on Flame Gun and he now rode a copybook race to win the Champion Hurdle, Fare Time staying on up the hill to win by four lengths from the Irish hurdler Ivy Green.

Clair Soleil provided a Festival double for Gerry Judd and Ryan when Fred made all the running to win the Spa Hurdle. Fred ended up by winning five races at the three-day meeting and was just a little unlucky not to have won the Golld Cup on Linwell.

After his victorious Cheltenham week, Fred rode Mr J. U. Baillie's staying chaser Done Up to win over three miles at Hurst Park; he reported that he had never had a harder ride but that the gelding was an out-and-out stayer. Ryan prepared him for the Whitbread Gold Cup. Not long afterwards Fred rode in a novice chase at Leicester. His mount Charles Brandon fell heavily at the second last fence and Fred sustained a fractured skull. He did not ride again that season, missing the last two months, and losing the jockeys' championship to Tim Brookshaw.

Ryan now had to find a replacement jockey for Done Up whom he knew would be a punishing ride. He chose the hurdle race jockey Harry Sprague who was on the point of retiring from the saddle. Ryan felt that his busy style would suit the lazy Done Up. It was an inspired choice.

The 1959 Whitbread was run on very heavy ground; Ryan knew that this would provide just the conditions his stayer would revel in and he warned Sprague not to give up but to keep persevering to the finish. The partnership very nearly came to an end at the first of the three quick railway fences, but under hard driving Done Up steadily won back the lost ground. Harry Sprague was virtually running on his back and as they turned for home the lazy stayer was in with a chance. They challenged the leader Mandarin at the second last fence and both horses touched down together at the last. Though Done Up was tiring and hanging, Sprague got him organized and induced him to make one last effort which carried him right up to Mandarin, whom he beat by a short head on the line.

Fred Winter would have been proud to have ridden such a race but the effort completely sapped Harry Sprague's strength and he almost passed out during the long walk back through the members' enclosure. Harry had put everything into his last big race winner and for a rider who had made his name over hurdles it was ironic that it should have been a steeplechase that gave him his great moment of glory.

Ryan rushed through to the back of the members' enclosure to greet his two returning heroes. Harry Sprague had just been sick and he revealed to Ryan that he had lost his teeth; would he please try to find them? Ryan missed the celebrations in the winner's enclosure, spending those moments scrabbling about in the dirt for Harry's missing top set, which he eventually found.

Done Up had been bred by his owner, Mr J. U. Baillie, whose Crimborne Stud was close by Hawkhurst Court, where Ryan had started his training career. John Baillie presented Ryan with a painting by Peter Biegel of the exhausted horse and rider returning to scale, which vividly illustrates the leg-weary chaser and the jockey in some distress.

In 1957 it had been the Whitbread which had cost Ryan the trainers' championship; this year Done Up had clinched the title.

During the season John Sutcliffe senior sent Ryan most of his string of horses to train. One of the heaviest gamblers of the jumping game, Sutcliffe, who eventually trained in Epsom, was a selling-plate wizard. Most of his winners were ridden by his son, John, who partnered thirteen winners for Ryan and ended the season as the leading amateur rider with eighteen wins to his credit.

To Ryan's relief, Fred Winter recovered from his head injury and was back in time for the start of the 1959–60 season, though the stable drew a blank at the first Newton Abbot meeting.

During Fred's absence, Ryan had come to realize how essential he was to the success of the stable, and how much he had depended on Fred for the past ten years. Quite apart from Fred's absolute integrity, he possessed physical strength that few jockeys could equal. He was built like a boxer – a pocket Hercules – but had no trouble with his weight; he kept himself fit and as a result had the power and endurance to keep a tired horse going with hands and heels and the strength of his own body. His vigorous finishing effort was achieved through his legs and thighs, and the rhythm and movement of his whole body.

The horses never came home with whip marks; the whip was swung – the horses were slapped, not cut. They were never soured by being flayed with the whip. Even horses that had been given hard races soon recovered. Fred was a valuable partner, and Ryan hoped that he would continue to ride for many more seasons.

With Fred in the saddle the winners continued: the big grey, Staghound, and the Grand National hope, Dandy Scot, both won good races at Newbury, and there were doubles at Wye, Cheltenham and Kempton. But somehow the big races eluded them; there was not a single four-figure prize in the season's results. Though Fare Time won the Oteley Hurdle again, he went wrong during his Champion Hurdle preparation and was unable to run. For once, both Ryan and Fred drew a blank at the Festival meeting.

At Aintree, Scarab dead-heated for the Lancashire Hurdle, and Davy Crocket won the Coronation Hurdle, but in the first televised Grand National, Dandy Scot became unsighted at the Canal Turn first time round and fell.

Fred was unhurt and walked across to the high scaffolding tower nearby, where the BBC camera and commentator were positioned, and where his wife, Diana, and Dorothy Price were watching the race. He enjoyed a grandstand aerial view of the second circuit, and later assisted the two ladies – now suffering from acute vertigo – down the ladders to safety.

So ended a rather disappointing season for both trainer and jockey. Ryan had saddled thirty-seven winners of £11,487 and finished in sixth place on the trainers' list. Fred Winter, who had been leading jockey throughout the season, lost his title when Stan Mellor rode a double on the very last day of the season and pipped Fred by one winning ride. Stan Mellor was to remain champion for the next two seasons.

The 1960–61 season began quietly; there were no West Country fireworks, and it was not until October that Sky Pink became the first winner at Cheltenham.

Ryan knew that he had some really promising material among his three-year-old hurdlers, and he unleashed the best of them, Cantab, in a maiden race at Chepstow, which he won on very heavy ground. Another win followed at Southwell before Christmas, and then, on 5 January, he saddled a significant double. Cantab, ridden by Josh Gifford, won at Stratford, and Tovaritch, ridden by Fred Winter, won at Hurst Park. Cantab was the first winner for the stable ridden by Josh Gifford, and Tovaritch the first winner that Ryan had saddled for his new Scottish owner, Lady Weir.

Lady Weir had been introduced to Ryan by Sir Archibald James, who encouraged her to have a jumper trained at Findon, even though her home was in Scotland. Tovaritch was her first venture. A few weeks later Ryan also saddled a backward gelding called What a Myth in a maiden hurdle at Plumpton, and on very heavy going the gelding trotted up. Ryan had originally bought the horse as an unbroken three-year-old from Ian Muir's Fawley Stud at Wantage for £400. Now he passed him on as a potential chaser to Lady Weir for £2000. Lucy Weir promptly gave a half share to Sir Archibald James. The partnership was destined to win the Cheltenham Gold Cup and £8129 in stakes. Not surprisingly, Lady Weir became one of Ryan's most loyal owners.

Josh Gifford was to prove a marvellous acquisition for Ryan. Apprenticed to Sam Armstrong at Newmarket, Josh had ridden fifty winners on the flat, but was now becoming too heavy to remain a flat race jockey. Josh's father had ridden over a hundred point-to-point winners, and Josh had started his racing life at Cliff Beechener's jumping stable, so he was quite at home among jumpers and his hunting experience proved a tremendous boon when he started to school over hurdles and fences. His style was the perfect marriage of flat racing and jumping; his positioning during a race was faultless and his judgement of pace was to become one of his greatest assets. In retrospect, Josh remembers that first win for the stable on Cantab with great affection, for it was the gateway to fantastic success.

Cantab was to become a very good hurdler. He had been bought in France from Dick Carver junior for £3000 on behalf of Miss Enid Chanelle, whose fashion house is known the world over. She was encouraged to start owning jumpers by Nat Cohen, who introduced her to Ryan. Cantab did her proud: in March he won the Triumph Hurdle — a pretty dramatic start for any new owner.

Ryan's hurdlers were in top gear that March for Eborneezer won another Champion Hurdle at Cheltenham. Yet it was a surprisingly disappointing season with only £16,379 won in stakes, and the Champion Hurdle and the Triumph accounted for half of that.

Ryan won the Triumph Hurdle again the following year with Beaver II, another French importation. Beaver II was a rig who had been altered and was only the size of a pony. He had come from the Strassburgers' stable, weeded out on account of his size and thrown in as a makeweight for another deal; he was absolutely free and, according to his homework, useless. Time was to show that he had been fooling everyone. Paul Kelleway had schooled him and told Ryan that he would one day be a top-class hurdler. Ryan did not believe Paul and the horse was sent to Ascot sales with a £50 reserve on his head. There was no bid and so Beaver II came home and continued his training.

At this point 'Lucky' Joe Sullivan appeared on the scene. He lived nearby at Worthing and always wanted to have a horse with Ryan. After following Ryan's advice one day at Windsor races, Joe won enough money backing winners to buy his first horse. When Joe arrived at Findon to discuss the matter, Ryan suggested he buy a horse being trained by Réné Emery. Fortunately for Joe Sullivan, the horse died before they could go to see it and Ryan sold him a half share in Beaver II for £500 instead. Joe received little encouragement from the Findon lads over his new purchase — they told him that the horse used to chuck his lad off every day and refused to work on the gallops. Paul Kelleway who rode Beaver II in his first race reported differently and was convinced that the little horse had ability; this was confirmed by Fred Winter who rode the horse next time out at

Birmingham where they were a close third in a hot three-year-old hurdle race.

Joe Sullivan did not have to wait long for his first winner; with Fred Winter in the saddle, Beaver II won at Birmingham early in the New Year and at Wincanton the following month. Joe Sullivan was a general dealer involved, at this stage in his career, in buying and selling gas works, but Beaver II was proving to be just as profitable as his normal business. When Joe heard that Ryan had entered Beaver II in the Triumph Hurdle, he was overjoyed for he longed to win a prestige race. But Ryan had other plans for the Triumph.

He had paid £6000 for a high-class French horse called Catapult II for Miss Enid Chanelle. The horse had finished fourth in the Prix de la Salamandre, the big two-year-old race in France; and there were high hopes that Ryan would saddle the winner of the Triumph for the second year running. So, against his better judgement, Ryan decided to let Beaver II take part. Catapult II had never run over hurdles in Britain before, but word had got round that Ryan had another ace, and the handsome colt started 7 to 4 favourite.

He was exceptionally headstrong and impetuous, and Fred let him make the running. Few were prepared for what happened next. Two flights from home Catapult II was tiring, and when a challenger loomed up on his outside Fred started to ride in earnest. However, no matter what he did, his cause was hopeless for the challenger was little Beaver II with Josh nursing a double handful, and they went sweeping past to win easily by six lengths. For the Hurst Park punters the wrong one had won. That arch villain Captain Ryan Price had done in again; he had put the public away and landed a coup!

The atmosphere in the unsaddling enclosure was distinctly cool. Miss Chanelle had parted with a great deal of money in order to lead in the winner for the second year running, and now she found that her trainer had scooped the limelight. It was acutely embarrassing for Ryan, who had really believed that in Catapult II he had a champion. He remains convinced that Catapult II was potentially the best horse he has ever trained over hurdles, but he had a hidden weakness. The following year Catapult II started favourite for the Schweppes. Again he had led the field a tremendous gallop and then faded when the Price second string, Rosyth, came sailing by to win. Later Catapult II dropped dead in his box; it appears that he had a heart defect which probably accounted for his failures in the top-class races.

Beaver II showed that his win was no fluke, for he went on to win the Grand Course de Haies at Auteuil in June 1962. On that memorable day Fred Winter also rode Mandarin to victory in the Grand Steeplechase de Paris, the dramatic occasion when the rubber bit broke early in the race, and Fred had to steer Mandarin round a twisting figure-of-eight course with only his legs and his whip as aids. After Paris, Ryan sold Beaver II to Mr (later Sir) Bernard Sunley, in whose colours he won the Mackeson Hurdle at Cheltenham; the price was £20,000.

Bob McCreery was Ryan's assistant at the time of the one and only strike in Findon's history. One day in 1961 the lads gathered in the tack room and refused to ride out first lot. A new lad had recently arrived from Willie Smyth's Arundel stable, and was using a minor complaint about the food in the stable lads' canteen as an excuse for causing trouble. Bob reported this to Ryan, who marched into the yard and called for the spokesman. The new lad came out and said his piece.

'Have you finished?' said Ryan.

'Yes,' said the lad, whereupon Ryan landed a haymaker on the point of his jaw which lifted the lad into the air and onto his back. Nobody bothered to count to ten, it was a complete KO: the lad was out cold.

'Who,' Ryan now inquired, 'is your next spokesman?'

Without a word the lads filed out of the tack room and went about their work. Ryan then turned to the head lad and told him to give the lad his cards, his wages and get him off the premises in two hours. The strike was over.

By this time James McLean's Gold Wire had won on the flat and also over hurdles, but the owner did not consider that the little gelding was big enough to tackle fences. He told Ryan that he wished to sell, and it was arranged that Teddy Knox of the Crazy Gang and Bob McCreery would take the horse over as joint owners.

Gold Wire had provided Paul Kelleway with his first win under National Hunt rules in a hurdle race at Taunton, and then on Boxing Day at Kempton Park, Fred Winter rode Gold Wire to victory in a steeplechase. The following year Bob McCreery was invited to take part in what was pompously billed 'The Championship of the World', a steeplechase for amateur riders to be run during a festival of racing in Madrid. 'We'd better take this on,' said Ryan, and so Gold Wire travelled to Spain and duly won the steeplechase. The subsequent party held at the Duc d'Alberquerque's lovely home went on for three days and nights. Apart from one year when he broke down, Gold Wire had won every single season up to the age of thirteen.

Now Bob McCreery was shocked to learn that Teddy Knox wished to cash in his share. Bob was furious that Ryan had confirmed with Knox that the horse still had a value. Bob had planned a quiet retirement in the Warwickshire hunting field for his favourite chaser. Bearing in mind Ryan's sentimental attachment to his old warriors, Bob found his attitude towards Gold Wire inconsistent. He arranged for a horsebox to collect his horse and sent him to be trained for a short while by Peter Walwyn. Eventually the gelding went home to Bob's Moreton Paddox Stud in Warwickshire.

Later, to dissolve the partnership, Bob sent Gold Wire to the Doncaster sales, bought him back for 1200 guineas, and promptly retired him. However, the little horse went so well in the hunting field that Bob brought him out of retirement and, at the age of fourteen, with Brough Scott in the saddle, the veteran chaser won at Sandown. In his career Gold Wire managed to win in six countries: Ireland, Scotland, Wales, England, France and Spain.

While Bob was at Findon, his father, General Sir Richard McCreery, had bought a top-class chaser called Granville for Bob to ride. The horse came from Willie Stephenson and Ryan rated him as the best two-mile chaser he had ever seen. In the Henry VII Chase at Hurst Park, Granville beat three previous winners and, with 11 stone 13 pounds, covered the two miles in 4 minutes 14 seconds, a new course record. Sadly, Granville then broke down and after that setback was never the same horse again. He too was retired to Bob's stud and kept Gold Wire company.

Gold Wire enjoyed a happy retirement at the stud, but in 1980, at the age of nineteen, he began to deteriorate because his teeth collapsed. Bob had him put down by injection, and his departure affected everyone. Two days later, Granville was killed trying to jump a ditch, presumably looking for his paddock companion.

During the 1961–62 National Hunt season Ryan achieved one of his three great ambitions. As a boy in Sussex he had set himself three targets: to train the winner of the Derby, to train the winner of the Grand National and to shoot a tiger. In March at Aintree Fred Winter and Kilmore made one of those dreams a reality.

The story of Kilmore began the previous year. Nat Cohen, the bewhiskered, urbane film producer, whose company was responsible for the *Carry On* series, had been a loyal supporter of Ryan's ever since his horse Alfarasio had arrived at Lavant. Nat and his two partners, Stuart Levy and Ben Rosenfield, had enjoyed many a successful tilt at the ring through Ryan's horses. One day Nat Cohen asked Ryan which horse Fred Winter was going to ride in the Grand National. Ryan was forced to admit that his staying chasers had not come good this season. Dandy Scot, his National horse, had gone wrong, and there was nothing for Fred to ride.

Nat Cohen was incensed: 'You have the best jockey riding in the world today, and you have not even got a ride for him in the greatest race in the world. You should find him one.'

'Can I use your money?' asked Ryan.

'Yes, as long as it wins,' replied Cohen.

That lighthearted conversation was the start of a search for a suitable horse that ended in a snow-bound field in County Tipperary. Ryan learned of Kilmore through Tim Fitzgeorge-Parker, then racing correspondent of the *Daily Mail*. Nat Cohen was in Hollywood at the time, and Ryan telephoned him there with the news that he had the opportunity of buying a Grand National horse in Ireland, and could he have permission to buy him if he proved suitable. Nat gave his approval, and Ryan took Bob McCreery to look at the horse which was trained by Mick Brown.

Vincent O'Brien was a neighbour of Brown's, and when he heard of the intended visit, he asked the party to lunch at Ballydoyle. Following Vincent's spectacular hospitality, everyone then staggered over to Mick Brown's stable to see the prospective Grand National winner.

It was intended that Bob should try the horse over a few fences, but the snow was thick on the ground, and he was only able to pop the eleven-year-old over three fences. Although he had raced for five seasons, and run in fifty-six races, Kilmore was as sound as a bell and looked more like a fresh horse than an old campaigner. Bob thought that he was even smaller than Gold Wire, his tough little chaser, but he had reservations about Kilmore being a National horse on account of his size.

Ryan loved the horse the moment he saw him. He thought Kilmore had a wonderfully intelligent head; he pointed out to Bob that he had not started racing until he was rising seven. It was a moment of decision, but Ryan did not hesitate; he had seen enough and he classified the gelding there and then as a future Grand National winner.

The deal was struck and Kilmore was bought for £3000 subject to the vet. Ryan sent a cable to Nat Cohen in Hollywood: 'CONGRATULATIONS, YOU HAVE A GRAND NATIONAL RUNNER.'

When Kilmore eventually arrived at Findon, Ryan wondered whether the Irish had switched horses. Kilmore appeared to have shrunk; he looked only pony size next to some of Ryan's chasers.

Kilmore ran in Nat Cohen's colours for the first time at the Cheltenham Festival meeting in the Kim Muir Challenge Cup. As the race was confined to amateur riders, Fred Winter watched from the stands. Kilmore, ridden by Mr Gay Kindersley, finished sixth to Nicolaus Silver. Fred turned to Ryan and laughed. 'So that is my National horse, you must be joking.'

That was Kilmore's last race before the National, so Ryan arranged for Fred to partner him in a school at Lingfield, where Fred realized that the little horse was a natural economical jumper. He retracted his remarks and felt he would at least get round in the National.

Even with the greatest jockey in the world on top, Kilmore was allowed to start at 33 to 1 for the 1961 Grand National. However, to Fred's delight he enjoyed a fantastic ride. The little horse jumped brilliantly, but ran all too freely. He was lying second at the Canal Turn on the second circuit, but weakened over the last two fences to finish a creditable fifth to the lightly weighted Nicolaus Silver.

Fred was bubbling over when he jumped off Kilmore. He said to Ryan: 'What a lovely little horse. The ground was too fast, and he ran too freely and he had a bit too much weight. Look after him and I will win it next year.'

Ryan trained Kilmore with one race in mind, the 1962 Grand National; all his work schedules were intended to get the horse to settle both at home and on the racecourse. His first race was at Folkestone in September, when he finished a good second to John O'Groats. He then returned to Aintree but fell at the sixth fence in the Becher Chase.

Kilmore's next races were disappointing. He ran poorly with 10 stone 4 pounds at Newbury in the Hennessy Gold Cup, carried 10 stone 5 pounds into fifth place in the Mildmay Memorial at Sandown, and then, after a two-month rest, promptly fell at the thirteenth fence at Lingfield, his 'prep' race for Aintree. In the Grand National the handicapper had dropped him by 10 pounds compared to the previous year, and he was set to carry 10 stone 4 pounds.

When Ryan and Fred inspected the course on the second day of the Grand National meeting, neither was particularly hopeful, for the going had dried out and was riding fast. That night Ryan, as was his custom, entertained the Grand National jockeys to dinner at the Adelphi Hotel. When the party broke up he went to the hotel entrance and was astonished to see that the streets were awash. There had been torrential rain and it was still coming down like stair rods. The rain continued all through the night. Every few hours Ryan went to the window to listen to the downpour that was altering Kilmore's chance for the better. It was still raining when the jockeys arrived at the course and Fred and Ryan again inspected the old turf. For the first time for many years the going would be soft and Fred felt supremely confident.

This time Fred was able to restrain Kilmore and he hunted round for the first circuit in the testing ground. He hugged the inside all the way and going to Bechers for the second time Fred was able to move effortlessly up behind the leaders. At the Canal Turn Fred had five horses in front of him, Fredith's Son who blundered at that point, Gay Navaree, Mr What, Nicolaus Silver and Wyndburgh. The race lay between those six, but before they crossed the Melling Road for the last time the Irish outsider Gay Navaree had shot into a clear lead. He was ridden by the Irish event rider Mr Tony Cameron, who had played his hand too soon. Between the last two fences Fred Winter now asked Kilmore for the effort that he had been nursing for four miles. Kilmore responded and he passed the leader going to the last fence, jumped it boldly and Fred knew the race was his. The veteran Aintree hero Wyndburgh came through to finish second, with a previous winner, Mr What, third. The first three horses home were all twelve-year-olds. Fred had ridden his second winner of the greatest steeplechase in the world and Ryan's childhood dream had come true.

The unsaddling enclosure was like a mad house. Ryan embraced Fred and in buoyant mood was interviewed on BBC Television by David Coleman. He revealed to the watching millions that he had trained Kilmore specially for the National following the horse's wonderful race the previous year. He told the story of the purchase, and regretted that the three joint owners were not able to be present as they were ill at home with flu. They had all had a good touch at 50 to 1 – it was great television.

A well-known trainer watched this and was overheard to say, 'Not a particularly glamorous Grand National, won by three Jews at home in bed with colds!'

Ryan gave every member of the press a personal interview, and left Aintree with the memorable words, 'Well that's the Grand National in the bag. Now let's get to Wye, I have a certainty there on Monday.' He was right, and several pressmen profited when Opening Bars won for Josh Gifford.

Ryan flew back to London Airport and drove home to Findon. As the car turned up the lane to Downs House it was ambushed by some of his staff. They diverted Ryan to a party in Kilmore's honour at the local – the Old Village House Hotel – paid for by Nat Cohen. After a gap of fifty years to the day, Findon had another Grand National winner, and Nat Cohen's dream of mounting Fred Winter with an appropriate horse had come to fulfilment, albeit a year late.

The following year, Kilmore, now aged thirteen, again ran in the Grand National but could only finish sixth to Ayala. In 1964 when fourteen and now trained by Sid Dale, Kilmore again took part at Aintree but fell at the twenty-first fence.

After returning to Ryan Kilmore won two more races and was then retired to a life of leisure roaming Findon Downs. He lived out in all but the severest weather and over the years had for company some very distinguished veterans of Cheltenham, Newbury and Newmarket: Hill House (who died in 1979), Le Vermontois, What a Myth, Persian Lancer, Major Rose, and Charlie Worcester.

Ryan loves seeing his old-age pensioners every day. Sometimes, after the flat racers have worked up the downs, the old stagers, usually led by Charlie Worcester, long-haired and woolly and just a little stiff, do their own thing in single file up to the top of the hill – just to show these upstarts how it should be done.

Seven years ago Kilmore began to show his age and Ryan was grateful to his neighbour Miss Tripp for having Kilmore in her paddock which was more sheltered than the open downs. In September 1981 Ryan finally decided that Kilmore should not be asked to face another winter and had him put down. Miss Tripp, who had cared for Kilmore with such devotion, was as distressed as Ryan.

Of his old pensioners Ryan said, 'These horses helped to make me famous and I will never forget them.'

10
The Rosyth Case

In the closing days of 1962, Downs House stables were doing very nicely, thank you. The Captain had just saddled his 900th winner; he had won the Grand National and the Champion Hurdle; he had also won several of the new sponsored races that had begun to appear in the race programmes. These were, in the early days, almost exclusively steeplechases. Amid a great deal of publicity, a new sponsored handicap hurdle was launched by the firm of Schweppes. It was to be worth almost as much as the Champion Hurdle and was to be called the Schweppes Gold Trophy. It was Schweppes who came to the rescue of the Grand National by putting up £7500 towards the prize money in 1960 and 1961.

The directors of Schweppes, however, did not feel that the firm had received enough publicity over the Grand National; the firm's name was not included in the title of the race. They doubted if they were getting full commercial value for their investment. They consulted their public relations advisers, and Andrew Hughes-Onslow was put onto the case. Andrew recommended that Schweppes should pull out of the Grand National and sponsor their own race, making it the richest handicap hurdle in Great Britain and Ireland.

The venture had a disastrous start. Because of the firm's connection with Aintree, it was decided to run the race at Liverpool. There were misgivings about allowing a large field of hurdlers to race round the tight Aintree hurdle course. With a field of forty-two, there was a lot of scrimmaging and bumping, and at the second flight Stan Mellor was severely injured when his horse, Eastern Harvest, fell. Stan was with the leaders at the time, and he was kicked like a football by almost every other runner. Present safety regulations now restrict the number of runners to twenty-four over the same course.

Stan Mellor suffered a fractured jaw, and only after intensive plastic surgery did he have his good looks restored. He became his handsome self in time to get married later that year, but the fall cost him the jockeys' championship. On his wedding day, the directors of Schweppes sent him a silver cigarette box, on which they had inscribed, 'To Stan Mellor for falling heavily twice in one year.'

Ironically, the jockey who won the championship that year – 1963 – was Josh Gifford, who also won the first running of the Schweppes on Rosyth.

Rosyth had been only one of six entries which Ryan had for the Schweppes. The prize money was equal to winning seven normal hurdle handicaps. The lure of the Schweppes was too much for Ryan, and he was determined to win it. On two occasions his efforts to do just that caused reverberations around the corridors of the headquarters of the National Hunt Committee.

All in all, Schweppes have received a tremendous mileage from the publicity that abounded after the race each year. At first the firm were concerned that the publicity was mostly bad; however, when three of the first four runnings of their race ended in inquiries, they maintained a dignified silence and left the matter to the stewards.

Someone stole the solid gold trophy when it was being exhibited in a Bond Street wine merchants a few weeks before the race. Even that created publicity, and though the present trophy is only a replica, it is solid gold like its predecessor.

Captain Ryan Price won four Gold Trophies for his owners, in 1963, 1964, 1966 and 1967. He also saddled Major Rose to finish second to Persian War in 1968, and Moonlight Bay to be third in 1973. It was the victories in 1964 by Rosyth and in 1967 by Hill House that caused all the trouble.

Rosyth was a chunky little short-backed chestnut colt. He was only just over 15 hands high, and had been trained on the flat for three seasons by Ryan Jarvis at Newmarket. Rosyth was by Admiral's Walk out of a Chamossaire mare, and had won three good handicaps as a three-year-old, but had completely lost his form as a four-year-old. Following the death of his owner, Mr James Bartholomew, Rosyth was submitted by the executors at Doncaster August sales and fell for 430 guineas to the bid of Mr John Sankey, a much respected and well-loved horse dealer from Ashford in Kent. Jack – as he was always known – dressed in the fashion of a bygone age. He always wore breeches and leggings, and carried a cane. He sent Rosyth to be trained by Ryan Price.

Mr Sankey had previously had a very good horse with Ryan. Creek had originally been owned by Baron Hatvany, but after the horse had failed to win a particular race when gambled on, the baron had instructed Ryan to put the horse into a seller. Before he won, Ryan had charged John Sankey to buy the horse at all costs. In November Creek duly won the seller at Wye, and Jack Sankey secured him at the subsequent auction for only 280 guineas. The grey gelding went on to win him sixteen races.

Rosyth though, was an entire, a full horse, and his runs on the flat as a five-year-old suggested that he had lost the zest for racing. Ryan discovered that he was so jarred up in his shoulder that he could not gallop. Rosyth was sent for a course of swimming off Selsey Bill. Horses love swimming, and the modern treatment of horses with such ailments as sprains and strains and deep-seated muscular disorders is frequently carried out at specially designed indoor swimming pools. Ryan preferred to use salt sea water. He used to tow the horses in a rowing boat. It worked wonders with Rosyth, who recovered his action in a very short time, and was soon put to schooling over hurdles. Many trainers would probably have had Rosyth gelded, but Ryan had enjoyed tremendous success with colts and as he wished to run Rosyth in the autumn, he left him as nature intended him.

Ryan loved the sleek coats and elegant good looks of the colts, and only had his jumpers cut as a last resort. Full horses such as Nuage Dore, Eborneezer, Cantab, Welcome News, Priorit, Sir d'Orient, Vermillon and Sy Oui won many races for him.

So Rosyth remained a colt and started his education at Findon by being schooled over hurdles by Josh Gifford, who was impressed at how quickly he learned. Within a month he was ready to run his first race. That was at Plumpton; starting at 25 to 1 in a novice hurdle, he showed promise when ridden by Buck Jones to finish fifth in a field of nine. The change of environment, the swimming treatment and the additional excitement of jumping hurdles seemed to cure the jade from Newmarket Heath. In his new stable the little chestnut had begun to thrive.

The following month Ryan ran Rosyth in a big field of maidens at Leicester. He also saddled Utrillo II, ridden by Fred Winter. Utrillo II – destined to win the Cesarewitch later that year – started favourite, but could only finish sixth. Rosyth, who had started at 100 to 6, was unplaced, but had jumped well throughout. It proved to be a useful education for next time out at Windsor with Josh Gifford in the saddle, Rosyth lost his maiden certificate by beating a previous winner, Vultrix, ridden by his owner, Sir William Piggot-Brown. The going had been extremely holding, but Rosyth had not put a foot wrong, and had stayed on strongly to win impressively by three lengths. Stamina was clearly his strong suit.

Following that win, Ryan took an exceptionally bold step by saddling Rosyth for a highly competitive handicap, the Imperial Cup at Sandown, one of the hottest hurdle races of the season. Here Rosyth carried the minimum weight of 10 stone, but ran a spectacular race to finish a close-up fourth. For a virtual novice to perform so well against seasoned hurdlers in only his fourth race in public suggested that Rosyth was something special. He had finished within three lengths of the winner, Antiar, and had run a great deal better than his more fancied stable companion, Charlie Worcester. Moreover, Rosyth had been unlucky in running, bumped at a crucial stage.

On the strength of that showing, Ryan decided to saddle Rosyth for the Schweppes Hurdle at Liverpool, even though it was run only five days after the Imperial Cup. Josh Gifford again had the ride, and making the most of his light weight, he again carried only 10 stone. They were with the leaders all the way, eventually running on strongly to win by a length. They had missed all the scrimmaging round the sharp Liverpool turns, which had caused some of the fancied horses to be obstructed. The joy of winning this huge prize money was marred by the news of the serious accident to Stan Mellor.

On the Saturday at Aintree, Ryan saddled the winners of both divisions of the Liverpool Hurdle – Pavot and Brocade Slipper. On the Friday, Walworth had been beaten by only a short head for the Lancashire Hurdle, and in the Grand National Kilmore – now thirteen years old – had completed the course to finish sixth. It was certainly a memorable Aintree for Findon.

Ryan had demonstrated that it was possible to win a competitive hurdle with a novice. What had surprised him was the remarkable rate of improvement that the strong little chestnut had shown in his two races in the spring. When he ran in the Schweppes, he sported a summer bloom on his coat. Rosyth was clearly a 'spring horse'.

Having won the Schweppes, Ryan recommended to his owner that he should cash the horse in. He was worried that Rosyth would now be asked to carry big weights in handicaps, and he doubted if his frame was up to the task. Also, after Mr Sankey had bought the colt, Ryan had been disturbed to learn from the colt's previous trainer, Ryan Jarvis, that Rosyth had broken a blood vessel after a race at Newmarket in July. Rosyth had done the same thing after running fourth in the Imperial Cup. Rosyth was duly sent to the Ascot sales in May with a £2000 reserve, but there was no bid for him and he returned home unsold. No one had been the slightest bit interested in him.

In September Ryan ran Rosyth in a mile-and-a-quarter handicap at Newbury, and he finished fourth. At Windsor, later in the month, he won over a mile and a half, but bled after the race. Though Ryan wanted to win the Schweppes again, he had only remote hopes that Rosyth would have a chance, and favoured the French colt Catapult II.

Everything depended on whether the handicapper gave Rosyth too much weight. It was encouraging that, in the November Handicap Hurdle at Liverpool, the handicapper raised Rosyth only 6 pounds, allotting him 10 stone 6 pounds. It was seven months since Rosyth had won over the course, and Ryan desperately wanted to run him with that very reasonable weight, if only to confirm the handicap. He had difficulty in getting the horse fit for whenever he tried to pack in some fast work the colt broke blood vessels. Though Rosyth had not run before that season, the betting public made him favourite for the Liverpool race. The colt looked well in the paddock – perhaps too well – but he never showed with a chance in the race, and did not improve out of the middle division.

Josh reported that the colt had made a hash of the first flight and had seemed frightened of every jump after that. On his return from Liverpool, Rosyth caught flu and for seven days he was a very sick horse. Mike Ashton, the vet, visited him every day, and for a while it was touch and go.

Following Ashton's advice to keep the horse on the move, Ryan next ran Rosyth at Newbury in the Berkshire Hurdle on 30 November. Rosyth was weighted by the conditions at 10 stone 10 pounds. Brocade Slipper had a pound more and was preferred to Rosyth in the market. Rosyth drifted in the betting from 6 to 1 to 10 to 1. The winner was Salmon Spray, who carried 10 stone 8 pounds and had a convincing victory. Rosyth ran another disappointing race and jumped so badly that he eventually finished tailed off.

A fortnight later Rosyth met Salmon Spray again, this time at Sandown Park. A 10-pound penalty for winning at Newbury brought Salmon Spray's weight up to 11 stone 4 pounds and he was now giving 3 pounds to Rosyth. At Newbury he had been receiving 2 pounds. However, the 5-pound pull in Rosyths favour made no difference. Neither did the application of blinkers, for the first time in a hurdles race, have any effect. Salmon Spray won again and Rosyth was a distant sixth, having made a hurdling error. In fact, he finished twenty-two lengths behind Salmon Spray.

In another fortnight, Rosyth had his fourth race of the season – the Kempton Park Hurdle at the Boxing Day meeting. The handicapper had dropped Rosyth, who was set to carry 10 stone 5 pounds, the lowest weight he had been allotted all season. He still did not win, but he ran a good deal better than before, finishing third, eight lengths behind the winner, Neapolitan Lou, to whom he was giving 8 pounds.

The Ripley Handicap Hurdle at Sandown Park, run thirty-five days before the Schweppes, was Rosyth's fifth run of the season. It was an ideal tuning-up race for the Schweppes. By now the handicapper had taken Rosyth's early season failures into consideration, and at Sandown the horse carried only 10 stone. The Ripley Handicap is vitally important when considering the Schweppes and the resulting stewards' inquiry into the running of Rosyth. The winner of the Ripley Hurdle was Salmon Spray; it was his third win in a row, and he carried 10 stone 10 pounds. He beat the favourite, Wilhemina Henrietta, by two lengths and Rosyth by nine lengths. Rosyth, receiving 10 pounds from Salmon Spray, finished sixth.

For the Schweppes, the handicapper, Captain Toller, allowed Rosyth 4 pounds for the nine lengths by which he had been beaten by Salmon Spray at Sandown. This meant that Rosyth was now receiving 14 pounds from Salmon Spray. Compared with their running in November, Rosyth was now 16 pounds better off.

For 1964, the Schweppes was transferred from Liverpool to Newbury, where it has been run ever since. The sponsors had had enough of the primitive Aintree facilities. The previous year the directors of the sponsoring firm had reserved a private dining room in order to entertain some private guests. They were surprised when, on entering the racecourse, they had to purchase badges in order to gain admission. The luncheon room was not so private either for it had to be shared with another party. The menu was Lancashire hotpot, made considerably less palatable by flakes of yellow plaster which wafted down from the ceiling from time to time.

So, at Newbury on 15 February, a field of twenty-four went to the post for a race worth £7639. Ryan Price saddled two: Catapult II, the favourite, and Rosyth, who started at 10 to 1. The stable's first jockey, Fred Winter, rode Catapult II and Josh Gifford rode Rosyth.

Just as at Liverpool, the field went off at a tremendous pace with Catapult II in the van fighting for his head, but fading quickly after the second last flight, and finishing in the ruck. He was later found to be lame. In this exceptionally fast-run race, ten seconds faster than average time, Josh Gifford had judged his effort to perfection. Biding his time, while the others scorched round, Josh demonstrated his superb judgement of pace. With only one horse behind him on the final turn, he cut through beaten horses like a knife through butter. Joining the leaders two flights from home, he swept on and was always beating Salmon Spray on the run-in. On their fourth encounter of the season Rosyth had turned the tables on his old rival, and won by two lengths. Ryan had now won both runnings of this most competitive handicap with the same horse. Behind him at Newbury were Magic Court and Another Flash, destined to finish first and second in the Champion Hurdle at Cheltenham one month later, and another subsequent Champion Hurdler, Salmon Spray, who won in 1966. However, on the day, and at the weights, Rosyth was their master.

Ryan was looking pretty pleased with himself when the press crowded round him in the unsaddling enclosure. But there was a distinct chill in the air when the stewards' secretary, Lieutenant-Colonel Christian, tapped him on the shoulder, and said the words that every trainer dreads, 'Captain Price, the stewards would like to see you.' So started a chain of events which, in three weeks' time, was to see Ryan disqualified from training.

General Sir Randle Feilden, the senior of the stewards on duty at Newbury, outlined the problem. The stewards considered that Rosyth had made abnormal improvement between his race at Sandown on 11 January, and the Schweppes Gold Trophy on 15 February. Abnormal improvement in thirty-five days. Sir Randle also made the point that Ryan had actually led Rosyth out of the paddock, and not the more fancied stable companion, Catapult II, which was favourite and was ridden by the first jockey, Fred Winter.

Ryan conceded that he had improved Rosyth, chiefly because the horse had naturally come to himself'. He explained that the colt had a tendency to break blood vessels, and that he had been forced to bring him along gently because of this. He assured the stewards that the horse had been run on his merits, and that there was nothing sinister or remotely significant about the fact that he had personally led the eventual winner out of the parade ring.

The Newbury stewards refused to accept Ryan's explanation, and referred the running of Rosyth to the stewards of the National Hunt Committee.

The following day in the *Sunday Telegraph*, John Lawrence agreed with the need for questions to be asked of Rosyth's trainer. He went on:

> Last time out at Sandown, Rosyth finished nearly 10 lengths behind Salmon Spray and met him on only 4 lbs. better terms this afternoon.
>
> The discrepancy is there for all to see and while there may be perfectly valid reasons unknown to the public for Rosyth's rapid improvement, it is not altogether surprising in the circumstances that his case has been referred to the National Hunt Committee.

Whatever the responsible press may have thought, Ryan simply could not see that he had transgressed any rules, and did not consider that there was a case to answer. 'No one understood that with a colt, they do not begin to come in their coats until the breeding season is near. Rosyth was the only entire ever to win the Schweppes. I had trouble with him all through the year. I could not get him as fit as I would have liked, for he kept on breaking blood vessels and I had to go easy on him.' Ryan's defence rested solely on these considerations. Yet one had to accept the fact that, in two highly competitive and valuable races, Rosyth had not broken blood vessels.

On the Saturday before the hearing, Josh asked Ryan if he wished to have a conference over the weekend concerning the evidence that they were going to present at the hearing. Ryan dismissed the idea, saying, 'What have we got to worry about? Rosyth is a spring horse, I couldn't train him all the year, he is entitled to improve.'

In retrospect Ryan realizes that it was foolish to be so confident and to appear before the stewards without carefully marshalled evidence. This bitter lesson did not go unlearned, and when later he was faced with yet another inquiry over Hill House, he enlisted the full force of the legal profession to help him coordinate his defence.

The inquiry into the running of Rosyth was held at 15 Cavendish Square on 20 February 1964. The stewards were Lord Cadogan, Lord Cottenham and Major David Gibson. Also attending were General Sir Randle Feilden, and the official handicapper for the Schweppes, Captain Charles Toller.

On this ill-fated day Josh and Ryan drove up to London together, stopped off for a drink at Jules' Bar in Jermyn Street, and presented themselves at Cavendish Square at the appointed time without a care in the world.

As witnesses Ryan called his own veterinary surgeon, Mr Michael Ashton, Ryan Jarvis, the Newmarket trainer who had trained Rosyth on the flat, and one of his owners, Mr J. U. Baillie. There was no previous meeting, and they all turned up independently at the National Hunt Committee headquarters at Cavendish Square.

General Sir Randle Feilden weighed in heavily with the case for the prosecution. He explained the reasons why the Newbury stewards could not accept the discrepancy in Rosyth's form in the Schweppes compared to his previous races. The General then listed the dates on which Rosyth had run: once on the flat and five times over hurdles. He revealed that, the day before the Schweppes, he was worried that Rosyth might win, and he had discussed the horse's previous form with the official handicapper, Captain Toller. He also told the National Hunt Committee stewards that he had ordered a saliva test after the Newbury race.

Sir Randle summarized his case: that the horse had run every fortnight; that Gifford had given evidence that the horse had been suffering from a cough, and that Captain Price had told him that the horse had broken blood vessels ten times. A great deal of emphasis was placed on the fact that, in the paddock, Price had ignored his better fancied runner, Catapult II, and that he had actually led Rosyth out onto the course. He made the point that Gifford had ridden the horse differently from when he had run at Sandown. The general also stated that there was stable confidence behind Rosyth.

Ryan could not believe his ears: at no stage did he ever have confidence in Rosyth; neither he nor the owner had placed a penny on him. There was nothing sinister in the fact that he had led out Rosyth – he could hardly lead out two horses at the same time. He pointed out the similarity in the way that Rosyth had run the previous year in the Imperial Cup at Sandown to the way in which he had performed before winning his second Schweppes.

Ryan became so incensed at the way in which General Feilden had unfolded his damaging statement, that Lord Cadogan had to caution him. Ryan recovered and said that the horse had mystified him, Josh Gifford and the vets with his poor running. After his races at Liverpool and Newbury, Ryan felt that Rosyth was 'pulling their legs', and he ran the horse in blinkers next time he raced at Sandown. The horse ran no better with them, and they were never fitted again.

Captain Toller, the handicapper, then explained that he had raised Rosyth by 9 pounds compared with the previous year's Schweppes. His view was that Rosyth, having been beaten by nine lengths at Sandown, produced for 4 pounds eleven lengths on the winner, an obvious discrepancy.

A word about handicapping here would not be out of place. The handicapper is attempting to weight all the horses to finish level. When Captain Toller made his weights for the Schweppes, he had the evidence of the Sandown race before him. In the Schweppes, he set Salmon Spray to give a stone to Rosyth. He had allowed Rosyth 4 pounds for a nine-length beating. This was not particularly generous and, in theory, if the two horses had exactly run their Sandown form at Newbury, then Salmon Spray would have beaten Rosyth by five lengths. However, we know that this did not happen, and on only 4 pounds better terms Rosyth beat Salmon Spray by two lengths. Rosyth's improvement of Salmon Spray was, therefore, 7 pounds, or, if you prefer it, seven lengths.

Put another way, at Sandown Rosyth had received a 19-pound beating from Salmon Spray, who had carried 10 pounds more and had beaten the other horse by nine lengths or 9 pounds. At Newbury, Salmon Spray – giving 14 pounds – was beaten by two lengths. He was 12 pounds better than Rosyth; still an improvement of 7 pounds.

Another horse – Neapolitan Lou – can be used as a link: he had finished fifth in the Schweppes, carrying the same weight as the winner, but was beaten by just under six lengths. The handicapper had a previous line to them both, for on Boxing Day at Kempton, Neapolitan Lou had beaten Rosyth – who was giving 8 pounds – by eight lengths. Allowing a pound for a length, Captain Toller set them both to carry 10 stone 2 pounds in the Schweppes. In the Schweppes, Rosyth can be said to have improved by 9 pounds on Neapolitan Lou.

It had always been Ryan's contention that a trainer's job was to improve his horses; that was precisely what he was employed to do. Ryan reckoned that a trainer who knows his job can improve a two-year-old by something like 10 pounds to a stone simply with one introductory race. A novice hurdler can be expected to show as much as a 14-pound improvement with one educational outing behind him. A trainer with a Classic prospect would be looking for at least a 21-pound improvement between the spring and the Derby. The stewards did not believe that it was possible to improve older horses the way that Ryan did without recourse to illegal methods.

Faced with an accusation of improving a hurdler by 7 pounds, Ryan could not see that the stewards had a case. If they were going to make a stand on 7 pounds, then in his view they were unaware of the facts of racing life. If a 7-pound improvement was illegal, it virtually meant that no horse could ever be allowed to win with a 7-pound penalty.

Lord Cadogan returned to his constant theme. If Ryan was so disappointed with the horse, why did he continue to run him, and why did Gifford ride him, and not Fred Winter? Ryan replied that Winter was his number one jockey and, therefore, rode his number one horse, Catapult II. Winter had never ridden Rosyth; Gifford had always ridden him.

Ryan was then invited to call his witnesses. Ryan Jarvis, who had trained Rosyth on the flat, gave evidence of the colt's career while in his care. He revealed that once after a gallop 'across the flat', and once after a race on the July course, Rosyth had broken blood vessels half an hour later when he had returned to his stable. As the colt had become inconsistent, he was weeded out and sold to Mr Sankey for 430 guineas at Doncaster August sales. He had advised his brother-in-law, Charlie Hall, who trained jumpers, not to buy the horse. Ryan Jarvis recalled that all the trouble with Rosyth seemed to stem from that first occasion when he had worked the horse perhaps too soon after he had contracted flu, and the colt had bled later from the nostrils.

Mike Ashton, Ryan's vet, told the stewards that he knew of Rosyth's tendency to break blood vessels, and that he had suggested to the trainer a course that had proved effective with another horse called No Worry who had an identical problem. This was to keep the horse light and active, and not allow him to become gross; to keep him going throughout the season. He told the stewards that, after Rosyth had won the flat race at Windsor in September 1963, he had been sick for a week, and he detailed the treatment that he had prescribed. Ashton also described the final gallop at Fontwell Park, on the Wednesday before the Schweppes, when he had witnessed the blood in the colt's nostrils. He confirmed that he had said to Ryan that, as it was so close to the race, there was nothing he could prescribe and that they just had to hope for the best. The veterinary surgeon also told of the occasion on 2 January 1964 when he had examined Rosyth thoroughly one day while Ryan was away, because the head lad had been worried by the colt at exercise. He had checked out the horse's heart.

General Feilden now referred to a discrepancy in Ryan's previous evidence. Ryan had earlier told the Newbury stewards that his vet had seen Rosyth ten times; in fact it now seemed that Ashton had only examined Rosyth three times. Lord Cadogan also remarked that, after Rosyth had broken a blood vessel in the Imperial Cup in 1963, the vet had not been summoned.

John Baillie, the owner and breeder, who had horses in training with Ryan, now gave evidence. He recounted Ryan's conversation with him about Rosyth, confirming that Ryan had confided in him his worry about the horse's loss of form. He knew that Ryan had advised the owner to sell the horse, and was adamant that press comment to the effect that the horse had been specially 'readied' for a second Schweppes was wholly false and misguided. He suggested that the bookmakers had their knife into Ryan following press comments that he favoured a Tote monopoly. Finally, John Baillie told the stewards that Ryan had advised him to back Catapult II. He showed the stewards his voucher and confirmed that he had not invested a penny on Rosyth.

Jack Sankey now repeated what Ryan had said to him. It was quite clear that something was amiss, and he had wanted to send the colt to the Equine Research Station at Newmarket for tests.

Lord Cadogan again asked Ryan why he had run the horse so often. Ryan's reply was that Rosyth would not exert himself at home, but was a great eater and doer, and spent the time at exercise jumping and kicking. The only way that he could tell if he was making any progress was by his performance on the racecourse. He had been following his vet's advice.

Ryan was now asked whether Rosyth had ever broken a blood

vessel in a race; the answer was, never *in* a race, usually about twenty minutes after it.

Then the stewards moved on to inquire into the betting on the Schweppes. Ryan was asked if he had backed the horse. The answer was an emphatic *no*, but some of the owners in the stable had backed him. The stewards then asked him what arrangements he had for backing the horse for the stable. 'I have never backed horses for the stable,' Ryan replied.

Continuing on the betting angle, Colonel Blair, the chief of security for the Jockey Club and the National Hunt Committee, confirmed that he could find no evidence of any bets made by either Captain Price or by Mr Sankey. There was nothing abnormal over the on-course betting market for the Schweppes, but there had been considerable activity in the ante-post market. Several owners in the stable had backed Rosyth. On 28 January Nathaniel Cohen had taken £500 for £30 and £350 for £20. Stuart Levy had placed similar bets and stood to win £5780 over a £20 double – Welcome News and Rosyth. Also, Stephen Simpson, a firm with which Nat Cohen was associated, had, on 3 February, taken £1000 for £70 and, on 13 February, £500 for £40 about Rosyth. There was a range of doubles, trebles and accumulators in which Rosyth was involved, with other horses also trained by Captain Price, such as Welcome News, Montgreenan (Lincoln) and Kilmore (Grand National). Colonel Blair quoted a possible £80,000 win, provided they landed the Spring Double as well. Ryan denied that the betting was remotely significant.

The stewards then adjourned, and later they recalled Mike Ashton for further questions. He was asked how many times did he know for sure that Rosyth had broken blood vessels. The only time he had seen blood in the horse's nostrils, Ashton told them, was when he had seen the horse at Fontwell after his workout for the Schweppes.

He simplified, in lay terms, bleeding, stating that there were two categories. Horses that bled from the back of the nostrils, when blood was apparent immediately, and internal haemorrhage, when the blood was not obvious for some considerable time.

The stewards then asked Ashton whether internal bleeding would have a detrimental effect on a horse, and Ashton replied that it was unlikely that a horse with that history would be capable of winning a race like the Schweppes. His opinion was that Rosyth had at some time blown out a hard, solid piece of mucus, and ruptured one of the vessels in the back of the nostrils, leaving a permanent scar and weakness, resulting in nasal haemorrhage.

Ryan was then challenged to state how many times Rosyth had broken blood vessels. He replied, three times; after winning a race at Windsor, at Liverpool twenty to twenty-five minutes after the race, and after the Imperial Cup. In fact, in three races in a row, and all in 1963.

Ashton then stated that he knew that there was something physically wrong with the horse, and he admitted that it could even be his heart. There was something wrong with his circulation, but precisely what was never discovered.

Lord Cadogan then questioned Ryan on the wisdom of running the horse on 30 November, only a month after the colt had been so ill, and pointed out that there were many contradictions in the case. In previous evidence, the trainer had stated that his vet had seen the horse ten times, whereas Ashton had only once seen the horse in the act of breaking a blood vessel. The stewards, he said, could discount coughing as the reason for Rosyth's poor form, and they could very nearly discount breaking blood vessels. In view of the horse's past history, Ryan needed his head examined for running him.

Ryan's reaction was that he was following his vet's advice to keep the horse going; he only had the one horse for Mr Sankey, and he wanted to try to win the Schweppes again for him. He remembered how the horse had suddenly 'come to himself' in February the previous year, so that he felt justified in taking a chance.

Major Gibson agreed that there was some sense in what Captain Price had said – the horse was clearly wrong. Why was there so much talk of broken blood vessels? Ryan said that he thought that this was at the root of the cause; clearly something was wrong inside the horse. Lord Cadogan followed on this line of reasoning. Would it not have been better, he asked, simply to have stated that there was something wrong with the horse instead of broken blood vessels and coughing? He was merely trying to explain, Ryan said, the mass of things wrong with the horse, and breaking blood vessels seemed the most likely cause of his poor performances.

Time was running out for Ryan and Josh; they realized that their defence plea was not making any impact. So Gifford made one last attempt to win the hearts and minds of the stewards. He had known that there was something wrong with the horse for, in the early part of the season, he would not go at all. Two years running he had come to form at the same time; he was a spring horse. Lord Cadogan asked what was a spring horse? Ryan replied that Rosyth had started to thrive; colts often do at this time of the year. Lord Cadogan then reminded Ryan that Rosyth had also won in the autumn!

While Josh and Ryan waited outside the inquiry room for the verdict, they felt that they had been defeated. Josh said, 'I don't think that they have taken any notice of what we have been saying. I think they had already made up their minds.'

Trainer and jockey were recalled, and Lord Cadogan informed them that the notice of their findings could not go in this week's *Racing Calendar*, but that the report would be published in a week's time.

He read them the stewards' statement:

> The stewards of the National Hunt Committee held their inquiry on Thursday, 20 February 1964. Having heard the evidence brought by Captain Ryan Price and J. Gifford including veterinary evidence brought by Captain Price, the stewards were unable to find a reason for the reversal of form of Rosyth between his previous races of the current season and the Schweppes Hurdle race on 15 February. They therefore withdrew Price's licence to train until the end of the season and declared him a disqualified person. They withdrew Gifford's licence until 31 March.

To this day Ryan cannot remember the full words of the sentence.

Muttering phrases like 'kangaroo court', Ryan and Josh left by the side entrance to avoid the waiting newsmen, Ryan convinced that he had not had a fair hearing. 'It is a crime to improve a horse and a far bigger crime to win too many races.' He regretted not having discussed his defence with either Josh Gifford or his vet. The future looked uncertain as they drove home to Findon.

Following their usual custom, no announcement concerning the judgement of the stewards or their sentence was issued from Cavendish Square. For legal reasons the stewards always wait until the issue of *The Racing Calendar* which enjoys the legal protection of a privileged publication. On this occasion a misunderstanding arose, for Ryan was convinced that he had lost his licence for ever.

Press comment, on the whole, was sympathetic. Many journalists referred to the indefinite period of suspension. In the *News of the World*, John Hislop wrote:

> The stewards do not make decisions of such gravity concerning

leading members of their respective branches of the training profession lightly. They have no axe to grind, acting according to their honest beliefs and in the interest of the sport in the light of the evidence before them. Without knowledge of this evidence further comment is impossible. But the practice of not naming a period for the loss of a trainer's licence, whether for life, a matter of years, or months, seems harsh and unnecessary.

John Lawrence (later Lord Oaksey) wrote in the *Daily Telegraph*:

> They [the stewards] are themselves an anachronism and their every act, however well intended, is inevitably examined for signs of injustice under the hard spotlight of public opinion. The indefinite nature of Price's disqualification appears to me and to many others to bear such signs. They should be removed without delay.

Looking back on the case with the advantage of hindsight, Ryan realized that his presentation of his evidence had been amateurish. His witnesses had failed to convince the stewards that, whatever was wrong with the horse, breaking blood vessels was probably the root cause. The stewards had eliminated that excuse.

Ryan wished that he had called Nat Cohen as a witness in order to repudiate the charge that they had landed a coup. Of course, Ryan had no idea that evidence of Cohen's transactions with his bookmakers was going to be presented. In retrospect, Ryan felt that, if the stewards were influenced by a £50 bet on a race like the Schweppes, then there was never going to be any hope for a gambling stable again.

Ryan felt that Colonel Blair's information was misleading, and the fact that an accumulator based on the Spring Double was seen as evidence of an organized coup was derisory. The sums involved were laughable: Cohen had invested £50, Levy £70, Stephen Simpson – a West End commission agent – £110, hardly a professional gambling coup. In Ryan's view, the information was not as important as the stewards seemed to think.

Lord Cadogan's inference that the stewards could very nearly rule out breaking blood vessels does not stand up to Ashton's evidence that the colt had ruptured his nasal vessels on his final workout for the Schweppes at Fontwell Park. Were the stewards right to rule out breaking blood vessels? On the other hand, was Ryan morally justified in continuing to race in public a horse that was clearly not at his best? Was a 7-pound improvement sufficient grounds for the inevitable reaction to the sentence, that Ryan was guilty of cheating with the horse? Ryan was convinced that General Sir Randle Feilden was incorrect in believing that there had been confidence behind the horse. He did not think that the evidence of either the owner, the trainer, the jockey, or John Baillie could lead to such a conclusion. He felt that he had let too many opportunities slip, simply because he did not have a legal mind to counter such a forcefully delivered accusation.

Ryan was convinced of his own innocence.

To Bill Scrimgeour fell the thankless task of finding new homes for some ninety horses, owned by forty-five different owners, ensuring that, wherever possible, the lad that 'did' the horse went to new quarters with him.

To begin with there was talk around the yard that Fred Winter, who was soon due to retire from riding, would be coming to Findon to take over. Fred had spent the night of the 21st deep in conference with Ryan. After much persuasion, Fred reluctantly agreed to take over the yard, even though this meant that he would retire earlier than he had planned. Ryan had been in constant touch with Major Derek Wigan, who had acted as go-between to the stewards. Major Wigan took the view that this would be flouting the intention of the stewards, and if Ryan wished eventually to get his licence back, then the stable must be dismantled.

That took everyone back to square one. Uppermost in Ryan's mind was the need to take no action which might jeopardize or delay his return to training. Acting on Major Wigan's advice, he then issued a statement to the Press Association that all the horses in training would leave his yard within seventy-two hours:

> My family and I will remain here at Findon, together with horses not in training and young stock. Pending my application to the stewards for a renewal of my licence to train, I shall retain my senior staff and I hope that the lads leaving with their horses will return in due course.

The following day, Don Cox, writing in the *Daily Herald*, scotched any idea that Fred Winter would take over: 'Findon not for me,' Cox reported Fred as saying. 'I intend to stick to my plan to set up as a trainer in Lambourn early next summer.'

Findon became a village of mourning as the long queue of horseboxes wended its way up the hill to the stables, watched by a sad and silent crowd of locals, to whom the master of Downs House was a formidable character who had brought fame and success to the village.

All of Major Wigan's horses went to Sid Dale, who had been Ryan's head lad before setting up on his own at Epsom; he also took the ante-post favourite for the Grand National, Kilmore.

While the horses were being loaded up into the horseboxes, Ryan had a telephone call from Jack Sankey to say that, during the night, thieves had broken into his home at Pounds Farm, Kingsnorth in Kent, and had stolen the solid gold Schweppes Trophy that Rosyth had won in 1963. Fortunately, the 1964 trophy was away at the engravers.

There was enormous press coverage of the dispersal. Photographers and journalists, representing most of the papers and agencies, had come to see the event. When the last horse had gone, they pressed Ryan for interviews and for photographs. In the atmosphere, charged with emotion, Ryan addressed them: 'Gentlemen – all I pray is to be allowed to train horses again. It is my life, and I want to do nothing to jeopardize just that.' Everyone then filed quietly away; sometimes even the press can be human.

Then suddenly the stable yard was quiet. Josh Gifford, a witness to all the activity, said, 'When all the horses had gone, the yard was like a museum. That was when it really hit the Guv'nor.' Ryan walked away to the highest point of the Downs to collect his thoughts.

When the announcement concerning the sentence of the stewards did appear in *The Racing Calendar* on 27 February, there was a glimmer of hope in the way that the notice was worded. It said that the stewards withdrew Price's licence to train until the end of the current season, and declared him a disqualified person.

John Lawrence, reporting in the *Daily Telegraph*, wrote:

> Many people, and particularly myself, owe the National Hunt stewards an apology for accusing them wrongly of too great severity in imposing an indefinite sentence. Yesterday's announcement makes nonsense of that accusation.

Clive Graham pointed out in the *Daily Express*:

> While the wording in no way implies that Ryan Price will be granted a licence if applying for the 1964–65 National Hunt season, the outlook is, perhaps, not quite as bleak as the trainer depicted.

The *Evening Standard* quoted a spokesman for the National Hunt Committee as saying:

> ... the fact that different wording has been used in the *Calendar* notice should convey that Price is not without hope of getting his licence back after the end of the season.

Back in the 'museum' at Findon, this news was received with quiet optimism. Ryan began to try to answer the two thousand letters of sympathy that he had received during the days of the case.

The following year Rosyth – now trained by Tom Masson at Lewes – ran for the third time in the Schweppes Gold Trophy. He carried 11 stone 2 pounds (14 pounds more than he had in 1964) and finished second to Elan, beaten by one and a half lengths. There was the almost inevitable inquiry over the winner, but Ryan wonders what would have been Tom Masson's fate had Rosyth managed to win the race for the third time. Someone suggested, ironically, that the Schweppes should carry a special prize for the trainer unwise and unfortunate enough to saddle the winner, which would come in handy by way of compensation when he lost his licence.

Before the 1965 Schweppes Rosyth had run three times without gaining a place. His sudden return to form confirmed Ryan's submission that he was indeed a 'spring horse'.

Rosyth retired in 1966, and stood at his owner's stud in Kent. His total winnings amounted to £20,528. He died in 1975.

11
Suspension

Cheltenham and Aintree, the two great events in the National Hunt calendar, passed by. Ryan watched both meetings on television. He saw Arkle win his first Cheltenham Gold Cup, and was disappointed when Kilmore – now fourteen years old and trained by Sid Dale – fell at the twenty-first fence in the National when up with the leaders.

For once Ryan had time to spare, time to think and time to make plans. Time was something he had not had very much of since he had left the army in 1946. The day-to-day routine of stables, travelling to and from race meetings, making entries and keeping owners informed left very little time for a private life. You made plans day by day. A week ahead was a very long time away.

Now, with no runners, Ryan probably had too much time for thinking. 'Suppose,' he asked himself, 'suppose I do not get my licence back, what then? Farming, breeding racehorses, perhaps.'

During the successful years Ryan had wisely bought the remaining land that made up the Findon training complex as it had existed during the days of Bob Gore. He had begun with the stables and fifty-four acres of paddocks in 1952. That was followed by the acquisition of Downs House, less the wing occupied by Gerry Judd.

One day, quite by chance, while browsing through the adverts in the local paper over breakfast, Ryan saw an announcement by the official receiver of the sale of a parcel of land at Nepcote Green, adjoining his lower stables. Ryan had to secure it. With Dorothy he rushed to Worthing where the auction was taking place and managed to make the final bid. Outside the auction rooms his relief at the purchase was tempered by an understandable anxiety as to how he was going to find the £17,750. He made an appointment to see his bank manager who had no hesitation in lending him the money.

The following year Ryan bought outright the freehold of the gallops and the remaining acres for £8100. The previous owner, Harry Davison, who had trained at The Vale, Findon, had now retired.

Ryan now owned almost 300 acres of the Findon training grounds, and he worked out how he could exploit this in the event of the stewards not restoring his licence. Downs House and the stables could be sold as a going concern, and Ryan could expect to receive a handsome sum for the two, as well as an annual income from the new inmate to use his gallops. This would mean that he would have to build a new home, and the paddock at Nepcote would be ideal for this purpose.

Adjacent to this paddock was the bottom yard of Downs House stables; this consisted of a large barn attached to six loose-boxes and a long building used as a pigsty, which could be converted to take a further twenty boxes. With a new house and these buildings, Ryan would have the basis of a small stud for breeding. 'I could always stand Rosyth here,' he thought.

Dorothy was enthusiastic; Downs House, for all its old-world charm, was not complete (Gerry Judd still occupied a wing) and did not lend itself to expansion or modernization. Together, Ryan and Dorothy began to pace out the paddock. In her mind Dorothy began to design a new and exciting house.

In July Major Derek Wigan arrived at Downs House. As an emissary from the National Hunt Committee, he brought startling news. The stewards were, it seems, prepared to grant Ryan a licence to train, providing he complied with certain conditions. He was not to train the cause of his troubles – Rosyth – nor was he to train for Nat Cohen, Stuart Levy, Ben Rosenfield or Pinky Taylor.

Why the stewards tied in the four men with Rosyth is obscure. Ryan believes that the connection was the successful coups that the men had enjoyed on some of his big race winners. They had won large sums on Chief Barker and Kilmore.

On one occasion, after Nat Cohen had looked round the stables, he became infected with Ryan's colossal confidence. He ignored part of Ryan's advice and bet a 'pony' each-way double on Welcome News in a race at Stratford and Rosyth for the Schweppes. However, he reported what Ryan had told him to Stuart Levy, and Stuart, who was one of the original 'mug punters', placed a 50-shilling yankee on four horses: in addition to the two that Nat had backed, he included Montgreenan for the Lincolnshire Handicap and Kilmore for the Grand National. With two 100 to 6 chances, one at 33 to 1 and one at 100 to 1, the odds against all four winning were so great that the bookmakers did not fill in the total amount on the voucher.

Nat landed his 'pony' double when both Welcome News and Rosyth duly won. If Montgreenan had won the Lincoln, then Stuart Levy would have won £64,000, which would have gone onto Kilmore. If Kilmore had won, Stuart would have received just over £2 million.

In fact, Montgreenan led the Lincoln field for 6 furlongs, then faded, which effectively killed the running accumulator. Kilmore was going well in the Grand National when he fell at the twenty-first fence. Stuart Levy landed just the double – £640.

Ryan's view was that anyone who considered that betting at that level was irregular or abnormal, or that it was 'hot' money or stable-inspired money, was being very naive. He thought it inconceivable, in the serious matter of the loss of a person's livelihood, that the stewards could be influenced by a 50-shilling yankee struck by an overoptimistic punter. Yet Ryan could not help feeling that this might have been the case.

Though Ryan was overjoyed at the prospect of training again, when he and Dorothy talked the matter over with Bill Scrimgeour, they were all concerned at the strings attached and deeply distressed that they were going to have to get along without Nat Cohen and his friends. Ryan wrote identical, formal letters to them all, informing them that he was unable to continue to train for them. He did not give a reason, feeling too embarrassed. Nat Cohen was incensed and asked for more details as to why he was being discarded. Finally Nat went down to Findon where he learned the truth.

Nat and his colleagues decided to leave the horses with Fred Winter, who had started to train at the late Charlie Pratt's old yard at Lambourn. Among the string was the little chestnut, bred by Sir Randle Feilden, called Anglo. Ryan had bought him from Jack Nicholls for £150 and the gelding became Fred Winter's second Grand National winner as a trainer.

During the later part of July, the horses that had been dispersed so quickly in February to other yards started to return with their lads and the yard began to seethe with activity. Everyone was infected with the same sense of purpose; the lads were prepared to sweat blood for the Captain. He had to succeed.

Apart from Nat Cohen's string and Rosyth, who was to remain with Tom Masson, the only horse that did not return to Findon was Mr Bernard Sunley's Beaver II.

Ryan desperately wanted to kick off with a winner, once his licence had been restored. He took Greenhills Lad to Lewes with high hopes, but the colt was not completely fit and could only finish fifth. Ryan's next runner was at Brighton on 4 August, when Sylvan's Boy – in the capable hands of Jimmy Lindley – won the two-year-old race. Ryan had won his first race since the Schweppes. On 12 August Ryan saddled his first National Hunt winner since Rosyth. This was Scarlet Cloak, owned by Brigadier Hardy-Roberts. Ryan was back in business.

Ryan had no runner in the Grand National, but he was the first to congratulate Fred Winter when Anglo became his second successive winner of the big race; but for the stewards' ban, Ryan would have been training him. Fred Winter enjoyed a fantastic season, ending up third on the trainers' list with thirty winners. Anglo was owned by Stuart Levy, who had not been in the Kilmore partnership. It was remarkable that the four friends – Nat Cohen, Ben Rosenfield, Pinky Taylor and Stuart Levy – should have two Grand National winners between them.

When Stuart Levy died he left legacies to both Ryan and Fred Winter, and he left Anglo's Grand National trophy to Nat Cohen.

In August the action started again in Devon, and again Ryan and Josh were in tremendous form. By Christmas 1966, Ryan had saddled forty winners – an unprecedented number even for Downs House. Clearly if the weather held Ryan was heading for a record total of winners – bar accidents or suspension.

After his enforced break, Josh Gifford seemed to be riding with all his old skill and dash, and in the autumn of 1964 he appeared to be heading for his third jockeys' championship. It was not to be for, on 30 November, he took a terrible fall at Nottingham on Reverando, owned by Christopher Collins, and broke his right thigh. It was the cruellest luck and Josh missed the remainder of the season. But that was not all, for just when the leg had mended, Josh played in a cricket match in Oxfordshire; on the way home he was involved in a car accident and broke the same leg again. The stainless steel plate which had been inserted into the broken leg was smashed, and the whole operation had to be repeated. Josh was out of action for fourteen months, and so missed the first half of the next season.

While Josh was away, Ryan divided the rides up amongst his stable jockeys – Buck Jones, Doug Barrott and Paul Kelleway. Buck was the son of the versatile and evergreen jockey, Davy Jones, who rode up to his sixtieth birthday. Doug Barrott was the son of Colonel Hornung's stud groom. As a boy Doug had learned to ride on the ponies owned by Major Derek Wigan, and he came to ride the Wigan horses. He excelled on the hurdler, Burlington II, on whom he rode six successive winners in 1965

Paul Kelleway came from Harry Wragg, and quickly established himself as tough, fearless and determined as a schooling rider. He formed a successful partnership with What a Myth on whom he won the Rhymney Breweries Chase and the Mildmay Memorial Chase.

Ryan's young riders did well, but once Josh returned with a winner at Windsor on 28 January 1966, there was now a constant stream of successes. In February Josh and Ryan won their third Schweppes Gold Trophy, with the virtual novice Le Vermontois. Three out of four was Ryan's score, only this time there was no unpleasantness, no inquiry, just a general delight that Josh had climbed back to the top.

Le Vermontois was one of the best hurdlers Ryan ever trained, though he managed to win a flat race with him at Alexandra Park in 1969. The gelding was always very difficult to train for, like Rosyth, he started to break blood vessels, and did not win another race over hurdles after the Schweppes.

Josh rode Walpole to win the Topham Trophy, and, though Ryan was leading trainer at the end of the season for the fourth time, Josh's accident meant that he was only sixth in the jockeys' list with forty-nine winners.

12
The Hill House Case

> When I hear a man applauded by the mob,
> I always feel a pang of pity for him. All he
> has to do to be hissed is to live long enough.
> H. L. MENCKEN

The seven-year-old hurdler Hill House owned by Mr Len Coville and trained by Ryan Price became the central cause of a racing sensation that rocked the racing world and completely overshadowed everything else that happened at Findon in 1967.

It was to become a *cause célèbre* and, from that fateful day in February, when Hill House won the Schweppes Gold Trophy at Newbury, until August, when the case was finally resolved, the gelding featured almost daily in the racing pages. Had novelist Dick Francis used the story as a plot for one of his highly successful racing thrillers, he would surely have been open to criticism that the twists and turns of the case were too far-fetched. But Francis, then writing a weekly racing column for the *Sunday Express*, enjoyed a very considerable scoop later in the year when he revealed – in advance of the official verdict – the cause of the trouble over Hill House.

It was through the recommendation of Bob McCreery that Ryan came to train Hill House in the first place. After a tremendous day's hunting with the Heythrop, Bob telephoned Ryan to tell him about the fantastic ride he had enjoyed on a hunter owned by Mrs Len Coville. Bob had been so impressed with the gelding that he urged Ryan to try the horse and to buy him. So Ryan duly arrived at the Covilles' home at Lower Slaughter in Gloucestershire. Coville, still a great man to hounds, had been a brilliant point-to-point rider and so had much in common with Ryan.

Ryan proceeded to give the hunter a thorough tryout over the hedges and ditches round the Coville farm. They jumped everything they could find. Ryan was immensely impressed and decided to pay whatever they were asking.

Back at the house the deal was struck and Ryan then asked about one of the horses that had accompanied them round on their 'tantivy'. Len Coville told him that it was a racehorse called Hill House, which had been trained by Bernard Van Cutsem on the flat as a two-year-old. He had finished second in the Buggins Farm Nursery, but had been returned as he had failed to train on. His temperament always seemed to get the better of him. Now a gelding, he was trained by Coville as a hurdler and he had already won a maiden hurdle in the West Country.

Coville then suggested to Ryan that he should train Hill House and get him ready to win a seller. 'Train him for me,' Coville said, 'and I'll give you a half share.' So Ryan took the hunter called Sebastian, who was later to win the working hunter class at the Horse of the Year Show, and became the greatest hunter that Ryan had ever ridden, and Hill House, destined to become the centre of a notorious turf story.

Years later Ryan was to look back on that fateful day. 'One horse gave me as much pleasure in the saddle as anything I have ever ridden; the other caused more anxious moments than any horse I have ever trained.'

When trained over hurdles by Coville, Hill House had run third at Newton Abbot in a maiden hurdle in April 1965, and then, two days later, had managed to win a similar race on the same course. Long before he arrived at Findon he had been handicapped. Now Ryan set out to develop his obvious talent without setting the alarm bells ringing again.

Ryan soon discovered that he had taken on a tricky customer. Some days Hill House would work on the gallops like a dream, then quite suddenly he would behave like a mule and refuse to go near them. There was nothing that his rider or indeed anyone else could do. Ryan loved such eccentrics and set out to try to discover the key. It was found that the gelding went most kindly for a young amateur rider from Kenya, Peter Murray-Wilson, who was on a visit to Findon to learn about training. Ryan also discovered that the horse was very quickly put off his feed by the bustle and activity of the busy stable yard, so moved him to the quieter yard with the two-year-olds. This course of action seemed to work and Hill House began to thrive.

Six weeks later Ryan was able to telephone good news to Coville: 'I do not know about winning a seller for you but I will win the Champion Hurdle.' Coville thought Ryan had gone mad, but in

October 1966 Ryan produced Hill House in a hurdle at Kempton and the horse ran well and finished fourth. He then took the gelding to Huntingdon and duly won the Cambridgeshire Hurdle. This is the race that Sir Ken always used to win every year as part of his preparation for the Champion Hurdle. Hill House trotted up.

Three weeks later he ran in the Mackeson Handicap Hurdle at Cheltenham. Here he started joint-favourite at 11 to 2 on the strength of his win at Huntingdon, which, according to the *Chaseform Notebook*, was impressive. They described him 'coasting to an easy win', adding, 'From his present mark in the handicap he should soon supplement that success.' Carrying a 10-pound penalty which put his weight up to 10 stone 10 pounds, Hill House did not win or even enjoy a very happy run. At the hurdle at the top of the hill just when the downhill dash was about to begin, the horse ahead of him swerved and Hill House was almost brought down, losing at least fifteen lengths. He went in pursuit, but his chance had gone and he finished just over six lengths back in fourth place.

After the race Josh was adamant that he would have won but for the interference and added that, if they handicapped him on that running, he would very nearly win the Schweppes, providing he did not run again before the weights came out. This plan fitted in well with Ryan's ideas, for the horse had run up light after his three races, so he asked Len Coville to take Hill House home for a change and for a spot of hunting to freshen him up for an attack on the Schweppes and the Cheltenham National Hunt Festival.

It was just the tonic that the horse needed. Usually, as he was brought up to peak fitness, something seemed to snap in his brain and he became unmanageable. Ryan said, 'When he was nine tenths fit he was brilliant, but ten tenths fit and he had gone over the hill. He just couldn't take it.' This is precisely what Van Cutsem had found when the colt, as he then was, was being trained for the flat.

Ryan sent for Hill House on 5 January 1967, and started to get him ready for the Schweppes. The horse had 'done himself' rather too well while he had been at Coville's and, with the January weather so atrocious, Ryan had not been able to put as much work into him as he would have liked before his preparatory race at Kempton on 4 February, just a fortnight before the Schweppes. The race was the Lonsdale Hurdle, which had provided an uncanny guide for the Schweppes – both Le Vermontois and Elan were beaten in it, but managed to win the big Newbury race. In 1967, however, things went sadly wrong; Hill House became very stirred up at the start of the race and, a warm favourite at 9 to 2, he dug his toes in and refused to race. It was a severe setback but it was decided to try again the following Saturday at Sandown Park when his owner would go down to the start and lead him in to the tape.

At Sandown Hill House now had to run a pretty respectable race to stand any chance in the Schweppes just a week away. He had not had a race proper since the Mackeson Hurdle at Cheltenham on 12 November, almost three months to the day. In the early part of the race he showed this by jumping very rustily and he made comprehensive mistakes at the fourth and fifth flights of hurdles. At halfway he was right out of contention, but Josh Gifford persevered with him and his jumping improved. Josh succeeded in getting him into the race with a chance approaching the second last flight. Though Hill House stayed on well, he was unable to improve his position any further and was fourth, beaten four lengths and a head by the lightly weighted winner Spartae. Subsequently, the *Chaseform Notebook* reported:

> Hill House, racing in the rear of the field, made two bad errors at the fourth and fifth flights – and consequently was still last three flights from home. Brought round the outside of the field, he had his chance two hurdles out but did not have sufficient extra, though staying on well to the end. No doubt he will improve a bit yet.

Josh reported that the horse had been sluggish early on, had then warmed up to his jumping, but between the last two flights simply blew up. Both trainer and jockey were satisfied with the horse's performance, considering he had not run for three months. Coville said that the horse had given no trouble at the start, and he suggested that he should lead him in at the start of the Schweppes. This Ryan agreed to and added that he thought a good stiff mid-week gallop would bring Hill House to his peak.

Naturally the press corps wanted to know Ryan's plans regarding the Schweppes. He was outspoken and told them, 'I will win.' There was no inquiry by the Sandown stewards; the horse had run into fourth place, as in the Mackeson Hurdle, and could not have finished any closer to the winner. In spite of this, there was an undercurrent of rumour; the notoriety that the big Newbury handicap had generated in past years was about to be reactivated. Some journalists sought official confirmation that the local stewards were satisfied with the running of Hill House, but the germ of the idea that there were storm clouds ahead was sown by one of the members of the National Hunt Committee.

Major Derek Wigan was a loyal patron of Ryan's stable; his wife owned Burlington II, a fancied candidate for the Schweppes. Major Wigan, no doubt fearing for the future of his talented trainer, warned Ryan that in his view if he won the Schweppes with Hill House, he would be in serious trouble with the stewards. Unfortunately, this conversation was overheard by the *Daily Mail* racing correspondent, Tim Fitzgeorge-Parker, who wrote on the Monday under banner headlines: 'Trainer warned: your horse must not win.'

The article went on:

> If Hill House wins the £7500 Schweppes Gold Trophy at Newbury races next Saturday, there will be a stewards' enquiry. Mr Ryan Price, who trains the horse at Findon, Sussex, has been given this warning by a member of the National Hunt Committee. Mr Price, who has won three of the four previous races for the Schweppes Gold Trophy said: 'I'm fed up. I've been advised not to run Hill House. They've told me that if he wins the Schweppes, I'll be warned off for life.'

The significant word in that paragraph is 'they'. Who were 'they'? Was Major Wigan acting as an emissary from the National Hunt Committee, or was he warning Ryan as a private individual? Had it been a message from the turf authorities, then it would have been an extraordinary way of maintaining discipline.

On the Sunday, Major and Mrs Wigan had visited Downs House in order to see their horses. The Major once again repeated his warning to Ryan and again to Bill Scrimgeour. Major Wigan then pressed Ryan to switch Josh from Hill House to Burlington II and Ryan agreed to make the change, and then informed the Press Association of his decision.

On the Monday when the article in the *Daily Mail* appeared, the telephone never stopped ringing all day. Ryan then issued a statement contradicting the *Mail* report:

> At no time has he received either a threat or a warning from any representative of the National Hunt Committee with regard to the running of Hill House last Saturday at Sandown, or a suggestion as to its future running. The stable are planning for Burlington II and Hill House to take their chance in the Schweppes Gold Trophy.

There the matter lay until Wednesday, as Josh Gfford was away riding at Leicester on the Monday and Tuesday. Before going racing at Fontwell, Josh rode Hill House out at Findon, and at breakfast reported to Ryan that he thought the horse was extraordinarily well; that the race had really done him good, and by Saturday he would be ready to run for his life. Josh added, 'I want to ride the winner of the Schweppes and that means Hill House.'

At Fontwell Races there was a distinct atmosphere when Ryan informed Major Wigan of Gifford's decision to switch back to Hill House. The racing press had a field day as the various parties were seen huddled in small groups around the racecourse. Tim Fitzgeorge-Parker wrote: 'Biddlecombe rides Burlington II.' In the *Evening Standard*: 'Gifford will ride Hill House.' No sooner had Josh made his fateful decision than he had a crashing fall on Colonel Wood. He was concussed but, though he missed his other booked rides, he left the course assuring everyone that he would be fit for the Schweppes. Throughout, Ryan's attitude was one of injured innocence. 'My conscience is clear, I have nothing to fear.'

Clive Graham, perhaps still smarting from the fact that Ryan had put him off tipping either Rosyth or Le Vermontois, when they won the Schweppes, wrote a critical article in the *Daily Express*, which ended: 'Whatever the result, Ryan Price must surely be value for a five-figure job on the publicity staff of Ssch... should he decide to retire!'

There was an atmosphere of expectancy at Newbury. Ryan, jaunty and confident in his sheepskin coat, gave Josh the leg-up on Hill House and led him from the paddock. This was Ryan's standard procedure, and there have been many guesses as to why it was necessary for the trainer to lead his horse out onto the course from the parade ring. General Sir Randle Feilden had made much of this when the Rosyth inquiry was being heard. Some have suggested that Ryan did this so that the jockey could not impart any information to punters lurking by the paddock exit. Others suggested that Ryan 'gave them something' before they went down to the start!

The true reason is that Ryan preferred to go out with the horse rather than to watch the race with the owner and have to undergo a postmortem afterwards if the horse was beaten. Trainer and owner would therefore appear from different directions following a win, and everyone was happy. Beaten horses and beaten owners do not mix well with beaten trainers! In this instance the owner, Len

Coville, was not even in the parade ring, for he had already gone down to the start where he was to lead Hill House in to the tapes, just as he had done at Sandown.

The previous year Ryan had received a generous reception when he trained Le Vermontois to win his third Schweppes. There were, however, very different scenes at Newbury following the fifth running of the race. The crowds began booing even before Hill House had jumped the last flight, and by the time that the horse had reached the post, the cheers and jeers had reached a crescendo. Though Hill House was entirely alone on the run-in, Josh Gifford rode a finish as if the hounds of hell were on his heels, and won by twelve lengths. Josh was convinced that he had heard a horse coming up behind him, but he was mistaken and, to his immense surprise when he looked round after passing the post, his nearest challenger was well behind.

They were standing twenty deep at the unsaddling enclosure, and a vociferous and ignorant section of the throng was quite literally giving Ryan 'the bird'. It seemed almost inevitable that there was to be an inquiry, and when the stewards' secretary, Lieutenant-Colonel John Christian, tapped Ryan on the shoulder, one of the crowd shouted out, 'He'll have to be Houdini to get out of this one.' While the stewards deliberated there were incredible scenes outside the weighing room.

Inside, things were not going Ryan's way. The Newbury stewards on duty that day were Major General Sir Randle Feilden, General Sir Richard McCreery and General Sir Miles Dempsey. 'It was the day of the generals.' Though the junior from a military point of view, Sir Randle Feilden was in the chair for the inquiry. He asked Ryan to explain the great improvement in the horse in a week since Sandown.

Ryan did not at first give a clear answer to the question, but referred to the fact that he had wanted to run the horse at Kempton a fortnight earlier, but that the horse had refused to start. He then pointed out that Hill House had made two mistakes at Sandown, and had blown up – a racing expression to denote that a horse was found short of wind, and was therefore short of condition. 'But,' Ryan agreed, 'he has improved.' General Feilden then referred to the fact that Hill House was only fourth at Sandown, beaten one and a half lengths by Get Stepping. Now he had won by twelve lengths. Ryan again explained that his horse had hit a couple of hurdles at

Sandown, and before that he had not run since November, when he had finished fourth in the Mackeson Hurdle.

The handicapper responsible for the Schweppes weights, Captain Charles Toller, was invited to give his opinion. He mentioned that although, before Sandown, the horse had not run since November, the improvement was obvious. Ryan again insisted that Hill House had blown up at Sandown.

Sir Randle then informed Ryan that he himself had seen the Sandown race, and insisted that the horse had improved. Ryan told the stewards that he realized after Sandown that Hill House was short of work when he ran there, and that he had done a tremendous amount of work with him during the week.

General Sir Richard McCreery than asked Ryan whether he had fancied Hill House at Sandown. Ryan replied that he thought he had been straight enough to win. He had looked marvellous, but lost the race when he blew up.

Gifford was not asked for an opinion, and the trainer and jockey were asked to wait outside.

Colonel Blair, the Jockey Club chief of security, and Mr Geoffrey Hamlyn, the representative on the rails of *The Sporting Life*, were then called. General Feilden asked Hamlyn whether there was any unusual betting on the Schweppes. Hamlyn's evidence seemed to influence the stewards. He reported that, at first, Burlington II was the more fancied of the two Price runners, and he recorded a lot of money for both horses with some of the leading layers, but that right at the end a man whom Hamlyn believed was connected with the stable had £4000 to £400 on Hill House. Apparently this backer, whom Hamlyn did not know personally, was connected with the Price stable, and, according to Hamlyn, was one of their 'putters-on'.

Price and Gifford were recalled, and Gifford was questioned for the first time. Sir Randle asked him if he had ridden the horse in both races. Gifford's sole contribution to the inquiry then was delivered loud and clear: 'Yes, sir.'

General Sir Randle Feilden had virtually conducted the cross-examination single-handed. Sir Miles Dempsey had remained silent throughout, and General Sir Richard McCreery had asked but one question.

General Sir Randle Feilden then informed Ryan that it was the view of the stewards that Hill House had made abnormal improvement, and as it was not in their jurisdiction to compare the two races at Sandown and at Newbury, they were reporting him and Gifford to the National Hunt Committee. Ryan then steamed away from the weighing room and straight out to the saddling area where Hill House was undergoing a routine dope test.

Ryan had to remain at the races for he was to saddle Major Derek Wigan's novice hurdler Regimental in the last race. Burlington II, owned by Mrs Wigan and deserted by Gifford, had finished unplaced in the Schweppes. Regimental was only third, and everyone went gloomily home.

The lights were on in the press room long after the crowds had left. Journalists are a pretty hard-headed lot, but they all realized that here was a news story of the first dimension. Would it turn out to be another Rosyth? And was Ryan now destined for oblivion having done the ungentlemanly thing in training four winners of this competitive hurdle? Few of the racing journalists could have realized that they would still be writing about the Hill House affair seven months later, or that it would become one of the great talking points in National Hunt racing.

Ryan went sadly home with the memory of the ugly and distasteful scenes around the weighing room in his mind. At the recent Sandown meeting there had been a spontaneous outburst by a section of the crowd after Scarlet Cloak had won the handicap hurdle run over 2 miles and 5 furlongs. Scarlet Cloak, owned by Brigadier Hardy-Roberts, had won at 100 to 8, but in his previous race at Kempton over three miles just seven days previously, the same horse had run unplaced when a well-backed favourite; presumably those who had supported the horse at Kempton, but had failed to back him at Sandown, suspected trainer and jockey of dishonest conduct. There was a stewards' inquiry, but Ryan had given an explanation that satisfied the Sandown stewards.

Lady Weir wrote to Ryan to express her sympathy at the reception that he had received. She described how she and her daughter had found themselves in the centre of a howling mob by the unsaddling enclosure. A man dressed in a windcheater, with dirty baggy trousers, was yelling abuse at Josh and Ryan at the top of his voice. Lady Weir wrote: 'It is so revolting that anything such fun, so exciting and so beautiful as National Hunt racing should have attracted such riff-raff.'

All through the weekend, the telephone at Downs House rang incessantly as owners with horses in the yard sent their congratulations, which turned to sympathy when they heard the news of the inquiry. One of the first greetings telegrams made Ryan chuckle. It said: WELL DONE ON YET ANOTHER YOU KNOW WHAT, RUTH AND CHARLIE SMIRKE.

Bryan Marshall sent a message of congratulations and good luck, and Peter O'Sullevan, holidaying in Famagusta, sent: CONGRATULATIONS ANOTHER GREAT TRIUMPH STOP DOUBTLESS THE MINI MINDS ARE YAPPING STOP GENIUS HAS ALWAYS BEEN PERSECUTED   PETER O'SULLEVAN.

One of the few redeeming features of adversity is that it assists you to draw up a list of your true friends. Ryan had plenty of support and gained considerable encouragement from the many letters that now began to arrive by every post. Bill Scrimgeour sifted them out into various headings: some were from colleagues and professionals offering advice, some came from members of general public with no stake in racing. There was much intelligent and practical comment.

John Sutcliffe senior, then training at Epsom, wrote offering to send the stewards an account of a discussion that he had had with Ryan during the running of the Spring Hurdle at Sandown. There Ryan had become agitated when Josh had fallen behind on Hill House. Sutcliffe gained a clear impression that Ryan wanted Hill House to win. Ryan had shouted out, 'Catch hold of his head, Josh, and get the so-and-so jumping.'

Ryan was delighted to hear from Bob Turnell, the trainer of the big grey gelding Get Stepping, the horse that the Newbury stewards had used as a link between the Sandown race and the Schweppes in order to measure the improvement by Hill House. Bob now reported that he thought that Get Stepping had gone in the wind and that it was not Hill House's improvement that had been abnormal, but the form of Get Stepping that had altered for the worse. Would the information be of any help, asked Bob?

The following day John Lawrence (as he then was) reported this fact in the *Daily Telegraph*. The headlines said: Get Stepping mishap may be clue to Hill House affair.' It was an important breakthrough for Ryan.

Still the letters kept arriving. One came from an inmate of HM Prison, Camp Hill, Newport, Isle of Wight. Written on prison notepaper, it was a long and sympathetic letter sending encouragement and good luck.

Lieutenant-Colonel Walter Skrine, ex-Commando and amateur

rider extraordinary, wrote: 'It gave me the greatest joy that you had made the Schweppes a four-timer. Lord bless you, you rub salt in the stewards' wounds.... I thought you were wronged cruelly in Rosyth's year, but this time it looks like being an even greater injustice.'

Tim Fitzgeorge-Parker of the *Daily Mail* wrote from Ireland that Paddy Prendergast had suggested the Newmarket trainer Bernard Van Cutsem (who had trained Hill House as a two-year-old) might give vital evidence about the horse's form and erratic temperament.

Rex King sent a most encouraging letter warning Ryan not to lose his 'cool' when he appeared before the stewards. He wrote: 'I don't know what the *hell* all the fuss is about, and my emphatic view is that the Newbury stewards have been stampeded into their action by the "baying" of people "talking through their pockets".'

The Reverend Cronin wrote from a parish in Staffordshire asking to know the exact time of the hearing before the National Hunt Committee, so that he could say mass for a favourable result.

Mr A. E. Sharp of Southampton wrote to point out that all the races at Newbury on that particular day had been won by wide margins, probably due to the holding nature of the ground.

1.55	won by	a head:	10 lengths
2.25	won by	7:	15 lengths
3.00	won by	12:	short head
3.30	won by	15:	8 lengths
4.00	won by	8:	12 lengths
4.30	won by	1:	5 lengths

One of the most respected race-readers and judges of form, Tommy Watson, who helped to compile the *Chaseform Private Handicap*, wrote at some length to show how he had handicapped Hill House after the Sandown race, and after the Schweppes. He enclosed his actual workings for the Schweppes, and wrote: 'You will see, therefore, that for my book Hill House improved by just over 7 pounds from Sandown to Newbury – and this was a horse who had had only one race in public in three months. It does not seem surprising.'

A remarkable letter arrived from a Mr Frank O. Beard BEM. It was a copy of a letter addressed to the stewards. As an ex-jockey, who served his apprenticeship with Mr R. J. Colling, he felt it was his duty to acquaint the stewards with some facts. He then charged both the press and the National Hunt stewards with influencing public opinion well before the day of the Schweppes through an article in the *Daily Mirror*, which stated that the stewards had warned Price that, if he won the Schweppes with Hill House, there would be an investigation. He accused the stewards of dropping behind the times. He continued:

> In Ryan Price we have a man who has mastered the art of training the racehorse. You simply must realize and awaken yourselves to the fact that we have a man who can present an animal on the day of the race in perfect physical condition, trained to the minute, and ready to give its very best performance on the hour and for the race for which it has been trained. . . .
>
> In conclusion, it will be a sorry day for all of us if we allow bigotry, stupidity and the kind of pre-race activity that I have had the misfortune to witness in the case of Price, Gifford, and Hill House, used as a means of destroying a man who has become England's greatest trainer, and all because some out-of-date, out-of-touch and thoroughly vindictive people cannot accept the fact that we have a phenomenon in our midst. The decision is yours – may I suggest that the National Hunt Committee bury personal feelings for the day, and wake up to the real facts. No Gestapo tactics please.

It was quite an extraordinary letter, but it certainly mirrored the feelings and fears of those who were attempting now to provide Ryan's defence.

The Monday morning newspapers on the whole were sympathetic towards Ryan. The *Daily Express* however was one exception. At this time its fine writers Clive Graham (The Scout) and Peter O'Sullevan exerted an enormous influence on the racing world. Clive and Peter were also racing commentators for the BBC, setting a standard that was hard to match; both had a tremendous following.

Before Peter O'Sullevan had left on his annual holiday abroad, he had warned his readers to keep an eye on Hill House for the Schweppes. Bill Scrimgeour was horrified to see that, in Peter O'Sullevan's absence, his colleague Clive Graham was actually siding with the stewards. In desperation Bill cabled Ryan's absent friend: 'URGENT O'SULLEVAN GRECIAN HOTEL FAMAGUSTA HILL HOUSE BY TWELVE LENGTHS ALL HELL LET LOOSE HOPE YOU ARE RETURNING SOON BILL.'

On receiving Bill's *cri de coeur*, Peter wrote to Clive giving a detailed summary of the horse's case. Peter said, 'This horse has form and FORM.' He suggested that, as the horse had been trained with one aim in view, the outcome posed the question: 'How good can a trainer afford to be?'

Clive replied: 'I find it difficult to gild the halo you propose and question whether racing can afford the image created by Captain Ryan Price,' adding, 'Even George Todd described it as the act of a very stupid man.'

Peter's acknowledgement of that letter widened the temporary rift between what was regarded as the most powerful and influential team ever to have operated in racing journalism. The breach was soon healed, however, over a glass or two on Peter's return.

Ryan now gave careful thought as to which solicitor he would engage to prepare his defence and to marshal his evidence. One of his most loyal owners was Mr Cambell Nelson, and he and his wife insisted that Ryan should take the very best possible advice there was available. They strongly recommended James Buckley of Macfarlanes. It proved a wise choice, but Buckley first checked out Ryan and Bill Scrimgeour before accepting the case.

On Monday, 27 February, Ryan saw Buckley for the first time, and the following day Buckley dispatched a rough draft of Ryan's statement for the forthcoming inquiry. Buckley then began to sift the flood of evidence that was arriving by every post. The inquiry was to be held on 7 March, and both the BBC and the ITA had agreed to release video recordings of the races that Hill House had taken part in, at Cheltenham, Sandown and Newbury. The letters from John Sutcliffe senior and Bob Turnell had been sent to the stewards, together with a letter from Bobby Beasley, the rider of Albinella in the Schweppes, confirming the scrimmaging that had put paid to his chance in the race. Bernard Van Cutsem had agreed to appear in order to present details of the two-year-old career of Hill House and the colt's neurotic temperament.

Ryan felt confident that, with all this expert and responsible evidence, he could refute the assertion by the stewards that Hill House had made *abnormal* improvement. He felt sure that he could prove that the improvement was within acceptable limits, within Tommy Watson's estimate of a 7 pounds improvement between the two races.

On the morning of 28 February, Ryan was in Bill Scrimgeour's office by the stable yard. The telephone rang; it was a call from the Jockey Club chief investigations officer, Mr Robert Anderson, and he had news that made Bill's spine tingle. Anderson told Bill that the dope test on Hill House, taken after the Schweppes, had turned out to be positive for the steroid cortisol, and there was to be an inquiry.

Bill passed the phone to Ryan, who listened in grim silence. Ryan then put his hand over the mouthpiece of the phone and said, 'Bill, have we ever fed the horses on cortisol?' Bill shook his head.

Ryan then said to Anderson, 'We have never given our horses anything like that. Would you like to come and test the horse again here?'

Anderson left the phone and returned, saying, 'The senior steward, Lord Willoughby de Broke, is not interested in any tests other than that one taken on Hill House at Newbury.'

Coming at this particular time, the effect of the news was shattering, and it deeply affected everyone who had spoken up for Ryan. On Buckley's advice the news was kept from the stable staff, but Ryan personally telephoned all those who had agreed to give evidence on 7 March to tell them the news.

In those days a positive dope test generally meant that the trainer was automatically warned off, and even Ryan's most optimistic supporters now felt that his cause was hopeless, and that there would be yet another dismantling of Downs House, Findon – possibly for the last time.

Buckley now attempted to gain time in order to pursue scientific and veterinary inquiries into this new, and to Ryan totally unknown, factor. It was agreed with the stewards that the inquiry on 7 March should go ahead as planned, but would restrict its activity to obtaining evidence of the security aspect of the case, and that no conclusions would result.

One person who did not sit down in despair was Lady Weir, for on hearing the news concerning cortisol, she determined to discover who the leading experts in this field of medicine and science were.

For Ryan and Dorothy Price, these were desperate and anxious days. Daily Ryan walked the Downs with the dogs, to try to puzzle it out. What a curious twist of fate had brought the horse to his attention. How ironic that one the the stewards now sitting in judgement was the father of Bob McCreery, on whose suggestion he had gone to Coville's home. Recalling the way in which the Rosyth case had been handled, Ryan thanked his stars that this time he had James Buckley on his side. Ryan knew in his heart that he had not given Hill House anything that would show as cortisol.

He completely trusted his staff, but whatever was cortisol? And how on earth had it got into Hill House?

The Newbury stewards resumed their inquiry at 42 Portman Square on Tuesday, 7 March. General Sir Randle Feilden explained that the purpose of the second hearing had been brought about by the further evidence of the analyst's report on the official test on Hill House. Ryan had been advised by Buckley to hold in abeyance his defence regarding the presence of cortisol.

The stewards then set out systematically to try to discover whether anyone had been physically able to gain access to Hill House in order to administer a drug. A week before the inquiry, the chief investigations officer of the turf authorities, Mr Robert Anderson, had visited Downs House, and had interviewed all the relevant members of Ryan's staff. An ex-Scotland Yard Flying Squad inspector, Anderson produced a complete dossier on every aspect of the security at the stable. He took the view that, due to the excellent security arrangements, the possibility of an outsider getting at Hill House was almost nil.

As a preliminary but vital question, Ryan was asked if he had given any medication to the horse. He denied categorically that he had given anything by way of medication to Hill House.

The course of the investigations then covered the routine involved in the handling and travelling of the horse to the race meeting, and the stewards called the lads responsible, as well as Ryan's travelling head lad, Owen Davies, and the security staff at Newbury racecourse. One or two unusual factors emerged. The lad who cared for Hill House and rode him at exercise, Peter Murray-Wilson, whose father was a friend of Ryan's, was not a stable lad, but a visitor from Kenya, learning the art of training. He did not, therefore possess a stable lad's pass, nor did his name appear on the obligatory list of stable employees which had to be submitted to Weatherby's, the stewards secretaries. The stewards then found that no one in the yard on the morning of the race could remember whether there were one or two blacksmiths 'plating' the horse with racing plates.

Mr Coville, who was in attendance, clearly began to feel a sense of frustration at the apparently long-winded attempts to try to apportion blame to someone for having administered a drug. The stewards seemed so certain that a drug had been administered. Were they not jumping to conclusions? Could the presence of cortisol not be through natural causes? Sir Randle would not be drawn, and he asked Coville to agree that the presence of cortisol was a fact that everyone must accept. The General then pointed out that the hearing had merely been a 'summary of evidence' and as there was a positive result from the analyst, there was a *prima facie* case which must be referred to the National Hunt stewards.

Ryan then formally asked the stewards for more time in which to carry out further tests on Hill House. The General offered as long as was required. The stewards would not press for a particular day, but asked Ryan to inform them when he was ready.

Coville then asked whether he could run Hill House in the meantime. Before the stewards could reply, Ryan interjected that the horse would not run again. Coville reacted strongly to this, saying that there were plans for the horse to race in France, and that as he was joint-owner he had a say in the matter. Ryan then invited Coville to come and collect the horse the next morning. This certainly indicated the degree of tension which existed between Ryan and the blustering Coville.

The inquiry was over. It had virtually eliminated any possibility that some outside agent had succeeded in getting into the stables to dope the horse. There had been no burglary, no break-in; all the padlocks had been cleared, none had been tampered with. Only those persons who had normal and rightful access to Hill House could possibly be suspected. Ryan trusted all of them, and so the inquiry, far from solving the problem, merely deepened the mystery.

Ryan, aided by James Buckley, now began to put the defence case together. There were two parts: first, on the subject of the 'abnormal' improvement in the horse's running they had to attempt to show that Ryan had broken no rules of racing in his public preparation of the horse; second, they must try to prove that Hill House had not been doped, but that the cortisol discovered in the routine sample was there through natural causes.

To support the first part of the case, Buckley had asked the BBC and ITA to provide television recordings of the races that Hill House had run in. These were first shown in the most unlikely of places, an upstairs room in the Elysée Restaurant in Percy Street. I attended, and as there were no sound commentaries on the film it was decided that, in order to bring out the various points for the defence, someone should be there to back up the films. I, therefore, became the first racing correspondent ever to give evidence at a stewards' inquiry in support of a trainer.

The charge concerning cortisol defeated everyone. If doping had been done it must have been an inside job. Here, Ryan showed his almost naive trust in his staff. 'There is no way that anyone employed by me would do such a thing, so do not waste any time on that subject.'

As soon as the positive report for Hill House had been received at Findon, Ryan had commissioned Dr E. C. G. Clark, an eminent scientist based at the Royal Veterinary College in London, to check the reserve sample of Hill House's urine held at the forensic laboratory. On 10 March, Dr Clark wrote to the stewards to the effect that he had, in collaboration with Mr Michael Moss, the director of the forensic laboratory, examined the sample of urine AB 810 from Hill House. He went on: 'I find that this sample contained hydrocortisone [cortisol]. I cannot be dogmatic about the amount of this compound present, but should estimate it to be of the order 10 to 20 micrograms.' The official test had been confirmed. So Ryan now knew the worst, but Dr Clark had reported to Buckley that he was not at all impressed by the method that was used to measure the quantity discovered.

The next job was to determine what level of cortisol (if any) were present in Hill House now, almost a month after the Schweppes. Without any of the stable staff or Ryan being given advance warning, samples were taken from the horse on two separate occasions. These were then analysed by Dr James at St Mary's Hospital. Both samples contained hydrocortisone in excess of the sample taken officially at Newbury. Even more significantly, a third sample taken from one of the horses stabled at the Royal Veterinary College field station was also analysed. This too also contained hydrocortisone in a similar quantity to that found in Hill House's Newbury test. These results exceeded Ryan's wildest hopes, but the tests at Findon had been made without any outside supervision, and were not carried out in a secure situation. Buckley now informed the stewards of the results obtained and, as further tests were needed, suggested that it would be better from everyone's point of view not to rush matters.

The stewards now stated that, in the light of the private tests carried out at Findon, they were prepared to grant facilities for Hill House to be kept at the Equine Research Station at Newmarket, and for tests to be taken there by Dr Clark. A condition was that the horse should be entirely under the control and care of the ERS staff.

Both Buckley and Ryan considered this a perfectly reasonable request, but a new element now entered their calculations: the attitude of the other joint-owner of Hill House, Mr Len Coville. Relations between his solicitors and Buckley had been cool, and now Coville began to rumble. The last thing that anyone wanted was for the joint-owners to fall out at this stage. Coville raised objections immediately. He wished the horse to be sent to a licensed trainer, and wanted to know who was going to pay for all the tests and for the keep of the horse. He also wanted the horse to run in the Scottish Champion Hurdle at Ayr on 22 April.

On 7 April, Buckley replied to the stewards' invitation to send the horse to Newmarket. He wrote: '... after further discussions with our client's advisers and the owners of the horse, it is not now felt that any useful purpose would be gained in sending the horse to Newmarket as, apart from any other reasons, in view of the fact that it will not be possible to keep the horse in training, no conclusive sampling could be carried out.'

The next hurdle to overcome was the written reports from Ryan's expert advisers. The stewards wanted their evidence put forward by way of written memoranda; this Buckley flatly refused to do. He proposed to introduce the expert evidence at the main inquiry. He put forward a date, 5 May, as one convenient for his expert witnesses, and also asked for a list of the witnesses that the stewards proposed to call. Weatherby's then wrote back to confirm that the stewards' advisory committee would be present at the forthcoming inquiry.

Once the date of the inquiry had been telephoned to Len Coville, Ryan, to his consternation, learned that Coville would be abroad on holiday, and that 5 May was inconvenient for him to attend. Weatherby's, in a strongly worded letter to Coville, explained why the inquiry had been convened at that time; first, to enable Captain Price to gather further evidence, and, second, that the date arranged was the only one for some time which was available to the stewards, their advisory committee, and for Captain Price's expert witnesses to attend. Coville agreed to postpone his holiday, but his uncooperative attitude was to continue to the end of the case.

Buckley now had the final report of his expert veterinary witnesses. He admitted to Ryan that the report gave him indigestion, and he realized that it was going to be an extremely difficult task for a layman in law, as Ryan undoubtedly was, to be able to present his case and to organize his witnesses. Buckley then wrote to

Weatherby's to raise again the question of legal representation at the forthcoming hearing. This matter had come up in February, when the stewards had turned it down. Buckley suggested that this was an exceptional case, which, in fairness to Captain Price, demanded that he should be represented.

Weatherby's replied the following day. The decision was again no. Ryan would have to battle it out on his own. However, Buckley would be present at the hearing, but outside the room where the inquiry was to take place. There was nothing to stop Ryan coming out in order to ask him a question.

Meanwhile, Lady Weir was tirelessly working behind the scenes. She wrote to Ryan to say she had remembered a celebrated case in Australia where a horse that was positive for cortisol in a dope test was found to have produced the substance naturally.

Another letter came from a trainer in America, and told of a similar case to Hill House. The horse was Star Ice, and following a positive test for cortisol, it was found that he, too, had manufactured the substance naturally. The stewards had taken over the horse and conducted their own tests. The New Jersey Racing Commission kept Star Ice under lock and key with a twenty-four-hour guard on his stable. The horse was then sent to another stable and apparently the harder he was worked, the more cortisol he produced. After eighteen months of testing, the turf authorities dropped the case.

It could easily prove to be that Hill House was a similar type, a highly nervous and excitable individual who, when he was tuned up for a big race, began to produce cortisol in massive quantities. That was all very well, but how could Ryan possibly prove that to the satisfaction of the stewards?

The preparation of his case, and the legal fees that Ryan was now incurring, gave him cause for concern. Here, Lord and Lady Weir showed their loyalty and generosity, for they offered to assist in any legal expenses that Ryan might be liable for.

Lady Weir had been an outspoken critic of the way in which Ryan had been treated over Rosyth in 1964. She had been exercising her considerable energy in the scientific detection of the mysterious substance cortisol. She now wrote to Ryan enclosing a letter to her from Dr G. F. Marrian, director of research at the Imperial Cancer Research Fund. As Lady Weir said in her letter: 'We have now struck oil.'

Dr Marrian wrote:

'The facts, to the best of my knowledge, are as follows. In man, and in many other animals, cortisone, cortisol, and a number of closely related compounds, are normally secreted by the adrenal glands. These compounds, and some of their metabolic products, appear in the urine, and under conditions of stress the amounts of these compounds in the urine are increased.

While it is possible that cortisone and cortisol may not have been identified in horse urine, it is highly probable that they are normally present. Certainly, a number of closely related compounds have been found normally in horse urine.

Ryan compared that comprehensive statement with the terse typewritten report of the stewards' advisory committee on Sample AB 810:

> The urine sample AB 810 contained cortisol (hydrocortisone).
> Cortisol was administered to the horse prior to the race, in a dose sufficient to improve racing performance.
> Cortisol is not a normal nutrient.

Ryan just could not believe his eyes. One panel of experts stated that cortisol was *not* a normal nutrient; another eminent scientist said categorically that it was normally secreted by the horse.

On 28 April, Ryan received an official summons from the stewards for the inquiry on Friday, 5 May. They asked Ryan to attend in his capacity as trainer of Hill House, and as a half-share owner. The allegations as listed were significant:

> (i) that you administered or allowed or caused to be administered or connived at the administration to the horse of a substance (other than a normal nutrient) which could alter its racing performance at the time of racing, contrary to rule 165(1) of the National Hunt Rules.
> (ii) that you are the trainer of the horse and that the horse ran in the Schweppes Gold Trophy and was found on examination under Rule 66(1) to have received a substance (other than a normal nutrient) which could have altered its racing performance at the time of running of the said race.
> (iii) that the horse when it ran in the Sandown Spring Handicap Hurdle was not run on its merits, contrary to Rule 132.

The letter then listed the persons from whom they were prepared to hear evidence.

So now Ryan knew the extent of the charges against him. They were quite specifically charging him with administering the substance cortisol, and for the first time it was suggested that Hill House had not run on his merits in the Spring Handicap Hurdle at Sandown. There was no mention of abnormal improvement, but a more definite and damning accusation that he had caused the horse to be stopped at Sandown. Here the stewards were most surely putting their necks on the block, for the senior steward on duty at Sandown on the day in question had already stated that the stewards were satisfied with the running of Hill House. Major W. D. Gibson, in response to a pressman's query, had confirmed that he had seen the patrol camera film of the race three times, and the stewards had taken no action. That had certainly cleared the air and removed any suspicion that the horse had not been run on its merits there. A later statement from the National Hunt Committee confirmed this, and was widely reported in the papers.

Still, in spite of a feeling that the weight of evidence was in his favour, Ryan was only too aware of what could happen at these 'Star Chamber' courts, where the stewards were prosecutor, judge and jury. It was Captain H. Ryan Price versus the Establishment, and following the sentence meted out to him after the Rosyth case, Ryan felt uneasy.

The third inquiry into Hill House was held by the stewards of the National Hunt Committee – Lord Willoughby de Broke, Lord Leverhulme and Captain H. M. Gosling – on Friday, 5 May, at 42 Portman Square.

As soon as Ryan arrived in his most discreet and sober grey suit, he heard some disappointing news. Dr Clark, the chief witness for the defence, was ill with a severe attack of flu, and was confined to his bed on doctor's orders.

In his absence, the stewards began by hearing evidence concerning the first part of the charge relating to the running of Hill House. The fateful story unfolded. The starter at Kempton, who was on duty when Hill House failed to start, gave evidence which confirmed that the jockey had made every effort to start, but that after another horse had kicked out at him Hill House became unruly and, when the field was released, refused to race. Then the camera patrol films and the BBC and ITV tele-recordings of the relevant races were shown.

Next, the official handicapper for the Schweppes Gold Trophy, Captain Charles Toller, gave his evidence. When asked for his assessment of the improvement that Hill House had made during the week between his Sandown race and the Schweppes, he replied that his own estimate was an improvement of twelve lengths.

Other handicappers now gave evidence, and the significant point was made that, in subsequent races following the running of the Schweppes, three handicappers had, quite independently, raised Hill House by almost identical margins in the scale. For the St James Handicap Hurdle at Kempton on 11 March, Mr Meredith had put Hill House up by 24 pounds, Mr Sheppard had given the horse 12 stone 4 pounds in the County Handicap at Cheltenham at the Festival meeting, and Mr Harter had raised the weights to 12 stone 3 pounds in the Imperial Cup at Sandown, an increase of 21 pounds. These savage increases were the penalty for a twelve-length win. However, they were only an assessment for future handicaps; any measurement of the improvement that the horse had shown in the week between Sandown and Newbury was virtually impossible, for the only horse that ran in both races with Hill House was the big grey Get Stepping, and he was suspect. He never ran again that season, and had a hobday operation for his wind.

Ryan's reply to the arguments over the poundage was that it was different going at the two racecourses, coupled with the ridiculous pace at which the Schweppes was run, which he said magnified the improvement. The jockey judged the pace to perfection and, throughout the final half mile, was pulling over beaten horses that could scarcely raise a gallop.

In retrospect, there is strong suspicion that it was only moderate horses that Hill House defeated so easily. None of the five horses cut much ice in their subsequent races, as the table shows. Only Albinella came out and won in Ireland, having finished fourth in the Champion Hurdle.

Order of finish Schweppes	*Subsequent races*
1 Hill House	Did not run again
2 Celtic Gold	Fell
3 Beau Caprice	0–0
4 Duneed	0
5 Oberon	3–0
6 Albinella	4–won–0

Just before the stewards broke off the proceedings for a short lunch break, James Buckley sent a message to Ryan that Dr Clark had arrived – against doctor's orders – and was ready to give evidence. Ryan breathed a sigh of relief; without Dr Clark he would have no cornerstone for his scientific defence.

The veterinary and scientific experts who formed Ryan's witnesses were Dr Clark from the Royal Veterinary College, Mr P. Daykin, of Organon Limited, and Dr V. H. James of St Mary's Hospital, together with Mr Michael Ashton, the Findon vet. Ranged up against them, in the red corner as it were, the stewards' advisory committee, consisting of Professor R. J. Fitzpatrick, Dr F. A. Alexander, Dr D. C. Garratt and Mr M. S. Moss.

Ryan then read a long and detailed statement tracing the actions that he had taken after learning from Weatherby's that the official test at Newbury had proved positive for cortisol. He then described how random samples had been taken from the horse while at Findon, and that these had been analysed by Dr James at St Mary's Hospital. One batch had shown a higher content of cortisol than the official Newbury sample. In fact, Dr James had also analysed a sample of urine taken from a horse at the Royal Veterinary College, and that also contained cortisol. The crux of Ryan's defence was that the hydrocortisone (cortisol) which the forensic laboratory stated it had found in excessive quantities in Hill House was naturally secreted.

Mr Michael Moss of the forensic laboratory now gave details of his analysis of sample AB 810. He explained that the sample contained a quantity equivalent to approximately 5 microgrammes from 180 millilitres of urine, and that because there were losses on purification, the actual quantity present was probably between ten to twenty times higher. He maintained that although cortisol is a naturally occurring hormone, it is not normally present in horse urine; the result, he insisted, was therefore positive.

Did Mr Moss agree that hydrocortisone was *never* present? Moss now retracted his remark; what he meant was that hydrocortisone was not normally detected by the methods of analysis that he used. He added that he had never obtained a positive reading for cortisol, unless it had been administered on its own or as part of a related compound.

Lord Willoughby now pressed Moss for an answer as to whether cortisol could not be present *unless* it had been introduced from outside sources. Moss answered in the affirmative, but with the qualifier that it was not normally detectable in the tests that he used. Every test had its sensitivity, and in normal horse urine the quantity was always below the limit for the test.

Once again, Lord Willoughby asked Mr Moss for an assurance that cortisol cannot be found or is never excreted in a horse's urine. This time Moss admitted that it was not possible to say that it was never present, only below the detection limits of the test.

Now Dr Clark described how he had worked alongside Mr Moss at the forensic laboratory, and he now confirmed that the substance found in sample A B 810 was indeed cortisol, and that the amount found in the reserve sample was 1.56 microgrammes. He advised the stewards that the amount one found was never the amount one started with. In this type of analysis, there were certain definite losses. He used Mr Moss's estimate of the losses involved in the process, and though he was in no doubt that cortisol was present, he was very unhappy about exactly what the quantity was.

It was now the turn of the stewards' advisory committee, and Professor Fitzpatrick weighed in with some solid evidence supporting Moss's tests. The committee had questioned Moss thoroughly regarding his methods, and they were absolutely satisfied that although cortisol had not been found in hundreds of other cases, it was present in this case. They confirmed the statement on the charge sheet that cortisol was not a normal constituent of urine. They had asked Moss to describe the *pattern* of the analysis, and from this they were able to conclude that this cortisol was not derived from another commercially available substance. They eliminated the possibility that the cortisol was produced by a substance stimulating the gland which secretes cortisol normally. They eliminated the possibility of the cortisol being produced in the urine by the gland being stimulated physiologically under the stress of racing. The excretion pattern was typical of cortisol and of cortisol alone, and the most reasonable assumption was that cortisol was *administered* to the horse, either by injection or by mouth. The figures suggest that a dose of approximately 1 gramme was compatible with a therapeutic dose.

This, then, was the basis of the prosecution case, and it sounded ominous delivered as it was by such an eminent veterinary professor with such resounding confidence.

Lord Willoughby now attempted to clarify how cortisol had been introduced, and whether it could be implanted under the skin. This, according to Professor Fitzpatrick, would be an unusual method of administering cortisol. Lord Willoughby was trying to establish whether an implant could give a lasting or more permanent effect, and remain in the system for longer. The answer was that it was possible. The stewards then heard a discussion as to the method by which cortisol could be administered to a horse, and the time factor involved in the clearance of the substance from the horse's system.

Now came the sensational and important piece of solid expert evidence from Dr Clark. He challenged outright the statement of the advisory committee that hydrocortisone is not normally excreted by the horse, and he challenged the statement that it must necessarily appear to have been administered in this case. He outlined just how he proposed to bring evidence to show that hydrocortisone is a natural substance normally secreted by a horse. So, after all the skirmishes around the fringes of the case, this was to be a head-on confrontation between two expert witnesses, both eminent scientists and leaders in their own field.

Dr Clark received support from Mr P. Daykin, a research worker in the pharmaceutical industry. He, too, was surprised to hear that the expert committee would not accept that hydrocortisone was a normal constituent of urine; it was an established fact that hydrocortisone is found in the urine of men, dogs, monkeys, rats, mice, indeed, all the species that one can think of, and it would be surprising indeed if it were not to be found in the urine of horses. Mr Daykin suggested that he and Dr Clark should complete further tests on Hill House, and on other horses, and have the results analysed by Dr James.

Dr James, who had analysed the samples taken from Hill House at Findon, explained just what he had found. In the first sample he discovered cortisol to a concentration of 11 microgrammes per 100 millilitres of urine, and in the second 7 microgrammes per 100 millilitres. Both figures were corrected for analytical recovery. The third sample, from a non-Thoroughbred, contained 3 microgrammes per 100 millilitres. He went on to explain the differences in the testing methods, but stated that the values which Mr Moss obtained in collaboration with Dr Clark were not significantly different from the values that he obtained on subsequent samples.

Dr James stressed that the analytical method that he used was stringent, and that the samples had been measured quantitively and completely, and correctly for analytical losses. He was in no doubt that the random samples which he examined contained an amount of cortisol which would seem to be higher than the limit of sensitivity which was earlier suggested by Mr Moss.

The discussion now ranged freely between the experts and became highly technical. The outstanding issue on which neither side could agree was the amounts found in the various tests and the losses incurred on purification.

A misunderstanding arose over the ten to twenty times error that Mr Moss was describing in his tests, compared with the 10 to 20 per cent error that Dr James was referring to – vastly different figures. Moss continued to maintain that he had discovered in his tests an amount fifteen times higher than a normal sample on a horse that had not been given cortisol. He argued that if this was a high normal concentration he would have expected to have found, in the hundred or so tests that he had done, intermediate concentrations between zero and what he found in the sample. He had, though, never found cortisol before.

Lord Willoughby questioned Moss on this and Moss confirmed that he had only found cortisol when it or an allied substance had been administered. Lord Willoughby relentlessly pursued this line of questioning, and he referred Mr Moss to his own report that he had found 5 microgrammes from 180 millilitres and questioned whether this was twenty times higher than the amount that Dr James had found in his tests. Moss said that to find 5 microgrammes he would lose between ten and twenty times that amount in purification.

Mr Daykin pointed out that 5 microgrammes per 180 millilitres was the equivalent of 3 microgrammes per 100 millilitres which was the amount that Dr James had discovered in the horse chosen at random from the Royal Veterinary College. He also made the significant point that the *normal* secretion of hydrocortisone in the urine of horses had not been established. There simply was not sufficient evidence to say what was normal and what was not normal.

Dr Garratt, the analyst on the advisory committee, explained the analytical side of the test methods used by Mr Moss. During the course of the test he discovered between 50 and 100 microgrammes of a compound which was probably hydrocortisone, but in order to determine that it was hydrocortisone he went through an enormous number of purification stages to get a true assessment. This reduced the quantities found from between 50 and 100 microgrammes to between 7 and 11 microgrammes.

Lord Willoughby challenged by recalling Mr Moss's statement that he had found 5 microgrammes. Dr Garratt corrected him by pointing out that it was 5 microgrammes of *purified* material.

Ryan felt that his future was now in a delicate balance. It all hung on whether Lord Willoughby de Broke and his stewards were satisfied by Professor Fitzpatrick's confident assertion that, because Mr Moss had found cortisol, it *must* have been administered. Dr Clark came to Ryan's rescue by maintaining that hydrocortisone was to be found in horses' urine in small and variable quantities. He could not give a figure for it, but he felt that more work should be done in that field, and he offered to collaborate with the advisory committee in order to get a true answer. The discussion then became technical once again, far beyond the comprehension of laymen.

Again Dr Clark brought the inquiry back to the defence plea. They were attempting to prove that the horse was still excreting a high level of hydrocortisone, and that it would go on doing it under any conditions that the stewards cared to arrange. He then suggested that Hill House should be tested under controlled conditions, and that samples should be taken by Mr Moss and Dr James for analysis, and then the two analysts could get together in order to see how the results stood up. Mr Moss was against this, but he was overruled by Lord Willoughby who explained that the stewards had to be satisfied beyond all doubt that what he had discovered in the horse could only have been given him for the purpose of making him go faster for the purpose of the race.

The stewards then conferred in private, and after recalling Ryan and Len Coville, announced their findings. They accepted that Dr Clark believed that Hill House was an exceptional horse in the amount of cortisol he excreted, and he stated that the stewards were prepared to give facilities for the horse to go to the Equine Research Station at Newmarket for no less than four weeks, during which time samples of urine could be taken and tested. These tests would be carried out jointly by Mr Moss and by Dr Clark, who could call in any of the expert witnesses present at the hearing.

Both Ryan and Len Coville agreed to this, and they now worked out the details for the horse's training and feeding while at Ballaton Lodge. Ryan, in response to a question by Lord Willoughby, expressed himself completely satisfied with the way in which the inquiry had been conducted. Coville agreed that he had received a very fair hearing. The stewards then adjourned the inquiry so that further tests could be carried out on Hill House.

It had been some day, and Ryan went away with James Buckley to report on the proceedings. Certainly, Lord Willoughby de Broke had leaned over backwards to give Ryan's witnesses a fair hearing. It was now up to that highly volatile and unreliable character Hill House.

By now the press were getting restless at the apparent inability of the stewards to come to any decision about the Hill House case. On 11 May the *Daily Sketch* headline stated: 'Ryan Price case has gone on too long.' Its opening paragraph went on: 'The sword of injustice has been hanging over Captain Ryan Price of Downs House Stables for eleven long weeks.'

Dick Francis in the *Sunday Express* asked: 'Why the delay? – This Price trial should end now.'

Richard Baerlein in the *Observer* wrote: ' ... it's time that Price had a decision.'

The next scenes in the saga were enacted at Ballaton Lodge in Newmarket. Hill House travelled there on 13 May, was stabled under prearranged security and was cared for, exercised and fed by one of Noel Murless's most experienced lads, Tom Isaac.

Ryan had outlined a training and feeding programme for Isaac to follow. The gelding was to be given one and a quarter hours' exercise each day, with work over a mile at half speed on Wednesdays and Saturdays. Twenty pounds of lightly bruised Canadian oats were to be given in four feeds with a full mash on Wednesdays and Saturdays. He was to have his own hay as supplied to Findon. This routine continued for four weeks with Mr G. A. Hudson, a veterinary surgeon from Bury St Edmunds, keeping a watching brief on behalf of Ryan and Coville.

Random samples of urine were taken at periodic intervals; these were divided into two. One part was analysed by Mr Michael Moss at the forensic laboratory, and the other was sent to Dr James at St Mary's Hospital.

Dr James informed Ryan of his results, which confirmed that Hill House – even under lock and key – was still manufacturing his own cortisol. Dr James attempted to discover what Mr Moss was unearthing, but Moss refused to release his findings. Buckley then wrote to the stewards' solicitors asking for Dr Clark to be informed of the Newmarket analyst's results, and this was promised. However, even as late as 9 June, Moss had still not informed Ryan's experts of his findings. Ryan also became suspicious when the stewards asked for a blood test to be taken from Hill House before he left Newmarket. It was eventually agreed, after Dr Clark's intervention, that the blood samples would be deep-frozen and retained in reserve at Newmarket.

On 9 June the cause of all the trouble left Newmarket in Ryan's horsebox and returned to Findon. On 14 June Len Coville collected Hill House and took him home to Gloucestershire.

That same week Dick Francis went down to Lower Slaughter and succeeded in obtaining an exclusive interview with Len Coville. On the following Sunday, the fruits of that meeting were emblazoned in banner headlines in the *Sunday Express*: 'Hill House makes his own "drug".' It was a very considerable scoop, and Coville talked frankly and openly. Considering that the final inquiry had not even been convened, it was a dangerous outburst, but then Coville was concerned only for his reputation. Ryan, with his livelihood at stake, maintained a dignified silence. Dick Francis was under no doubts as to what the result of the tests at Newmarket meant: '... suspicions that dope was administered before the Schweppes Gold Trophy can die a much overdue death.'

Before that could become a fact the stewards' advisory committee had to meet Ryan's experts; this they did informally on 17 July. It was a long meeting. There was finally an agreed statement by both parties; the advisory committee admitted at long last that there was a strong probability that the level of hydrocortisone could have been a natural phenomenon. Both parties agreed that the abnormally high level of cortisol could indicate that it was administered *or* that this particular horse showed a natural variation from the normal excretion of cortisol. They added that the scientific evidence did not permit distinction between the two possibilities.

So finally the advisory committee had been won over by Ryan's scientists and analysts. It took a further three weeks, though, for the stewards finally to let Ryan off the hook.

The time that the case was taking to resolve was causing many journalists concern. Among them, Michael Williams, who wrote an extremely telling article headed:

INQUIRY INTO AN INQUIRY
Someone has tampered with the bran of Lord Willoughby de Broke, Lord Leverhulme and Captain Miles Gosling ... the three stewards who nearly six months ago began an inquiry into the running of Hill House.... The three executive stewards have shown an abnormal lack of improvement in their ability to clear or otherwise, the name of Hill House's trainer, Ryan Price, or his jockey, Josh Gifford.

> There are a number of suspects, though neither Captain Price nor Gifford are among them. Extensive clinical tests will have to be made on Lord Willoughby de Broke, Lord Leverhulme and Captain Gosling and are, I understand, likely to take some time.
>
> One danger remains. By the time the inquiry into the inquiry is completed, no-one will remember what the first inquiry was all about.'

The end was now in sight, and on 8 August the final inquiry was held at Portman Square. It took the stewards just twenty-five minutes to wrap up the case. For legal reasons the stewards would not release the text of their findings in advance of the publication of *The Racing Calendar*.

This time, though, Ryan was smiling and confident when he left Portman Square. On his behalf James Buckley issued a statement to the waiting press and the Press Association. It said:

> The stewards informed Captain Price, Mr Coville and J. Gifford at the resumed inquiry into the running of Hill House that the case against them was dismissed and their names and the names of Captain Price's stable staff were completely cleared of all allegations relating to the running of Hill House at Sandown and Newbury on 11 and 18 February this year.
>
> They also stated that they were fully satisfied that nothing other than a normal nutrient had been administered to the horse prior to the Newbury race. It is understood that the stewards will publish their full statement in *The Racing Calendar* of this week.

The following day the press had a field day. Peter O'Sullevan in the *Daily Express* called it:

SIX MONTHS' ORDEAL
The Hill House case which finally closed yesterday – with complete honourable discharge for all concerned – may both revolutionize the method of racehorse dope testing and alert trainers as a body to the need for legal representation. After Ryan Price had affirmed 'it is an ordeal I would not like to have to undergo again', Lord Willoughby de Broke looked towards his fellow stewards, Lord Leverhulme and Captain H. M. Gosling, and assured the Hill House connections: 'I can assure you that goes for us too.'

Jack Logan in his weekly column in *The Sporting Life*, after quoting from Peter O'Sullevan's article, remarked that Peter had also suggested that a poorer trainer might have 'gone' for lack of funds to prepare or sustain his defence. Logan wondered whether this might make the Levy Board consider whether a legal-aid system might not be a better investment for the little men of racing than, for instance, the building of another new stand at a superfluous racecourse. 'Quite clearly,' Logan ended, 'a new system of trial – and appeal – should be introduced by our turf authorities: and I still hope that a reference of the whole Hill House affair to the Ombudsman may lead to the reform of the present creaking machinery.'

Ryan's legal expenses amounted to £10,000, so Peter O'Sullevan's suggestion that a lesser man might have 'gone' for lack of funds was perfectly valid.

All the evidence from the various inquiries which had dragged on for 171 days were compressed into 1000 words in *The Racing Calendar*.

10 August 1967

NATIONAL HUNT NOTICE
NEWBURY FEBRUARY MEETING, 1967
SCHWEPPES GOLD TROPHY HANDICAP HURDLE RACE

On February 18th, 1967, the Stewards of the Newbury February Meeting were of the opinion that Hill House, the winner, had made *an abnormal* improvement in the seven days since the Sandown Spring Handicap Hurdle Race on February 11th. They, therefore, reported Captain H. R. Price, the trainer, and J. Gifford, the rider, to the National Hunt Stewards.

Mr. L. A. Coville, half share owner of Hill House with Captain H. R. Price, was later informed of the proceedings and became a party to them.

Samples of saliva and urine were taken from Hill House after the race (referred to below as A.B.810).

Following a report from the National Hunt Committee's Analyst that the urine sample had contained a substance other than a normal nutrient the Newbury Stewards held a further enquiry on March 7th, 1967, as a result of which they referred the analytical report to the Stewards of the National Hunt Committee.

On March 20th a letter was sent on behalf of Captain H. R. Price, trainer of Hill House, requesting from the Stewards of the National Hunt Committee permission for the horse to be sent to the Equine Research Station at Newmarket for tests to be made on it before the Stewards fixed the date for their enquiry. This request, which was granted, was however later withdrawn by Captain Price and the enquiry was fixed for May 5th. Immediately prior to the hearing the owners and trainer of Hill House again asked for an adjournment for further tests to be made on the horse.

The Stewards refused this request but indicated that, should it appear in the course of the enquiry than an adjournment was necessary, this would be granted.

At the enquiry the Stewards saw films taken of three races in which Hill House had taken part:—

The Mackeson Handicap Hurdle Race at Cheltenham on November 12th, 1966, the Sandown Spring Handicap Hurdle Race on February 11th, 1967, and the Schweppes Gold Trophy at Newbury on February 18th, 1967.

They also heard evidence from the following:—

Mr P. Bromley, Commentator for the B.B.C. at Cheltenham on November 12th, 1966, and at Newbury on February 18th, 1967;

Major W. D. Gibson, a Steward of the Sandown Park February Meeting, and Major-General Sir Randle Feilden, who was present at that Meeting and was Senior Steward at the Newbury February Meeting;

Captain C. B. Toller, the Handicapper at the Newbury February Meeting, and Mr J. F. A. Harter, who compiled the weights for the Imperial Cup, Sandown Park on March 18th, after the running of the Schweppes Gold Trophy;

Lt.-Colonel J. M. Christian and Lt.-Colonel R. T. Inglis, Stewards' Secretaries at both the Sandown Park February Meeting and the Newbury February Meeting, and Mr B. van Cutsem, who had trained Hill House as a two years old.

Expert evidence was then given on the analysis of the Newbury sample.

It was the opinion of the Scientific Experts called by the owners and trainer that the substance discovered in the analysis was a substance normally produced by Hill House, and in fact by any horse, and that it could affect the horse's speed in a race. It was denied that any such substance had been administered to the horse.

At the request of Captain Price and Mr Coville an adjournment was agreed to for the purpose of taking further tests from Hill House over a period of time in conditions of rest and also after exercise. The samples taken were to be available to the experts on both sides and analytical findings were to be exchanged.

Hill House was sent to the Equine Research Station at Newmarket from *May 13th to June 9th* where the tests were carried out and the horse was under the care of an independent stableman acceptable to all concerned.

The experts in the case, having completed their analyses, met on

Ryan with Penry (mounted) and Joe and Anne at The Downs

Fred Winter clearly in a distressed state thanks Beaver II after winning the Grand Course de Haies (the French Champion Hurdle) at Auteuil

Beaver II winning at Auteuil. On the same day Fred Winter rode Mandarin to win the big steeplechase

Chief Barker (D. Walker) beating Space King (P. Robinson) in a rough, driving finish for the Manchester November Handicap. Walker never rode another winner

'Boggy' Whelan representing Ryan helps Dennis Walker to unsaddle Chief Barker. The diminutive apprentice could not reach the girths. Note the white paint on Walker's right boot following collision with the rails

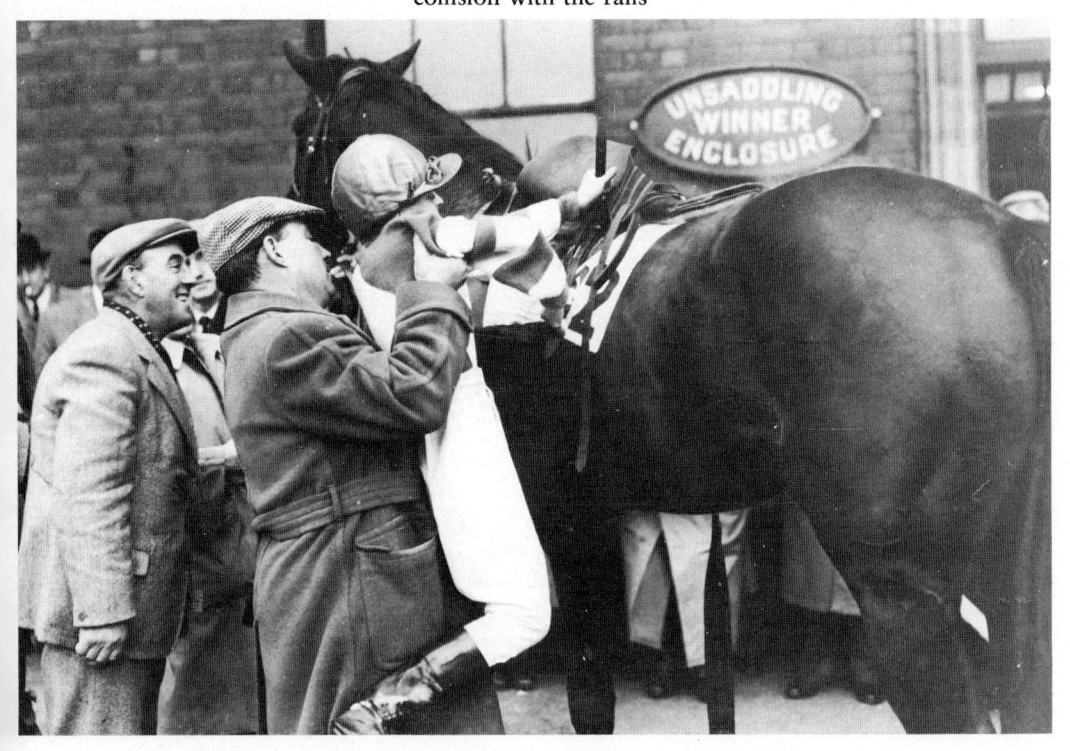

Below left Charlie Worcester ridden by Josh Gifford, winning the Mackeson Gold Cup at Cheltenham, heralding Dorothy's happy return to National Hunt racing

Below right Bob McCreery after riding Gold Wire to victory in Madrid. This remarkable gelding won in six different countries

Left Gold Wire (F. Winter) left, winning the George Williamson Chase at Hurst Park. Knucklecracker (A. Freeman) centre and Pouding (P. Madden) right

Above Hill House (J. Gifford) jumping the last flight before going on to win the Schweppes Gold Trophy at Newbury – the crowd had already started booing

Right Hill House led by Mrs Covell returns to a noisy reception after winning the Schweppes. Snowy Davis on the right

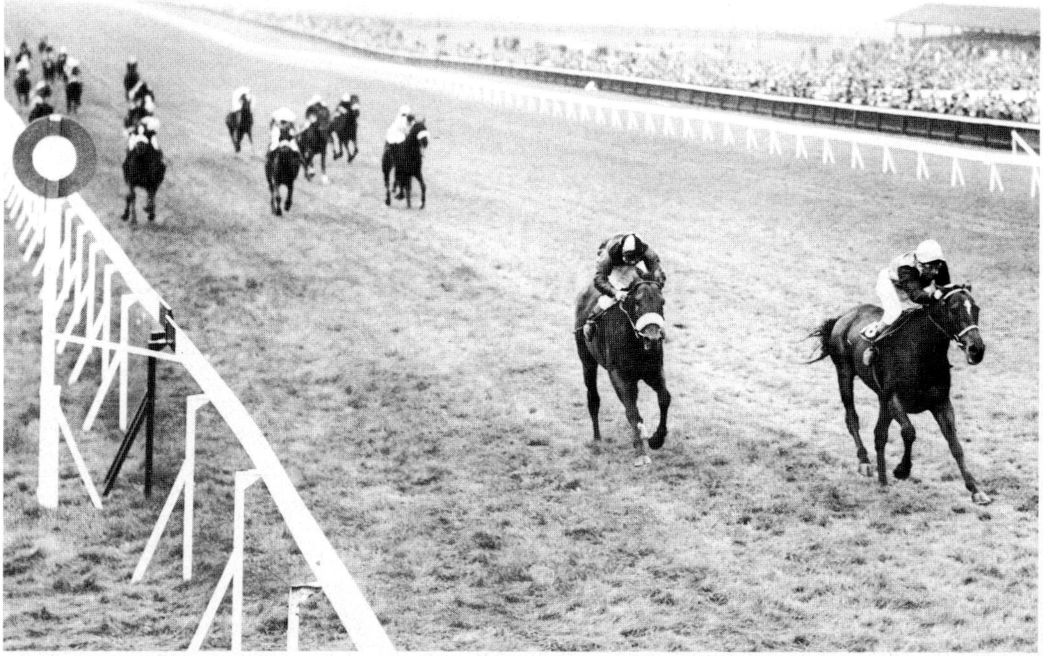

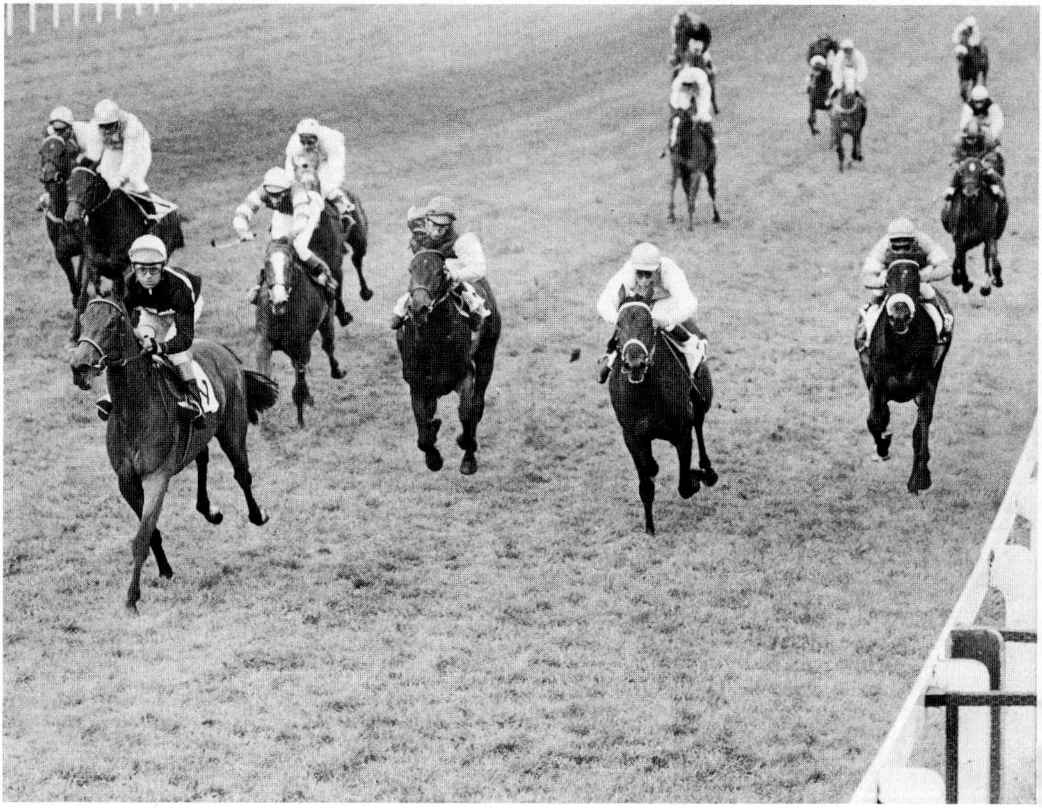

Opposite page above Persian Lancer wins the Cesarewitch five years after his narrow defeat in the race as a three-year-old. Ryan describes this as his greatest training feat

Opposite page below Ginevra wins the Oaks in style. 'Be last at Tattenham Corner and you will win the Oaks' were Ryan's instructions to jockey Tony Murray – carried out to perfection

Right Sandford Lad (Tony Murray) winner of the 1973 William Hill Sprint Championship

Below Major Rose (Lester Piggott) beats Frog in the Chester Cup

Below A Royal Ascot joke: Nat Cohen, H.R.P. and Sheik Essa Al Khalifa in the winner's enclosure

Right Bing Crosby at Soldiers Field with Ryan

Stoke Mandeville Horse Show at Ascot. Second in the team event: H.R.P., Bob Champion and Willie Carson

July 17th to consider their findings and reported to the Stewards of the National Hunt Committee as follows:—

"The Meeting considered the investigation of the horse Hill House when kept at the Equine Research Station, Newmarket, during 4 weeks in May and June. Analytical results for urine samples collected intermittently during this period were presented by Dr James and Mr Moss. Results for other (normal) horses were also presented for comparison.

It was agreed that for the first 48 hours after admission of Hill House, the urine contained abnormally high concentrations of cortisol. These were of the same magnitude as that found in sample A.B.810 obtained from this horse at Newbury Racecourse on Saturday, February 18th, 1967. After the first 48 hours at the Equine Research Station, the concentration of cortisol in the urine of Hill House fell to approximately one third of the initial concentration but remained consistently higher (about 4 to 5 times) than that found in the urine from apparently normal racehorses. This abnormal excretion of steriod occurred under security conditions which were as effective as reasonably possible and which were agreed by Mr Moss and Dr Clark before the investigation commenced.

Sample A.B.810 was considered in the light of this investigation.

There is agreement that Sample A.B.810 contained an abnormally high concentration of cortisol. This high concentration in sample A.B.810 indicates either

(a) that cortisol (or a substance interfering with cortisol metabolism) was administered to the horse, or

(b) that this particular horse, Hill House, shows a natural variation from the normal excretion of cortisol.

The scientific evidence does not permit distinction between these two possibilities.'

The enquiry was re-convened on August 8th, 1967, and the Stewards came to the following decisions:—

(1) They accepted the above agreed report submitted to them by the Scientific Experts on both sides.

(2) They accepted the explanations of Captain H. R. Price, the trainer and joint owner, Mr L. A. Coville, the joint owner, and J. Gifford, the rider, of Hill House, as to the horse's improvement between February 11th and February 18th. They found that no substance (other than a normal nutrient) had been administered to the horse.

The Stewards, therefore, dismissed the case.

After the Hill House verdict journalists in many papers launched 'in depth' features on the case and all its extraordinary aspects. The *Daily Mail* was infatuated by the part that Major Derek Wigan had played and reminded its readers that one of the paper's correspondents had pursued Major Wigan to his holiday island of Elba where he had been presented with a request to answer twelve questions. The major declined, but gave them a prepared statement to the effect that he had already made a full statement to the senior steward of the National Hunt Committee and was not prepared to make any further statement or comment.

The Sporting Life's veterinary correspondent in an article on 22 August wrote that the Jockey Club must now revise their rules on doping. He felt that there was at least one aspect of the system of dope testing which needed careful scrutiny. This was the question of whether or not the stewards or the scientists that advise them were in a position to interpret the exact significance of the results obtained from the analysis of samples.

He went on:

> It is generally recognized in scientific circles that in many instances too little is known about the body processes of the horse to allow for firm predictions about their physiology or function.
>
> Against this background the capacity to interpret with any degree of accuracy is extremely limited.
>
> ### WHAT IS NORMAL?
> For instance it would be interesting to know what the Jockey Cub experts considered to be the normal excretion rate of cortisol, and how far values outside these limits could be considered abnormal.
>
> As the analyst becomes more proficient at detecting the levels of various natural substances in the urine and saliva, so the stewards may, to some extent, become prisoners of their own system.

The late J. L. Manning in the *Daily Mail* wrote:

> ### HILL HOUSE EXPOSES RISK OF RACING INJUSTICE
> Hill House's long inquiry went so near to an unjust decision that the arbitrary procedure of secret turf tribunals urgently needs revision. In the end the finding was correct, but how slender was the thread on which the outcome hung is shown in the National Hunt stewards report in yesterday's *Racing Calendar*.

He went on:

> ### NO APPEAL
> A private organization's private investigation of a matter of public importance ended with limited information for the public. There was

more information than usual, but it was still inadequate.

Although at stake were the integrity of racing and the reputation, livelihood and property of individuals, this was a trial of persons without legal representation,* without sworn evidence, without the subpoena and examination of all witnesses, without the compulsory production of documents and without the right of appeal.

Len Coville sent Hill House to Doncaster sales, to dissolve a partnership, on 26 October 1967. The gelding was bought by the Scottish bookmaker, John Banks, for 12,700 guineas. The horse was sent to Malton to be trained by Frank Carr, in whose care he remained for the 1967–68 National Hunt season. Hill House ran twice and failed to start on each occasion. He whipped round with Gerry Scott at Ayr and a week later did the same with Jimmy Morrissey in the Schweppes at Newbury. He was dope-tested by the stewards on both occasions but their findings were never revealed.

John Banks then retired Hill House and sent him to Harvey Smith to be trained as a show jumper – without any success. Hill House eventually ended up at Findon with Ryan's other old war horses out on the downs. In 1980 this mercurial animal contracted colic and Ryan had to have him put down.

The traumatic months of the affair seemed, outwardly at any rate, to have had little effect on Ryan. His constant belief in his own innocence helped him through.

Dorothy took the events more thoughtfully and Ryan's ordeal left a far deeper wound. She had felt so sure that this time Ryan would be disqualified for good and the prospect of a future without racehorses haunted her constantly. She considered that there was a vendetta against Ryan. It was a long time before she could be induced to go racing again and then she only went when she had a runner. After Hill House nothing could ever be the same again.

Years later, when Dorothy's good young horse Ruisselet had pulled up in a steeplechase at Newbury, Ryan was summoned before the stewards. The gelding had clearly gone in the wind, but Dorothy felt 'the shivers of past ghosts' while Ryan was in with the stewards.

*This was a powerful article by a fearless campaigner for fair play. J.L. was not absolutely correct in saying that Ryan had no legal representation. He had James Buckley as counsel but Buckley was not allowed into the room where the hearing was taking place. This procedure was altered in March 1969 when, after Hill House, all trainers were legally represented at Jockey Club hearings.

13
The Lure of the Flat

After the tempestuous days of the Hill House inquiry, the 1967–68 season was rather an anticlimax. Ryan dropped down to sixth place on the trainers' list with only forty-three winners; the only important races that he captured were the Mackeson Gold Cup with Dorothy's chaser Charlie Worcester, which netted over £4000, and, the following season, the Cheltenham Gold Cup with What a Myth, owned by Lady Weir.

Dorothy now decided that it was time to start thinking about their new home at Nepcote Green. An architect was commissioned and given a set of priorities: 'The children come first, the dogs second, and Ryan and I third.' As the architect had just designed a house round a parrot for an eccentric old lady in Worthing, he did not envisage any great problems. The new house was to be spacious, with plenty of windows, rather like a villa on the French Riviera.

The building work was started in the autumn of 1968. Soldiers Field, as the house was named, was built by Cowley Brothers, a local firm for whom Ryan had trained in the past. They were between contracts and the house was completed in six months, with Dorothy in constant attendance.

In February 1969 Ryan, Dorothy, the children and dogs moved the half mile from Downs House which now became the home of the Downsman and his wife. Bill Scrimgeour, who had lived in the flat in what is now Josh Gifford's yard, moved in too. Later a self-contained flat was added, and a spectacular sun room where Dorothy grows the most exotic and beautiful potted plants.

Lady Weir was one of the first owners to be shown round and she greatly admired Dorothy's planning. Later that evening, she telephoned to tell Dorothy how much she had enjoyed seeing the new home, but added that it lacked one important feature, a swimming pool. She suggested that it should be sited near the orchard, and that it was to be constructed at once, at her expense.

In 1968 Ryan delivered his customary assault on the Schweppes Gold Trophy; although Major Rose had not run since October 1967, he very nearly brought it off. Persian War beat him by only half a length, and then went on to win his first Champion Hurdle. Ryan did not enter Major Rose for the Champion Hurdle. Instead he mapped out a flat-racing campaign for this great-hearted stayer.

Such was the public confidence in Ryan and his big-race jockey, Lester Piggott that Major Rose started favourite for the Chester Cup, even though he had not run since the Schweppes. Lester won by half a length to land a fair gamble. The runner-up, Ryan was pleased to see, was Frog, owned by his 'Chief Inquisitor', General Sir Randle Feilden.

Major Rose was never a particularly robust horse, but he was easy to train and he became stronger with age. Ryan had bought him as a three-year-old from George Todd for £200. Here was yet another horse in the long list of inexpensive purchases which became great money spinners. 'Money never bought a great horse,' is one of Ryan's favourite sayings, and he took immense delight in winning big races with horses which cost 'a row of buttons'.

After the Chester Cup, Major Rose ran in the French Champion Hurdle at Auteuil, but it proved an abortive venture and Josh had to pull him up. Ryan rested the Major until the autumn when his target was the Cesarewitch. The previous year, with Doug Smith riding, he had finished second to Boismoss, but now, with Lester Piggott in the saddle, Major Rose enjoyed his finest hour and, carrying 9 stone 4 pounds, which was 18 pounds more than he had carried twelve months before, he won comfortably.

Ryan also captured the Royal Lodge Stakes with Dutch Bells, owned by a Dutchman, Mr G. Van der Ploeg, founder of the House of Holland. Eventually Ryan lost the horse, which was sent to be trained at Epsom. Later the Dutchman returned to the fold and Ryan trained a brilliantly fast filly Truly Thankful to win the Queen Mary at Royal Ascot for him.

Ryan was exceptionally patient with 'difficult' owners, especially if they owned good horses. One day Van der Ploeg tackled Ryan about his training account: 'It seems that I am paying £5 a week a horse more than any other owners.' 'That's true,' Ryan retorted, 'you are more bloody trouble than any of the other owners.'

In 1969 Ryan again challenged for some of the big flat races, Lexicon winning the Ascot Stakes and Quarryknowe taking the National Stakes at Sandown. It was significant that, in the two years 1968 and 1969, Ryan's flat-racing winnings amounted to £37,567, compared to his National Hunt total of £42,441 for the two equivalent seasons.

Ryan was enjoying his invasion of the rarefied atmosphere of flat racing; Dorothy less so. The summer travelling was so much easier, the prize money greater, and there was an end product: a flat racer that had been successful could be sold either for stud or for racing abroad. There was not the same amount of injuries to horses and the flat racers returned from races fresher and could run again sooner than the jumpers. Ryan also had the complete respect of the top flat-race jockeys. He began to plan his switch to the flat.

Ryan has always been a man of instant judgement and sudden decisions, but even with *his* track record it was an astonishing offer he made to Josh Gifford in February 1970. The scene took place in Ryan's sitting room. Josh, relaxed and off duty, admitted to Ryan that he was enjoying riding less and less. The previous May, he had married the show jumper, Althea Roger-Smith and perhaps his thoughts were now centred on setting up a home, retirement from the saddle, and acquiring a training stable of his own.

Josh was one of the bravest of the brave – he gave every horse a terrific ride; but he had endured two serious racing falls and a car accident. Ryan recalled a day at Fontwell Park when Josh was still an apprentice, on loan from Sam Armstrong. Ryan was schooling horses after racing, and Josh had a crashing fall. Rather than admit to Ryan that he was hurt, Josh rode another horse in a school over hurdles. Later that day when Josh went for an X-ray, it was discovered that he had broken his collarbone.

Josh had been champion jockey on three occasions, and his injuries had probably cost him two more titles. He had ridden 642 winners, mostly for Ryan, who now had a premonition about Josh's future. 'Josh, you must give up riding immediately – you have done enough. I am giving up training jumpers and concentrating on the flat. I will move all my flat racers down to Soldiers Field. I will sell you Downs House, the stables and a paddock, and you can take over all the jumpers. Thank you for all the winners you have ridden for me; the place is yours. We will have The Downs valued and you can have four years to pay.'

Josh was taken completely by surprise. He had planned to go on riding for a couple of seasons until he found a yard and collected some horses together. Now here was Ryan offering him a yard of forty jumpers as a going concern. He felt he was not quite ready for such a responsibility and asked Ryan to carry on for at least another year. Ryan would have none of it, however, and implored Josh to give up immediately. But Josh wanted to ride in the Grand National, so Ryan agreed to stay on until the race.

Josh took twenty-four hours to consider the matter and discuss it with Althea. The next day he returned with the news that he had decided to accept Ryan's offer.

Josh had The Downs valued at £25,000, Ryan at £35,000. In the end they compromised at £29,000. Josh would pay £9000 down, and the balance in equal instalments over the next four years.

In the Grand National Josh rode Assad into seventh place. It was his last ride. A few days later he took over at The Downs. By then Ryan had moved most of his flat-race horses down to the yard near Soldiers Field. Some of his staff – mostly the heavier lads or those who preferred the winter game – remained with the jumpers, including Snowy Davis who had travelled horses for Ryan. Ron James stayed on as Josh's head lad. Ryan took Geoffrey Potts as head lad as well as Tommy Winters, Norman Freeman and Albert Allen.

Work now started on building new boxes; as the stables were finished so more horses arrived from Downs House and other sources. All the yearlings had been broken by Ryan's lifelong friend from Sussex, Roy Trigg.

There was little change in the stable routine except that Ryan did not drag the flat racers about the downs so much as the jumpers who were often out for two and a half hours. Findon had always been a centre for jumpers – no great flat-race horse had ever been prepared on those rolling downs. But Ryan knew that the gallops were severe and that his 6 furlongs against the collar was the equivalent of a mile on the level.

That great Yorkshire trainer Dobson Peacock, when asked what he did with his horses to get them fit, replied, 'Well, I walks and I trots.'

'What do you do after that?'

'Then I trots and I walks.'

All roads lead to Rome and one of the greatest trainers of jumpers, Tom Dreaper, never had his string out for longer than half an hour.

It is Ryan's contention that the modern horse does not possess the bone or substance or constitution of those of fifty years ago and he places the blame firmly on the studs. 'They are breeding horses in chicken runs now; the youngstock are not given enough space to use their actions.' Before the war Fred Darling would visit Lavington Park Stud in order to view the yearlings that he was later to train. He would bring his hack down and would gallop round the paddocks with the yearlings. After a few days he had marked down the good movers and earmarked the ones he wished to train.

Ryan also decries modern feeding methods: 'Cake, nuts and pellets have replaced the traditional oats, bran, good hay and linseed. Many paddocks are "horse sick" and in some cases poisoned with fertilizers.'

The dice was thrown. Ryan had turned his back on the National Hunt sport that he had dominated for so long. 'If I don't succeed,' he had warned Josh, 'I'll be back training jumpers again.' Secretly he thought he might have left the change a bit too late. He had been leading National Hunt trainer on five occasions. His jockeys had been champions eight times. What sort of an impact would he have among the top echelons of flat-race trainers?

It had always been Ryan's intention to switch over from jumping when Fred Winter retired in 1964. The arrival of Josh Gifford had changed that and Josh had carried him on for another six years. Ryan knew that he could prepare middle-distance horses and stayers – he had already won the Cesarewitch three times; it was the two-year-olds that were his biggest worry. 'I just didn't know if I could train them. In February I began to sort them out and I noticed that one of them by Hard Tack called Harland seemed much more forward than the others, so I concentrated on him.'

Ryan very soon received the answer to his question, for Harland, who had been bought as a yearling for 3000 guineas on behalf of Lord Weir, was his first runner of the season. Starting at 11 to 10 on, the colt won the first two-year-old race to be run in the south of England, at Kempton Park. Everyone seemed to know that Harland could go and the public had no inhibitions about Ryan's ability to produce two-year-olds ready to win first time out. Harland knew his job thoroughly and won by a length in the hands of Doug Smith's stable jockey, Tony Murray. This first two-year-old winner was to prove a happy omen for the string at Soldiers Field, and Ryan's first crop of yearlings bought at public auction through Jack Doyle's agency were to prove an outstanding collection.

Winning the Montgomerie Stakes at Ayr with Quarryknowe gave Ryan special pleasure, for this super, game colt was also owned by Lord Weir, who lived nearby at Montgreenan. Ryan was to saddle many winners at Ayr for the Weir family during the next few years, and never forgot the loyal support that they had given him in his time of need.

By midsummer Ryan was brimming over with confidence. He saddled another potentially useful two-year-old called Cornuto at Brighton. Ryan considers this colt was, on that occasion, the biggest certainty that he has ever had. He booked Bill Williamson to ride, and his orders in the paddock made 'Weary' Willie, as he was known, suddenly taken notice. 'For goodness sake *do not* win too far with this one.' Bill was unable to comply with instructions and, sitting with a double handful, won by five lengths.

During his first season Ryan used the best of the jockeys that were available – Lester Piggott, Bill Williamson, Pat Eddery and Tony Murray all rode winners for the stable. Lester won the Pilgrim Stakes at the local Goodwood meeting on a very smart filly, Super Honey. This was a hard-fought win and Ryan rested her until the Newmarket October meeting, where she was only just beaten by a neck and two short heads in the Cheveley Park Stakes.

Ryan's best two-year-old colt was undoubtedly Good Bond, who ended the season by winning the important Horris Hill Stakes at Newbury. However, another promising colt was Levanter, who had been most impressive when winning the Houghton Stakes at Newmarket.

Though Ryan finished well down the list of flat trainers, he was extremely satisfied with his 1970 season. His total winnings were over £25,000, he had produced eleven two-year-old winners and, in Good Bond, Super Honey and Levanter, he had three potential Classic horses. He waited for the new flat-racing season to start with growing impatience.

14
Ginevra

Ryan's transition to the flat was beginning to bear fruit. He began the 1971 season by saddling Good Bond to win the Ascot 2000 Guineas Trial, and Super Honey – who thrived on a busy spring schedule – won both the Princess Elizabeth Stakes and the Nell Gwynn Stakes. On both occasions she was ridden by Lester Piggott, who subjected her to exceptionally hard races.

In the 1000 Guineas, Super Honey ran her customary game race, but was overwhelmed by Altesse Royale, trained by Noel Murless, who beat her by half a length. In the Nell Gwynn Super Honey had beaten Altesse Royale, and the improvement that Noel Murless had wrought did not escape Ryan's admiration: 'Noel improved Altesse Royale by 8 pounds compared to my filly, but then he was training her expressly for the 1000. I never believed that my filly was a Guineas mare. We were delighted to win two Classic trials which enhanced Super Honey's value, and being second in the Guineas did her no harm.'

Later in the season, Super Honey was sold privately for over £40,000 to Bertram Firestone as a potential brood mare.

Ryan's Derby colt, Levanter, turned out to be his biggest disappointment as a trainer. Levanter won the Craven Stakes, but then failed in the Chester Vase. After the race the colt was found to be lame. He had punctured the frog of his hoof – probably on one of the steel pins that hold the coconut mats over the road crossing. There was little time now before the Derby, and the colt had missed two important gallops. Ryan managed to get him to the post for the Predominate Stakes at Goodwood, which he won after some extra tender riding by Piggott. Ryan realized that a Derby attempt was hopeless and, sadly, he took the horse out of the big Epsom race. Levanter never ran again and, the winner of three of his four races, he was retired to stud. He now stands alongside another ex-Findon inmate, Cornuto, at the Semley Stud at Shaftesbury in Dorset.

In August Good Bond landed an enormous gamble when winning the Northern Goldsmiths Handicap at Newcastle under 9 stone 8 pounds. However, the most significant event in the autumn was Ginevra's win in the Tankerville Nursery at Ascot in October. Ginevra was extraordinary. She had been bred by Lord Suffolk, but, with her rather light frame, the filly had not attracted any attention, and had been led out of the Tattersalls sales ring unsold at 1300 guineas. Two years later she was to attract rather more attention when she passed through the same ring.

Charles St George and his partner, Peter Richards, bought Ginevra privately from Lord Suffolk on Champion Stakes day at Newmarket. They nearly missed the race – won by Lorenzaccio in the St George colours – because they stopped off at the stables to view two fillies – one by Shantung and one by Hook Money – that Lord Suffolk had failed to sell. Mick Rogers, the Irish trainer, spent twenty minutes listening to the Shantung filly's heart beat. He simply could not believe his ears: the beat was spectacularly strong. He recommended to the prospective purchasers to buy the Shantung and forget the Hook Money. Later, at the races, Charles St George clinched the deal with Lord Suffolk and bought the filly, later to be named Ginevra, for £2000. Half an hour later Lorenzaccio beat Nijinsky in the Champion Stakes, and as Peter Richards had taken 1000 to 60 about the winner, he had won his share.

The partners sent the filly to be trained by Ryan at Findon, but several days later were concerned when Ryan telephoned to ask if there had been a mistake in the yearlings. 'This filly is only a 13.2 pony.' After checking with the breeder that the correct filly had been sent, they got back to Ryan. By then Ryan had changed his tune: 'Never mind, if they have sent the wrong one. This filly has grown two inches in a week. I'll keep this one. She's a ballerina and I love her; she's a racehorse.'

The initiation of the 'ballerina' to the racecourse was entrusted to that consummate horseman, Jimmy Lindley, who gave the highly strung filly a perfect and easy introduction to racing. Gently ridden, she finished a creditable fourth and seemed to be thoroughly enjoying herself. Next time out the filly was a warm favourite and, ridden by Ernie Johnson, she won a maiden race at Newmarket. This was Peter Richards's very first success as an owner, and two races later he was back in the same enclosure with his second winner, Irvine, trained by Henry Cecil.

For her next race Ginevra returned to Newmarket for the important Cherry Hinton Stakes. This time Lester Piggott was the rider, but for reasons that were not readily apparent, the filly took a violent dislike to him. She refused to allow him to mount and when all the other runners had left the paddock, Lester, in desperation, cornered her against the rails and hit her with his whip. Ginevra never forgot this and though she finished third, she did not show her usual dash. Next time out, at York, it was the same story: Ginevra simply would not have Lester on her back at any price. She threw him in the paddock, broke loose, careered round behind the saddling boxes and disappeared into the gents lavatory, where she was finally captured. Ryan gave Lester a leg-up again; the filly took off with him on the way to the post, and in the race she bolted, led for 4 furlongs and then tired. On dismounting Lester announced that he would never ride the filly again – a statement which the partners and Ryan received with equanimity.

Tony Murray was given the ride in the Tankerville Nursery, and Ryan's instructions to this quiet, accomplished horseman were to let the filly settle and only to produce her in the last furlong. 'Just see how many horses you go by.' Murray followed instructions to the letter, and won by two short heads 'going away'. Ryan was thrilled at the finesse which Murray had shown in his cool handling of an erratic filly.

He kept Peter Richards in the unsaddling enclosure for half an hour, during which time he told him, in the language of a door-to-door salesman, the talent, ability and devastating turn of foot that his filly possessed. Warning the joint-owners of the fine balance between her brilliance and her temperament, Ryan was still talking about the filly when the placed horses arrived from the following race. Ryan's last words to Peter Richards were, 'Make no mistake, this is a Classic filly, and ridden that way she will win you the Oaks next year.' When Peter Richards telephoned Charles St George that evening, he repeated what Ryan had said. St George thought that Ryan was out of his mind.

For 1972 Ryan at last had a retained stable jockey – Tony Murray, who had ridden twelve winners for the stable the previous season while riding for Douglas Smith. Tony Murray was a product of 'Frenchy' Nicholson's apprentice school, from which Pat Eddery and Paul Cook had emerged to stardom.

Ryan had always been a close friend of Doug Smith, but a misunderstanding arose over Murray's decision to accept Ryan's offer of a retainer. Douglas Smith complained to Ryan that the first he had heard of the move was when he had read it in the press. Murray was under the impression that he had informed his previous employer, but it took a good deal of diplomacy to smooth the affair over.

Having excelled on Ginevra at Ascot when she won the Nursery, Tony Murray's first ride on the filly as a three-year-old was a nightmare. Ryan dispatched them to Newcastle to contest the XYZ Handicap over $1\frac{1}{4}$ miles. Watching the race on television, Ryan was shocked to see the filly bolt from the stalls and lead the field at a breakneck pace, virtually out of control, until she blew up 2 furlongs out and came home very tired. When Tony Murray returned to Findon he was given a severe lecture on the correct way to ride the filly. In his defence, Murray pleaded that Ginevra had become very worked up just before going into the stalls, and that once the race had started she had bolted.

The quiet daily routine started all over again, but Ryan felt that all the good work of the winter had been undone. Ginevra possessed the high-mettled temperament that he so admired. She had the explosive energy of a stick of dynamite. When the fuse was lit she could go off in any of the four points of the compass. A training pattern was evolved to try to get her to relax and channel all her nervous energy in the right direction. She needed very little work, but if she was allowed to play 'the madam', she might just as well go straight to stud. She was always worked quietly on her own, and spent much of her time walking quietly over the downs in the company of another filly.

When she did work, she floated along like a graceful ballet dancer. Sometimes, though, she would dig her toes in, freeze like a statue and suddenly bolt off in any direction that suited her fancy. When she returned to the stables, she was turned out, wearing a light sheet, with a small, quiet, black, shaggy Shetland pony. At first, she behaved like a rodeo act, but when she saw the little pony cropping grass, she too dropped her head and did the same.

The Lingfield Oaks Trial was chosen as Ginevra's next race. Ryan led her out onto the course and Murray cantered her slowly to the start, where he managed to keep her away from the other runners. Ginevra remained cool and was loaded into the stalls last of the six runners. In the race she was amenable to restraint and Tony was able to settle her easily at the rear of the small field. They were fifth of six entering the straight. Murray made his move 2 furlongs out and, though Ginevra swished her tail, she went through with her run to win by a length. It was a perfect trial for the Oaks.

Ryan's assistant at the time was Peter Hudson, and to him must go a great deal of the credit for the stable's first Classic. One day at breakfast, Peter had voiced his misgivings about the noise and bustle of Epsom, and he wondered just how Ginevra would react to the crowds and to the long walk to the start. 'You'll find out for yourself, because you are going to lead her down,' was Ryan's reply.

In spite of all the care that was taken when Ginevra worked, her final spin on the Wednesday before the Oaks was a disaster. As she was being pulled up after effortlessly covering 7 furlongs, she suddenly stopped, reared up and deposited her lad on the gallop. Loose, with her reins and stirrups flapping, she set off at an extended trot on a tour of the downs. With head and tail erect, she jumped the rails at the top end of the gallop and disappeared from view.

All hands were mustered to intercept her. An hour later she was found quietly cropping grass on the central reservation of the dual carriageway that bypasses the village of Findon with cars passing at seventy miles an hour on either side of her.

When the filly was safely in her stable, Ryan and the vet examined her. Miraculously, there were no visible injuries, and scarcely a hair was out of place. 'That's the Oaks up the spout for certain,' thought Ryan. The unfortunate lad who had ridden her was in despair. All they could do now was hope and pray.

Ginevra travelled to Epsom on the morning of the race. Tom Winters was pleased at the way that she had taken the journey, and now everyone waited rather anxiously until the time came to saddle her. Again Ryan led her on the parade where she spent a lot of time looking up at the crowds in the grandstand. She began to get a little damp. As Ryan turned her round for the canter to the start, he said to Tony Murray, 'Be last at Tattenham Corner, and you *will* win the Oaks.'

Peter Hudson was waiting for the filly in the paddock, and he now led her through the gates, across the road and down into the dip and up the hill to the mile and a half start. The other jockeys were helpful, and when Ginevra reached the start she was remarkably calm.

So far, so good, thought Peter Hudson, but he could sense that the filly's self-control was under severe pressure. If there was any delay at the start she might boil over. At one stage she suddenly backed away from the stalls and stood frozen like a statue. They left her alone until she was ready to move, and when it was her turn to enter the stalls, she walked in like an old sheep. There was no delay; the gates clanged open and Peter Hudson saw that she had started with the others and that Tony Murray had her at the rear of the field, exactly where he wanted her to be.

After all the prerace tension, the Oaks was straightforward. Tony Murray, riding a calm and confident race, obeyed instructions to the letter. He was last at the 6-furlong point and came down Tattenham Hill hugging the inside rail. Once in the straight he was able to move through the field on the inside. Striking the front a furlong from the post, Ginevra quickened like a champion and sprinted past her rivals; she won by a length and a half.

Peter Hudson – his morning coat tails flying in the wind – was running like a hare back to the paddock, but Ginevra beat him to it. He heard the commentary wafting out from the loudspeakers saying 'Ginevra's challenging'. It was not until, hot and breathless, he reached the unsaddling enclosure that he learned the filly had won the Oaks.

Ryan was in his element. Sporting sun glasses and wearing his top hat at a jaunty angle, he greeted the owners with the words, 'What did I tell you! You didn't believe me.'

Charles St George tried to get Ryan to have a celebration drink, but Ryan, who never drank on a racecourse, refused. 'I have to fly in that helicopter over there to Warwick where I will saddle the winner of the Warwickshire Oaks, and what is more, she is a better filly than yours.' With that, he disappeared. The partners were well into their second bottle of Bollinger when Ryan returned unexpectedly. Just as the helicopter had been about to take off, he had learned on the radio that Warwick races had been abandoned.

Ryan accepted the offer of a drink, and Charles St George was anxious to know the name of the wonder filly that was due to run at Warwick. Three bottles of Bollinger later, he learned not only that the filly's name was Star Ship, but that he and Peter Richards had become the filly's new owners. The price was £40,000 or the prize money that they had just won in the Oaks. As Peter Richards left Epsom he was a little unsure as to whether or not they had been conned by surely the greatest horse-coper in the business.

It took just three weeks for their investment to mature. Carrying Charles St George's black and white colours, Star Ship won the Ribblesdale Stakes at Royal Ascot. Later the filly won the Lancashire Oaks and, after an injudicious ride, finished seventh in the French St Leger. It is doubtful whether she was in fact better than Ginevra, who, after winning the Oaks, finished third in the Yorkshire Oaks, third in the St Leger, and fourth in the Prix Vermeille to San San, who went on to win the Arc.

Ginevra was both Ryan's and Tony Murray's first Classic winner. Ryan's blind faith in the volatile filly had been vindicated, even though after the Oaks she never won another race. The filly won £37,870 in stakes, and at Tattersalls' December sales she was sold for 106,000 guineas to the Heron Bloodstock Agency for a client in Japan. This was then a record for a filly out of training.

When Sister Rose wound up the season by winning at Newmarket, she closed down a remarkable year for the Findon fillies. In addition to Ginevra and Star Ship, Ryan had trained Truly Thankful to win the Queen Mary Stakes at Royal Ascot. Ryan's total was seventy winners of stakes worth £108,093. He finished third in the trainers' list to Dick Hern and Vincent O'Brien.

The string went into winter quarters with a wonderful season behind them. The outlook for 1973 was promising, for Ryan had charge of a two-year-old which had won at Ascot, Goodwood and York – Sandford Lad. He was at this moment the apple of Ryan's eye, one of the most exciting prospects that he had ever trained.

15
Sandford Lad

At this time Bill Scrimgeour, or Bill 'Scrim' as he was known, began to feel the pressure of racing's bureaucracy and suggested to Ryan that they took on an assistant secretary to help out. Martyn Stewart, fresh from Lancaster University, was interviewed and appointed without further reference to Ryan, which illustrates the sway Bill held in the Findon power game.

On his first day in harness Martyn was getting to grips with the form book when Ryan swept into the office. 'Who the hell is this?' he asked. Martyn was introduced. 'Never mind the form book lad, we make our own form here,' bellowed Ryan. After that rather awesome start, Martyn settled down and became particularly adept at unlocking the secrets of the form book. In time his skill at reading it helped to have the right horse in the right race at the right time, and he became one of Ryan's greatest assets.

To start with Martyn had to learn to deal with the difficult owners such as Mr Van de Ploeg, who would always phone on Mondays to suggest what entries should be made for his horses. Bill refused to speak to him so Martyn had tactfully to take down endless lists in the knowledge that the Captain would completely ignore the owner's instructions.

Martyn recalls the day that Van der Ploeg and friend arrived unannounced at Soldiers Field and asked where they could get some coffee. To Martyn's horror Ryan directed them to the local café!

When Tony Murray left Findon in 1976 Martyn went with him to France to act as secretary and chauffeur. His place at Findon was taken by Rolf Johnson who came from the *Timeform* organization. Martyn had known Rolf at University. Later Rolf moved to Toby Balding's stable at Wayhill. After an absence of eighteen months

Martyn returned to Findon in the autumn of 1978, following short spells with Stan Mellor and Ryan's ex-jockey Paul Kelleway at Newmarket. After an eventful ten years Martyn left Findon to train as an official handicapper with the Jockey Club – a clear-cut case of poacher turning gamekeeper.

Ryan was steadily working his way through the entire spectrum of high-class bloodstock. He had produced Classic fillies, a colt of Classic potential, long-distance handicappers, and now, in Sandford Lad, he trained a colt who might well win Pattern sprint races.

Sandford Lad had been bought for 1800 guineas at Doncaster sales for Charles Olley. This was to be one of the greatest bargains in racing. Sandford Lad was one of the first crop of the sprinting sire St Alphage and his dam had bred jumping winners including the useful hunter chaser, Doctor Zhivago. The big chestnut was a grand walker, but Ryan thought he would need time.

The manner in which Sandford Lad came into Charles Olley's possession demonstrates how much the laws of chance operate in the fortunes of racing. Ryan regards Mr C. T. Olley as his luckiest owner; yet this remarkable man came into racehorse ownership by mistake. Whilst attending a stable lads' charity boxing gala at the Hilton Hotel, he had the misfortune to have a yearling knocked down to him by accident. Mr Olley was actually waving to a friend, but found that he had become the owner of a yearling Thoroughbred racehorse that was being auctioned for the charity.

To his immense credit, Mr Olley decided to keep the colt, and he dispatched his son, Robin, to ask Peter O'Sullevan, who was attending the dinner, for advice on a suitable trainer. Peter gave two names – Scobie Breasley and Ryan Price. The following day Robin Olley telephoned Scobie Breasley at Epsom, but was disappointed to learn that the trainer had no room. They were luckier with Ryan; he would take the colt, and would be delighted to meet Mr Olley. When they did eventually meet, Ryan promised that he would win a race with Mr Olley's unlucky bid. The colt was called Dolly's Mate, and, true to his word, Ryan tuned him up to win a seller at Haydock, and landed a quiet little gamble in the process. To Ryan's annoyance, Charles Olley bought his horse in for 1400 guineas at the subsequent auction. Ryan was furious, but agreed to take the horse back. The following season Dolly's Mate won another seller at Bath, but this time he was sold at the auction for 1500 guineas.

Later in the season Charles Olley asked Ryan to buy a yearling filly, which he wanted to give as a present to his wife, who had not been well, and whom he wished to cheer up. After the Doncaster September sales, Ryan telephoned Mr Olley and told him that he had fulfilled his commission and bought a lovely filly by Golden Horus for 2500 guineas. Much to Olley's surprise Ryan then said, 'I've also bought a colt by St Alphage for you. He only cost 1800 guineas and he is big, strong and powerful. He may need time but he could prove to be a store horse for jumping if he is no good on the flat!' Charles Olley accepted the filly, but told Ryan that he did not want the colt. There the matter rested until Charles Olley received the bill of sale from the Doncaster bloodstock auctioneers for Lot 103 – the filly – and for Lot 304 – the chestnut colt. The total bill came to £4515.

Charles thought that he had made it quite clear to Ryan that he did not want the colt. To avoid embarrassment he then offered the colt to a friend of his who owned racehorses. His friend declined to take him as he already had three horses in training, and that, he considered, was enough.

One day, when Robin Olley was in the office, Charles brought up the subject of the Doncaster sales bill. Robin offered to take a half share in the colt, and so Charles said, 'Give me your cheque for £945 and he's half yours.' For four fateful days the future ownership of the St Alphage colt was in limbo, but in this surprisingly casual way the destiny of future wealth was decided.

Charles Olley sent off his cheque to Doncaster sales on 22 September, and the ownership was registered between Charles and Robin Olley – 50 per cent each. As a part of the Olley business in Essex is to supply sand for the Ford Motor Company, they christened their unseen colt Sandford Lad.

Ryan remembered the first time that he ever worked Sandford Lad. He had been pairing off his two-year-olds, and there was one horse left over. Ryan told the lad to jump in behind the last pair and to follow them up the gallop. So off they went with the big and backward Sandford Lad tracking two previous two-year-old winners. Towards the end of the gallop, the big chestnut cruised up on a tight rein and left the other horses standing. The lad had not moved a muscle, but Ryan had seen the big colt's raking stride and marvelled at the effortless way in which he moved.

Ryan's immediate reaction was consternation. His first instinctive thought was that the winning two-year-olds must be wrong; they must be sickening for the cough. When they returned to the stables he had their temperatures taken. To his relief and delight, they were normal.

Ryan now took a deal more interest in the 'store horse'. This had to be his fastest two-year-old. Sandford Lad had revealed his true potential in the nick of time, for in another three weeks he was due to be gelded.

When the Olleys went to Findon to see their string in training, they fell in love with the filly, who was named Golden Dolly. Ryan then took them to see the colt who at that moment was lying down in his box. 'There,' said Ryan, 'is a real racehorse; one day he will be a champion.' At this stage he certainly did not look like a future champion, and Charles Olley also wondered if he was on the receiving end of a gigantic 'con'.

Ryan could not believe that such a big and apparently backward horse could possess such tremendous speed. When he began his preparation for his two-year-old races, Sandford Lad was still not properly furnished. For that reason Ryan decided not to challenge for the hot Royal Ascot 'plums', but to aim his star at the Errol Stakes run on the Saturday after the Royal meeting. As a tuning-up race he chose the Berkshire Stakes at Newbury. From over a score of four-day acceptors, there turned out to be only four runners.

On the day Sandford Lad started at 14 to 1 – the outsider of the quartet – and, ridden with the utmost tenderness by Tony Murray, he was beaten by half a length. In fact, but for inexperience, he would have won. It was to be his only defeat in eight races.

At Ascot Sandford Lad was a short-priced favourite and he won by five lengths. At Goodwood Ryan adopted a similar procedure, opting for the lower standard Pilgrim Stakes, in which Sandford Lad only had to be shaken up to win comfortably. It was the same story at York: once Tony Murray had organized the colt's colossal stride, Sandford Lad won effortlessly.

Those three wins – all at five furlongs – were gained against weak opposition, but in the easiest possible way. Sandford Lad was allotted 8 stone 13 pounds in the Free Handicap which was 8 pounds below the top-rated two-year-old – the filly Jacinth.

Ryan set his sights on the sprint Pattern races, and though he was certain that Sandford Lad would prove to be a high-class miler, he absolutely refused to try his speedy colt over 8 furlongs for fear of blunting his exceptional speed. He told the owners, 'If he can win the big sprint races, he will be worth half a million as a sprinting sire.'

After the season the Mylerstown Stud in Ireland – where St Alphage stood – contacted Ryan with an offer for Sandford Lad. They were losing St Alphage and they wished to have his son as a replacement. The stud made a firm offer of £150,000. Charles and Robin went to Findon to discuss the matter with Ryan, who now outlined his plans for the sprinter's three-year-old career. Even though there was a distinct possibility that the horse might stay a mile, Ryan advised that he should be kept to sprinting. The partners decided to refuse the offer and to retain the colt.

It was eleven months since his win at York as a two-year-old before Sandford Lad ran again. During that time, as the season drifted by, there were many occasions when the Olleys regretted that they had not taken the cash offer. Just as Ryan was getting the colt on the move for his first race in April, the stable was struck with a virus. Sandford Lad caught it badly, and even when he appeared to have recovered, the after-effects were still apparent when he cantered. The virus had affected his wind. As the summer wore on Ryan saw countless opportunities pass by. He had planned to win the prestigious King's Stand Stakes at Royal Ascot – tailor-made for the colt – but he would not risk his crack sprinter.

The next target was the King George at Goodwood at the end of July. The problem was to find a suitable preparatory race; there was nothing in the calendar at this time that fitted the bill. In desperation, Ryan opted for a handicap at a night meeting at Doncaster, even though this meant that Sandford Lad would be asked to give away over 40 pounds to some of his opponents. The northern trainers were amazed that Ryan was asking his horse to concede so much weight.

At last Sandford Lad pleased Ryan in his work and he was dispatched to Doncaster. When Ryan arrived there he was concerned when Tony Murray reported to him that there was a large patch of soft going right across the sprint course, where the automatic sprinkler had run amok. Ryan looked glum when he told the Olleys this news. Ryan recommended to the partners that they should pull the horse out.

Charley Olley had endured so many disappointments that he was in favour of running; after all, he pointed out to Ryan, all the field had to go through the soft patch. Ryan took Charles Olley on one side and said, 'If this colt gets beaten here today we'll have wiped

£50,000 off his value in just about a minute; that's what it's all about, Charles.'

Charles Olley had his way. Sandford Lad ran and duly won by five lengths with 10 stone on his back. The Olleys were elated, and when, in the winner's enclosure, Charles asked Ryan what he thought of that performance, he noticed that tears were rolling down Ryan's cheeks. Ryan angrily wiped away such signs of weakness, but Charles Olley sensed the tension and realized that Ryan's words in the stable had been true. He did in fact own a champion. Sandford Lad was back from the wilderness.

There is no doubt that if Sandford Lad had not had that race at Doncaster, he would not have won the King George at Goodwood. Though he defeated two very smart sprinters – Workboy and Saulingo – in the Goodwood race, he had to be pushed right out to do so. It was the hardest race of his career so far.

Sandford Lad beat both these horses again at York in the Nunthorpe Stakes, as well as the four-year-old Balliol, The Go-Between and the best sprinter in the north, Rapid River. It was a rousing finish, but Sandford Lad was too strong for the field. His relentless stride broke the others one by one. He had posted a warning order that he was the champion sprinter elect. Ryan was beside himself with joy for he had re-established his horse in two important Group races.

By now Sandford Lad was beginning to interest breeders as a future sprinting stallion. Ryan received several discreet inquiries from the agencies concerning the colt's future. Then, out of the blue, came an offer of £400,000 from Charles St George. The partners did not consider for very long; they accepted the offer. St George was acting with Tim Rogers, at whose Airlie Stud the horse would stand when his racing days were over.

It was decided that the Prix de l'Abbaye run at Longchamps on Arc day was to be the colt's final race. However, when Charles and Robin Olley received the cheque for the horse, they were surprised that they only received payment for two-thirds of the amount agreed. The new owners had added a clause which gave them the option to purchase the remaining third *after* the Prix de l'Abbaye.

Nothing was left to chance for the final race. The Abbaye is run late in the season, but Sandford Lad had started late, and compared with some of the other sprinters he was virtually a fresh horse.

Ryan admits that he was more nervous before the Abbaye than at any time in his career. There was so much at stake. The good news was that Sandford Lad was drawn number one, easily the best draw. The bad news concerned the state of the ground, which was soft and muddy after heavy rain, conditions that the big colt had never before encountered. Ryan walked the course with Tony Murray, and they were both gloomy about the prospects. If Sandford Lad had not already been sold Ryan would have pulled him out of the race.

Tony Murray showed the stuff he was made of by riding the sprint course to perfection. Sandford Lad powered himself to another famous victory, and though he was not able to dominate the race in quite the same way as he had in the past, he still had two lengths to spare over Abergwaun at the post, with the rest of the field strung out behind.

In two seasons Sandford Lad had won seven out of his eight races and £25,713.53. As a sprinting sire his value was now £½ million. At stud the horse can earn £3000 for each annual nomination to him. At forty mares, this gives him an earning capacity of around £120,000 a year – far more profitable than running his heart out on the racecourse, with all the inherent risk involved when a Thoroughbred racehorse travels at over thirty-eight miles per hour.

As the champagne frothed and bubbled around the paddock bar at Longchamps, Ryan was in his element. He had had all the worry and frustration of the colt's continuing sickness after the virus. It had been his responsibility to bring the colt back into work and to race him again. He had served up the goods on the day and won three sprint Group races, and now, to cap it, he had presented the new owners with a final bonus – the Prix de l'Abbaye – making Sandford Lad the undisputed European sprint champion.

With his felt hat at a dangerously rakish angle, Ryan said to Tim Rogers, 'I've done my shift; now he's your baby.'

Within a few days Charles St George took up the option to purchase the remaining third share and Charles Olley received his cheque for £133,000 for the balance. He also received a third of the prize money from the Prix de l'Abbaye. For an initial investment of £1890, they had cleaned up to the tune of £425,000.

Postscript: Throughout his career Sandford Lad was looked after by George Kyle, one of the leading northern apprentice jockeys before he came to Findon. Ryan thought highly of Kyle, whose promising career ended tragically in a horrific car accident on the main Worthing road just outside the village. Kyle and the occupants of the other car involved were killed, Ryan's lightweight jockey, Chris Leonard, was seriously injured, and another lad, Andy Coles, broke a hip.

16
Giacometti

Following their successes with Ginevra and Star Ship, Peter Richards and Charles St George were to prove just as fortunate in their partnerships in other horses. A very good three-year-old called Rheingold had just won the Dante Stakes at York, and was a leading fancy for the Derby when Charles St George learned that the owner was willing to sell a portion of the colt. Peter Richards and St George then hurriedly formed an eight-man syndicate of Lloyds brokers, which eventually made a successful bid. The papers were only signed on the Monday before the Derby. To their mortification, Lester Piggott's riding of Roberto cost them the race by a short head. Later Rheingold won the Grand Prix de St Cloud and clearly had stallion value.

At the Newmarket sales the syndicate was now looking for another racehorse, paying particular attention to the stock of Fabergé II, the sire of Rheingold. One enormously impressive colt was picked out, but a vet for one of the leading bloodstock agencies which was acting for the syndicate 'spun him' as his heart beat was unsatisfactory.

On the morning that the colt by Fabergé II was due to be sold, Peter Richards and Charles St George were walking up through the sales paddock when they saw a particularly handsome colt being led round. The more they looked at him the more they liked him, and he turned out to be the Fabergé II colt rejected by the vet. On the spur of the moment they commissioned Jack Doyle to buy him. The breeder was expecting a sum of at least 25,000 guineas and was far from satisfied with the 5000 guineas Jack Doyle managed to secure him for.

The partners named their purchase Giacometti – after the famous Italian sculptor. They sent him to Ryan to be trained. It was a wise move, for he was just Ryan's type of horse – a bold, masculine, lengthy, powerful colt, and a delightful mover.

Ryan unleashed what he felt sure was a future champion in a minor race at Lingfield. Hard-held Giacometti won by twelve lengths, and it is rumoured that every member of the Findon staff was present to back him.

It was Ryan's unfulfilled ambition to win the Derby, and after that impressive first run, he began to plan his colt's career round the Derby the following June. Then, quite out of the blue, came an offer of £200,000 for a half-share in the colt. The bid had come from Sheik Essa Al-Khalifa, the brother-in-law of the ruler of Bahrain. The Sheik wished to become involved in English racing, and what better way to start than to bid for a proven colt with a huge potential? While the partners were considering this offer, Ryan telephoned them to say that Giacometti had worked so well that he was sure he would win the Gimcrack Stakes at York. In the light of that information, the partners decided to turn down the Sheik's offer.

Giacometti won the Gimcrack, but hardly in the style of a future Classic winner. He also won the Champagne Stakes at Doncaster but, again, his performance did not please and he seemed to falter in the last furlong, so that he was nearly caught close home by Snow Knight. Ryan was not dismayed, and Giacometti became the latest in the line of 'best horses that I have ever trained'.

The Sheik soon shrugged off his disappointment at not spending his £200,000 on a potential champion and, by way of consolation, Ryan sold him a plater – Barrow Boy – for £3000 and guaranteed that he would win a race for him.

All through the winter Ryan nursed hopes of a Derby win, and in Cornelius Horgan's (Ryan's assistant) capable hands, the big colt thrived; at evening stables his coat gleamed like polished mahogany.

In spite of winning two Group races, Giacometti had been given only 8 stone 11 pounds in the Free Handicap – 10 pounds below the top two-year-old Apalachee, trained by Vincent O'Brien. Charles St George also owned a share in Apalachee, and the colt was favourite for the 2000 Guineas. The form book suggested that Giacometti had a lot to find to be considered for the Classics, but Ryan seemed to know something that the form students did not, and he was supremely confident that he had a Derby winner in the yard.

Ryan was sure that Giacometti would stay a mile and a half, and planned to run him in the Lingfield Derby Trial and then the Derby; he did not wish to attempt the Guineas. Early in April, to Ryan's consternation, Charles St George wished to change those plans. He wanted to run Giacometti in the Guineas. Though Ryan did not know at the time, he believes that when news trickled back from Ireland that Apalachee was not working well, St George wished to activate his other chance in the 2000 Guineas.

Ryan now had less than a month to prepare Giacometti for the Guineas. As he had no suitable entries, Ryan took the colt to Arundel Castle gallops and gave him a searching test. Giacometti came through with flying colours. 'Never mind Apalachee,' Ryan told St George. 'Back this colt, he will win the Guineas *and* the Derby.'

In the Guineas Tony Murray delivered his challenge going into the dip, and had taken the measure of Apalachee, but tragically could not get Giacometti to quicken up the hill when Nonoalco came with a sustained run close to home. Giacometti was beaten one and a half lengths, running on.

When Ryan met Charles St George in the unsaddling enclosure Con Horgan recalls that he had never seen the trainer so disappointed. In contrast, St George was elated that he had an interest in the second and third. 'What merit is there in being second,' Ryan growled. 'Winning is what counts, no one wants to know the runner-up.' This heated exchange was overheard by the press corps and next day they made capital out of Ryan's forthright manner. 'Owner falls out with trainer over Classic defeat.'

In spite of this setback Ryan was still confident of winning the Derby, but though Giacometti was lying third at Tattenham Corner, he made no further headway, and finished in third place, three lengths behind Snow Knight, the horse he had narrowly beaten as a two-year-old in the Champagne Stakes. Giacometti appeared to lack the necessary stamina to last out a fast-run mile and a half, and so the mile-and-a-quarter Eclipse Stakes seemed the next logical race.

Before the Eclipse the partners had attempted to have Tony Murray replaced by Lester Piggott, but Ryan had dismissed the idea. In the race Tony found that he was riding a lifeless Giacometti, who ran very sluggishly all the way and eventually finished fifth to the outsider Coup de Feu. Whether the colt was short of work, whether he was suffering from a minor ailment, nobody ever knew, but it was one of the few really bad races that Giacometti had ever run. Tony

Murray was blamed, and the owners informed Ryan that, in future, Lester Piggott was to ride their colt. This all had an unsettling effect on Tony, who took it very badly. He appealed to Ryan for help, but Ryan pointed out that the owners paid the bills and could go outside the retained jockey if they wished.

After the débacle in the Eclipse, the partners did not really know Giacometti's distance, and deliberated whether to go for the mile-and-a-quarter races or risk a mile and a half in the King George. Much to Ryan's annoyance, Lester Piggott was dispatched to Findon to ride the colt in a gallop in order to find out. The envoy's diagnosis shook both Ryan and Tony Murray. Piggott's advice was to train the colt for the St Leger, over one and three quarter miles. It did not make sense. Murray perhaps received some consolation when in the St Leger not even the genius of Lester Piggott could get Giacometti past Bustino, who outstayed him to win by three lengths.

Giacometti had achieved the remarkable distinction of being placed in all three Classics open to him. What next? Lester assured the owners that the colt would win the Champion Stakes, and for once Ryan agreed with him.

The chief obstacle to Giacometti's winning the Champion Stakes was the brilliant French-trained filly Allez France, who, thirteen days before, had won the Prix de l'Arc de Triomphe. Ryan's travelling lad – Tommy Winters – witnessed the arrival of the filly at the Links Stables at Newmarket, following a disastrous journey by air to Cambridge Airport. During the flight the filly had gashed her leg, and Tommy considered the injury severe enough to prevent her running in the Champion Stakes. Tommy immediately telephoned Con Horgan at Findon, who then rang Charles St George at Newmarket. This was certainly hot news for Giacometti was currently on offer at 8 to 1. With Allez France withdrawn on the morning of the race, Giacometti landed this consolation prize in great style at 4 to 1. But, thanks to Tommy Winters's intelligence work, the connections enjoyed a considerable coup at double those odds.

During the winter Charles St George attended the wedding of Vincent O'Brien's daughter, Elizabeth, to Mr Kevin McClory. During the service Charles sat next to Robert Sangster. On his return to England St George told Peter Richards that he had sold Giacometti to Robert Sangster in church! The deal was confirmed the following week and Giacometti crossed the Atlantic to stand at Gainesway Farm Stud in Kentucky.

17
Enter the Sheik

Sheik Essa Bin Mubarak Al-Khalifa, brother-in-law and first cousin to the ruler of Bahrain, came to train with Ryan Price through an introduction by Joe Sullivan.

The man who had owned half of Beaver II was in Bahrain conducting the purchase of a powerhouse and a ship while trying to sell a floating barge! He met Essa Al-Khalifa, who intimated that he would like to become a racehorse owner in Britain but did not know a trainer. Joe recommended Ryan, and on his return to the UK suggested to Ryan that he should make contact with the Sheik.

One day Essa arrived at Soldiers Field and was shown round the stables. Essa immediately recognized that Ryan was a true lover of horses and dedicated professional. Ryan's advice to the Sheik to keep tight hold of his money and to spend no more than £3000 on the plater Barrow Boy to start with paid dividends, for, in due course, Essa entrusted Ryan with the sole task of buying his yearlings – a duty he discharged most diligently with Jack Doyle over the next few years.

After Barrow Boy had won two sellers, Ryan and Jack bought two cheap yearlings at Doncaster. One of them, Briar Patch, won three races. So the following year (1974) they outlayed 16,300 guineas of the Sheik's money on four yearlings – Jellaby, Denaneer, Shuwaiman and Bahrain Paddy. All four won races. In a distinguished career Jellaby won eleven, including four Group III events, and £85,823. He was then sold for £100,000 to go to stud.

Jellaby – a massively proportioned grey – proved to be a wonderfully game and consistent horse at a mile and a mile and a quarter. He was, however, robbed of his greatest victory by one of the most extraordinary incidents of the 1978 season. In the Lockinge Stakes, then Newbury's richest race, Jellaby led from the start and galloped his field into the ground. A hundred yards from the winning post the big colt stumbled and unseated Brian Taylor when at least four lengths in the lead. To make matters worse, the ruler of Bahrain was visiting London and was watching the race on television with a large party at the Dorchester Hotel. It was a shattering experience for them and for Essa, who took the misfortune in his stride.

Jellaby was looked after by Ryan's oldest lad, Albert Allen, then on the wrong side of seventy. Albert was one of Ryan's great characters. He had been a rear gunner in the RAF in the war, first in Lancasters and then in Coastal Command, and had worked for Ryan since Lavant. He seemed to have become a permanent fixture.

Albert adored Jellaby even though the big horse could prove to be an eventful ride when he was fresh. In that state one morning he suddenly threw up his head, catching Albert a severe blow in the face and shattering several teeth. For some time Albert, with his jaw wired up, could only take nourishment in liquid form through a straw. Eventually Albert could smile again with a brand new top and bottom set – paid for by the Sheik.

After his success with Jellaby, Essa again struck oil with his next crop of yearlings. Wahed was a brilliant two-year-old but failed to train on. However, M-Lolshan and Weth Nan more than made up for this disappointment. Together they cost less than £20,000 but won more than £185,000. M-Lolshan was third in the St Leger and won the Irish St Leger; Weth Nan was third in the 2000 Guineas and won a Group III race in France.

M-Lolshan was sold to Carlo d'Alessio to race in Italy and Weth Nan went to race in the USA. They and most of the Sheik's horses were named after legendary Arab horsemen.

Though it began inauspiciously with a long, cold, wet spring, 1975 was one of Ryan's most successful years. The two-year-olds were slopping through ground more suitable for three-mile chasers than dainty-actioned flat racers. The grass canters were cut to ribbons and, for the first time since Ryan began to train horses for the flat, the entire area of grass had to be reseeded in the autumn.

Ryan's first two-year-old runner, Treasury Bond, sent out to test the water at Brighton, was his first winner. This colt by Good Bond was owned jointly by Dorothy Price and myself. He was to prove one of the greatest bargains of the turf, for he cost only 200 guineas, yet won all his four races. It was a fairy tale for me as joint owner.

Ryan had been underbidder when Treasury Bond had been submitted as a foal by Mrs E. A. Ingram's Barracks Stud near Bletchley. At that time he realized 4000 guineas. Ryan remembered what a good-bodied colt he had been and was shocked at his condition a year later when he was submitted as a yearling in a draft of two colts and a filly. There was only one bid, the entire draft fetched a meagre 450 guineas, and Treasury Bond was sold to Ryan Price for just 200 guineas. Ryan knew that all he really needed was nourishment.

I was standing by Ryan's side, and when the hammer fell asked for a half-share in the colt. The cost was £113 including VAT. Within moments Ryan could have taken £1000 profit, for Charles St George also wished to buy a share, but Ryan told him that he already had an owner.

After surprising his trainer, jockey and joint owners by winning first time out at Brighton, Treasury Bond then went on to win at Lingfield, but soon afterwards contracted the virus. Off the course for three months, he returned in the Rous Memorial Nursery at Doncaster St Leger meeting and, despite his long absence, won with top weight of 8 stone 12 pounds.

Treasury Bond's fourth and final race was the Limekilns Stakes at Goodwood at the end of September. Torrential rain had made the ground a quagmire, but Treasury Bond, who had been in front for the last 2 furlongs, battled on to beat a useful horse, Silver Steel, to whom he was conceding a stone. Treasury Bond won by a head. Soon afterwards the meeting was abandoned owing to the exceptionally heavy going.

At the end of the season Treasury Bond was allotted 8 stone 7 pounds in the Free Handicap, and in December he was sold to race in the USA. He was entered for the Kentucky Derby, but, unfortunately, broke a bone in his knee and never raced again.

It later transpired that Treasury Bond was already a father. It seems that while turned out at grass as a yearling, he jumped a fence and covered a hunter mare in the next paddock.

18
Bruni

In 1975 the compact, powerful, grey colt, Bruni, promised to be the stable's brightest star. Attracted by his physique, Ryan had bought him cheaply as a yearling for 7800 guineas for Charles St George. He had also trained his dam, Bombazine, as a two-year-old. The previous season Bruni had only one introductory race, at Warwick in a 7-furlong maiden. Ridden by the apprentice, D. Noble, the horse started slowly but finished fast. *The Raceform Notebook* reported drily: 'He is one to bear in mind for the future.'

Bruni was not an easy horse at home; he was strong and impetuous, and once he got into top gear he simply bolted. Ryan gave the job of settling him to his best work rider, Mick 'Jerry' Germon, who was a superb horseman. Bruni never worked with other horses; he was usually sent for long hacks over the downs with a quiet horse for company. Although he was bred to stay, being by the French-trained Sea Hawk out of a Shantung mare, unless he settled, the horse would never conserve his energy. His training was, therefore, arranged accordingly.

There were no early indications in his three-year-old career of the way in which his future was destined. Bruni finished second in a maiden at Sandown, won at Salisbury despite disliking the firm ground, and was beaten in the Predominate Stakes – then over one and a quarter miles at Goodwood – by a good three-year-old, No Alimony, from the same stable as the eventual Derby winner Grundy. The margin was only a short head, and Charles St George now wished to run the colt in the Derby, replacing Tony Murray with Lester Piggott.

Ryan was against this from the start; he did not consider Bruni to be mature enough to withstand the hurly-burly of the Derby, and the firm ground would not suit him. He also felt that Tony Murray knew the horse better and would be distressed to be 'jocked off'. How right he was, for Bruni and Piggott had a miserable race. They were bored off the course at Tattenham Corner and carried wide; worse, Bruni returned home very shin-sore and sorry for himself and promptly went down with a virus. The Derby nearly finished Bruni. It took Ryan three months to get him back onto a racecourse. The entire stable went down with the virus, and in June, July and August Ryan only saddled twenty-five winners.

By the end of August Ryan was able to send Bruni to Sandown to contest the Friends of the Variety Club Stakes – his owner did not even bother to attend. Bruni showed that he had benefited from his rest by winning most emphatically in record time. When Charles St George read the reports of Bruni breaking Mill Reef's Eclipse course track record, he suddenly started to take an interest. Even so he was not particularly impressed with Ryan's assertion that he would win the St Leger with the grey. Ryan learned that St George was about to accept an offer of £40,000 for the colt the week before the St Leger. He managed to persuade him not to sell, saying, 'If you're that keen to sell him, I'll buy him myself.'

With Tony Murray back in the saddle, Bruni demolished the opposition in the St Leger with a sustained burst of speed that carried him clear of the field. He eventually won unchallenged by ten lengths. Tony had the satisfaction of looking round and seeing Lester Piggott on the runner-up, King Pellinore.

Ryan now wished to retire Bruni for the rest of the season, but the owner overruled that plan and declared him a runner for the Prix de l'Arc de Triomphe. Ryan was totally against Bruni's running in France, maintaining that the colt had gone over the top. Bruni ran anyway and though, for a brief moment, he flattered to win the Arc, he weakened to finish seventh to the surprise winner, Star Appeal. Ryan took his colt home wondering if he had a future as a four-year-old.

Bruni was really Ryan's unluckiest horse. In 1976 his career as a four-year-old was a series of agonizing near misses: he failed to hit the jackpot in the three really important races, the Hardwicke, the King George and the Arc.

As the new season dawned Ryan had a jockey problem. Tony Murray, who had formed such a successful partnership with Bruni the previous year, was again to be 'jocked off' in favour of Lester Piggott. He refused to ride any other horse owned by Charles St George.

In January and February Tony had been at Cagnes-sur-Mer in the south of France, riding for Charles Millbank, the British-born, French-based trainer. As February came to an end Ryan wanted Tony at Findon to ride work on some of the early runners, but Tony pleaded that he would be missing winners if he was to return then. Ryan issued an ultimatum – come back at once or else lose your job. Tony elected to remain in France and promptly signed a contract to ride for Millbank for the rest of the season. Within minutes Ryan had contacted Brian Taylor at his home at Newmarket and offered him the job as first jockey. Brian accepted without a moment's hesitation and rode out at Findon the following day.

Brian knew that he would not be on board Bruni but he sensibly accepted that embargo, and it did not prevent him from riding the horse in home work. Bruni was a most difficult ride, and Ryan felt that the handsome grey and Piggott did not hit it off together. They had had a terrible run in the Derby and Lester's method of holding the colt in check was to ride him with a very short rein – almost a 'half-nelson' stranglehold – which the colt seemed to resent.

The new partnership started well, however, with a smooth win in the Yorkshire Cup with Bruni on the bit like a champion, but in his next three races – all at Ascot over the mile-and-a-half course – the colt hesitated, and propped on leaving the stalls, losing ground. This frustrating habit certainly cost Bruni the Hardwicke Stakes, and probably the King George, for in this race Piggott was almost dislodged from the saddle on leaving the stalls and lost an iron. Together they gave away six times as much ground as they were eventually beaten by.

The King George and Queen Elizabeth Stakes was the race that Ryan really wanted to win, and he believed that he had now got Bruni cherry ripe for it. To this day Ryan believes that Bruni should have won the King George for, even allowing for the six lengths that he lost at the start, Ryan thinks Lester Piggott showed uncharacteristic indecision after both he and Pat Eddery on Orange Bay had suffered interference when a beaten horse dropped back suddenly on the final bend.

After the race Ryan was severely critical of the way that Piggott had ridden and was overheard by the press. Against Ryan's advice

Bruni had been prepared for the mile-and-a-half prestige races rather than for the Cup races. Ryan had gone along with this and trained his grey accordingly. He had put a tremendous amount of patience and effort into producing Bruni fit and ready to run the race of his life, and all this had been put assunder by what to him seemed an inept ride by a jockey who appeared to lack confidence in the horse. Ryan stormed away from Ascot and was home at Findon in record time.

Ryan put Bruni away for a short rest before a second attempt at the Arc. Though he won his preparatory race, the Cumberland Lodge Stakes, very easily, he again gave away an immense amount of ground at the start. In the Arc he ran an almost identical race to his effort the previous year, this time finishing fifth to the filly Ivanjica.

After the Arc Bruni was sent to race in the warmth of sunny California, but it proved a total disaster. He failed to win and, in the spring of 1977, returned to Findon a tired, jaded and very sick horse. 'I knew that the fire had gone out and the first thing I did was to have him dope tested. I did not know what they had been giving him.'

Ryan was then allowed to do what he had wanted to do the previous season, train Bruni for the Cup races, but it was a hopeless task — the horse had lost his sparkle. Though he finished first in the Henry II Stakes, Bruni lost the race on an objection to Grey Baron. Brian Taylor found his horse was hanging under pressure, and the disqualification was inevitable. Following that, Bruni was a distant fourth to Sagaro in the Gold Cup, second to his old rival Grey Baron in the Goodwood Cup, and then, finally, he broke down in the Doncaster Cup. His racing career was over and he had failed to enhance his stallion value as a four- or five-year-old.

Ryan's relationship with his owners varied considerably. He bitterly resented any interference with the running plans for his horses. He preferred to be left alone, and in this aspect Sir Charles Clore was ideal. Ryan had produced and developed Anne's Pretender, owned by Sir Charles, as a fine mile-and-a-quarter horse with stallion value. Following the disqualification of Trepan, the winner of the Prince of Wales Stakes at Royal Ascot, Sir Charles had just received an £11,326 windfall, and when the same horse was disqualified from the Eclipse Stakes, Anne's Pretender was moved up to take the third-place money — £1522.

After the Eclipse, Ryan planned to run Anne's Pretender at

Deauville in August, but a pulled muscle in the horse's quarters ruled that out. Ryan informed Sir Charles of this setback, but to his astonishment Sir Charles Clore's veterinary surgeon arrived unannounced at Soldiers Field to examine Anne's Pretender. After a few days' rest the horse had recovered his action, and at his slow paces appeared to be sound again. The visiting vet prescribed him fit to run at Deauville.

Later, a representative of Clore's informed Ryan that the horse was to be sent to be trained by Peter Walwyn, and a few days later left for Seven Barrows at Lambourn. When Anne's Pretender arrived Peter Walwyn saw that the colt was lame and telephoned Ryan. 'What is all this nonsense about running the horse at Deauville, the horse is lame.'

Ryan replied, 'Don't tell me; I have been saying that for the last week.'

At the back end of the season Peter Walwyn was able to run Anne's Pretender in the Champion Stakes, but he finished a long way behind the placed horses and was eventually sent to race in the USA where he was successful. It was a sad epitaph to a horse that Ryan had developed and raced to win three Group races, and to be in the frame in two Classics.

Relations with Mr and Mrs Sonny Enfield started well but finished badly. Enfield's wife was the owner of a very strong and powerful chestnut colt called Sir Montagu by Connaught.

Sir Montagu had run a pleasing first race as a three-year-old at Newbury in the spring but, when favourite for a five-horse race at Lingfield, the colt had failed to quicken in the last furlong and had been beaten a neck by a moderate colt called Leventis. Another defeat at Newbury meant that Sir Montagu was now low in the handicap. Then a chance discussion with Noel Murless about the Connaught breed gave Ryan an insight into the way that his stayer ought, in future, to be ridden.

At Salisbury Brian Taylor was instructed to go and win his race decisively 2 furlongs out. Ridden this way, Mrs Enfield's strapping colt won there, and later at Ascot and Goodwood. Then in the Ebor Handicap, carrying a 7-pound penalty, which took his weight to 8 stone, he defeated Alverton and Shangamuzo by eight lengths and one length.

Sir Montagu was one of the easiest winners of this notoriously difficult handicap, compensating for some near misses, notably

Woodside Terrace (second in 1958 to Gladness) and Eborneezer (third in 1959 to Primera).

Ryan had set out to win the Ebor and was thrilled with his fine horse; he was just the type to go on to win a Champion Hurdle. There was just one big worry: Sir Montagu from time to time put his stifle out, and so, when an offer of £80,000 for the horse arrived from an agency, Ryan advised the Enfields to take it. The deal was concluded, and as Dorothy owned a 20 per cent interest, it was a most profitable arrangement.

The buyer turned out to be Monsieur Paul de Moussac, and in his colours Ryan saddled Sir Montagu to finish a good second in the French St Leger, the Prix Royal Oak. The new owner was delighted, but the old owner was less than pleased to read in David Hedges' column in *The Sporting Life* that the selling price had been £100,000. It seems that Ryan's secretary had given this information believing that the figure was correct. This sparked off a major row between Ryan and the Enfields who believed that they had been cheated of £20,000. There was talk of Ryan being sued for the balance. Nigel Dempster for several days made copy of the Sir Montagu story in the *Daily Mail*, implying that there was to be an inquiry about the matter by the stewards. Ryan rather hoped that the Enfields would sue him, for it would have brought the truth out into the open. However, no writ ever came. When Sonny Enfield did eventually meet the new owner of his horse at Longchamp, his question, 'How much did you pay for Sir Montagu?' exacted the following reply: 'I do not know, this was all handled by my agent.'

While all the flak was flying Ryan kept his head down and said nothing, but he did consult his solicitor over the Nigel Dempster articles in the *Daily Mail*. Eventually it all blew over and Sir Montagu left Findon to be trained in France.

19
The Last Straight

Ryan's most significant achievement in 1978 was to have three highly placed horses in the international classifications – M-Lolshan and Whitstead rated eighty-three, and Obratzovy eighty-two.

Ryan's severe one-and-a-quarter-mile grass gallop round the outside of the Findon complex had tested even the stamina of Major Rose in a pre-Cesarewitch work out. Ryan has always been waiting for the horse that could get to the top and still be full of running. Of all the horses trained at Findon the chestnut Whitstead came closest to fulfilling that ideal.

Whitstead, by Morston, had been purchased by Keith Freeman at the Newmarket Houghton sales for 14,500 guineas on behalf of Mr Harry Demetriou, the owner of Olympic Casinos. At the end of the horse's two-year-old career, Ryan was sure that he had a Classic colt in Whitstead, and trained him for the Derby.

After Whitstead's first race in the Classic Trial at Sandown, Ryan felt that he had the Derby in the bag; he had slammed a high-class field which included the eventual winner of the Derby, Shirley Heights. Whitstead then managed to win the Lingfield Trial easily despite being only three-parts ready. He had been plagued with splints and always wore leather boots on his forelegs when being worked.

In the Derby, Whitstead had a terrible passage and was never a factor, though he finished well to take seventh place behind Shirley Heights. Ryan was despondent, but at least Whitstead had displayed stamina, and so the plan now was to run him in the Grand Prix de Paris and the St Leger.

Ryan was hoping for an easy surface at Longchamp; in fact the ground was as hard as a road, and though Whitstead made up an immense amount of ground in the last half mile of this gruelling race, the post came just too soon, and he was held by Galiani and Roi de Mai, beaten only half a length and a short head. Brian Taylor reported that the colt was never able to stride out on the ground.

Ryan decided on the Great Voltigeur Stakes at York for Whitstead's St Leger preparatory race. He was delighted when the colt won decisively. Sadly, that proved to be Whitstead's last outing. A fortnight before the St Leger he went lame with a comparatively minor injury: a piece of flint had become lodged between his protective work boots and his shin, and it rubbed a raw patch which went septic and created heat in the leg. When M-Lolshan and Obratzovy finished close up third and fourth to Julio Mariner and Le Moss in the St Leger, Ryan could be forgiven the thought that Whitstead would have won the last Classic.

Whitstead was retired to Side Hill Stud at Newmarket at £5000 a share, having won £47,525 which included one Group II race and two Group III races.

In the summer of 1978 Ryan lost two influential and valued owners, Philip Solomon and Bob Rowlands. Through his racing manager, John Muldoon, Philip Solomon had bought six choicely bred yearlings for a total of almost 150,000 guineas. He called them all with the prefix Galaxy and named them after the signs of the Zodiac. Three were sent to Ryan to be trained: at £64,000 guineas, Galaxy Leo, a half-brother to the sprinting stallion Steel Heart, was the most expensive. The others were Galaxy Gemini who cost 36,000 guineas, and Galaxy Libra, a colt by Wolver Hollow, who had realized 16,500 guineas.

The first of the trio to run was Galaxy Leo whom Ryan unleashed in a maiden race at Kempton Park in June. Heavily backed by Philip Solomon, the colt ran green and finished a disappointing seventh. Solomon was outraged at the colt's poor showing and when the jockey Brian Taylor revealed to owner and trainer that he had been so unhappy at the way in which the colt had moved going down to the start that he had considered withdrawing him from the race, Solomon was furious. All this was reported in the press the following day and Solomon removed all three horses from Ryan's care and sent them to be trained by Barry Hills. After being handled by no less than four different trainers, Galaxy Leo did manage to win a minor 6-furlong race and was sent to stud in Australia.

At the end of the season Solomon sold his entire string at Newmarket Sales, Galaxy Libra being retained by Barry Hills for 145,000 guineas. The colt eventually raced successfully in the USA finishing third in the Washington International in 1981.

Hardly had the dust settled over the Solomon affair than Mr Bob Rowlands, the owner of the smart sprinter Skyliner, fell out with Ryan over the colt's best distance. Ryan had produced Skyliner in fine shape for a cut at the Tote Free Handicap for which race the owner had placed substantial bets at 33 to 1. Unfortunately Skyliner, ridden by Brian Rouse, met a 'rod in a pickle' in the form of Remainder Man, who beat him by one and a half lengths. The winner went on to finish second in the 2000 Guineas, so Skyliner's connections were unlucky to meet such a good horse. Ryan had felt that the severe 7 furlongs at Newmarket had stretched the colt's stamina and he persuaded the owner not to run in the 2000 Guineas.

Back at sprint distances, Skyliner won the Gus Demmy Stakes at Haydock Park. But now Rowlands intervened. He wished his horse to run in the St James's Palace Stakes at Royal Ascot. Ryan told him that he was crazy; the horse did not stay 7 furlongs at this stage and so was unlikely to win at 8. However, Rowlands had his way and Skyliner ran a distant fifth to Jaazeiro at Ascot. After Royal Ascot, although Ryan's judgement was proved sound, Rowlands removed all his horses and sent them to be trained by Paul Cole at Lambourn.

The following season Skyliner won the Hungerford Stakes at Newbury over 7 furlongs, beating his half-sister, Slip the Ferret, trained by Ryan. In the unsaddling enclosure Ryan congratulated Rowlands, who handsomely admitted that Ryan had been right about Skyliner's correct distance. Ryan ruefully reflected on the irony of the situation: he had been right but had still lost the horse to another trainer.

While the winter storms raged across Findon Downs Ryan had sent a string of six horses to the sun in the south of France in the care of his assistant, Robert Baker. Robert, with his wife, Jane, who was Ryan's niece, did well at Cagnes-sur-Mer near Nice on the French Riviera. The horses won seven races and £36,384.

During their stay Robert and another driver took Weth Nan – a winner at Cagnes – by horsebox up the autoroute to Paris. He took one lad, Don Stacey, to care for Weth Nan, who was due to run in the Prix Edmund Blanc at St Cloud on 8 March. The journey took eleven and a half hours. Don Stacey remained with the horse but

Robert Baker then turned round and drove back to Cagnes, a round trip of 1100 miles. On the day of the race Robert and jockey Brian Taylor flew from Nice to Paris. To their delight, Weth Nan won the first Group race to be run in Europe in 1979. Weth Nan then returned to Findon with some other English runners, but Robert and Brian returned to Cagnes to a hero's welcome from the other French trainers and jockeys and lads.

The return trip to Findon was less pleasant. The horsebox left Cagnes-sur-Mer at 4 p.m. for Lyons racecourse – their overnight staging post. Halfway up the autoroute the horsebox's engine blew up and they were stranded on the motorway until a tractor arrived to tow them to the nearest garage in the depths of the French countryside. As there were no stables near, the horses had to remain in the horsebox all night. Next day at noon another box arrived to take them to Lyons which they reached at 4 p.m. that afternoon. Then the horses were stabled overnight at the racecourse; they had been cooped up in the horsebox for twenty-six hours.

On the following day Robert was able to exercise the string on Lyons racecourse, but because of torrential rain the sand track was almost washed away. At least the horses were able to stretch their legs before the formidable ordeal which lay ahead. The next stage was to take the horses from Lyons to Calais, where they met up with Andrew Smythe, who had flown from Lyons to London when the engine failure dramatically intervened to stop their progress home. The horses were put on Ryan's other horsebox and they returned to Findon via the ferry from Calais.

No sooner had the horses arrived at Findon than two of them were off again. Brennans Glen and Speed Bonny Boat travelled immediately up to Doncaster to fulfil their engagements there. Brennans Glen finished sixth in the Lincolnshire Handicap and Speed Bonny Boat was third in the 6-furlong handicap. Considering their experiences, both performed with considerable credit and proved Ryan's point that you can travel fit horses over exceptionally long distances.

It was a momentous experience for Robert and Jane Baker which they will long remember; so will Ryan, for all the arrangements for the rescue act had to be initiated from Findon.

Ryan's horses were well forward for the 1979 season. Glenhawk broke the ice on the opening day at Doncaster and Sandford Boy won the sprint on the Friday.

At this time the apple of Ryan's eye, as far as the three-year-old colts were concerned, was the chestnut colt Lake City. This lovely actioned free-moving fellow by a then unknown American sire, Annihilate 'em, had been bought as a yearling in the States by that astonishing judge of a horse, George Blackwell, on behalf of Mr Harry Demetriou. The previous season Lake City had won the Coventry Stakes at Royal Ascot, and now Ryan had high hopes of the 2000 Guineas. As a preparatory race, he had selected the Trial at Salisbury.

Torrential rain all day created atrocious ground on which to run a good horse. As he waited for the race to start, Ryan admitted to a fellow trainer that he was apprehensive. There was a power failure, with the result that there was no loudspeaker announcement that the race was off, nor was there a running commentary. Ryan's colleague then shook his arm and said, 'What are you worrying about, there's your horse and he's won.' Lake City won unchallenged by three lengths.

In the Guineas Lake City ran all too freely and though he showed in the lead at halfway, he gradually lost his position to finish tenth to Tap on Wood, ridden by Steve Cauthen. Ryan then ran him in the Mecca Dante Stakes where he was third to Lyphards Wish. On the strength of that run, Lake City took his chance in the Derby, showing up in the early stages, but again fading, to finish sixteenth.

At racing's great showcase, Royal Ascot, Ryan was again in the limelight, winning the Coventry Stakes with Varingo in the livery of PTP Plant Hire, whose chairman, David Mort, qualified for the title of being Ryan's most enthusiastic owner. Le Soleil had been the firm's first racehorse, but at this stage it looked as if Varingo would sweep the board in the forthcoming two-year-old events.

Romeo Romani, in Ryan's view the best-looking horse that he has ever had, was another of George Blackwell's purchases. Romeo won the Norfolk Stakes without a previous race and within twenty-four hours his owner had refused an offer of half a million pounds for the horse. With Obratzovy winning the Hardwicke Stakes, Ryan's Ascot cup was full.

Throughout the month of June the winners flowed. Winning the Scottish Derby with Serge Lifar gave Ryan particular pleasure, for the colt was owned and bred by Lord Caernarvon. His Lordship, however, viewing the race on television, was less than pleased with the way the jockey Brian Taylor used his whip on the colt, and asked Ryan not to put Taylor up on any of his horses in future.

Though no Classics went to Findon in 1979 Ryan saddled M-Lolshan to win the Grosser Preis Von Baden which netted over £47,000 for Sheik Al-Khalifa.

One extraordinary feature of the season was the high incidence of placed horses. The 140 places won a staggering £198,927, compared with the £204,235 earned by the sixty winners in Britain. Of the place money £30,000 was earned by just three horses, M-Lolshan and Obratzovy in Germany, and Varingo in France. All in all the horses earned over £400,000 for the season, a satisfactory year's work by any standards.

At the start of the 1980 season Ryan again took a string to Doncaster to open the flat. Rose Charter and Silly Abdul – ridden by Joe Blanks – finished sixth in their respective races, but Ryan was concerned at their condition after their races and he sent his intended Saturday runners home.

Ryan had felt uneasy when Glenhawk, racing in the colours of the *Daily Express* newspaper, had disappointed in the *Daily Express* Triumph Hurdle at Cheltenham's National Hunt Festival. The four-year-old had been up with the leaders all the way but dropped back suddenly two flights from home and finished very distressed. Immediately after the race Glenhawk had been sent to Mr Victor Mathews's stud for a rest. It appears in retrospect that Glenhawk may have been sickening for the virus.

On returning from Doncaster Ryan was alarmed to see that almost his entire string had runny noses, and some were coughing. Diagnosis eventually confirmed that Findon had the virus rhino Pneumonitis; it was to be there for two seasons. 'You cannot *train* sick horses, all you can do is to nurse them and pray that they will suffer no after effects.'

As ill luck would have it, the sickest horse in the yard was Bozovici – Ryan's best and most promising three-year-old. This colt by Queen's Hussar had been bred by Lord Caernarvon and sold to Harry Demetriou for 17,000 guineas. Bozovici had won the Sandwich Stakes at Ascot, the Gilbey Champion Racehorse Futurity at York and had been beaten by a whisker by one of the leading two-year-olds, Final Straw, in the Seaton Delaval at Newcastle.

During the winter Bozovici had been sold to the French owner, Madame J. Binet, but it was not until the end of May that Madame Binet was able to see her colt run. Bozovici finished sixteenth in the Derby and eventually won a minor race at York in August. Shortly after that he went to France.

It was not until 10 May at Lingfield that Ryan saddled his first winner, Glenhawk, one of only four winners for Findon in that month. The most significant contribution to the meagre prize money won during the season came through Mirror Boy, who won the Andy Capp Handicap at Redcar sponsored by the *Daily Mirror* newspaper. With Joe Blanks in the saddle, the colt ran in the colours of the *Daily Mirror* Punters Club, an enthusiastic body, managed with much flair by Noel Whitcombe. Mr Charles St George's Stanislavsky won a valuable sponsored race at Haydock, and a listed race at York in September, but that was about all there was to shout about in a season that is best forgotten.

In all Ryan had forty-eight winners and they won £134,000, an astonishingly good total considering that for most of the season Ryan was undertaking what amounted to a salvage operation. Only in the autumn did the winners begin to flow in. In October Ryan sent out thirteen winners, but he was running out of time and a difficult season ended when My Rajah won for Dr Pajgar in the dying days of the flat.

At least the 1981 season could not be worse than the previous one – so Ryan thought. How wrong he was; 1981 was to see the stable's fortunes slump to the lowest ebb since he had begun training exclusively for the flat in 1970. To have the virus two years running seemed a cruel act of fate, but other trainers, including Dick Hern and Peter Walwyn, had found that it took more than a single season to be free of the scourge.

There was certainly no clue of the impending disaster to be discerned at Doncaster, for Shangarry, ridden by Ryan's new stable jockey, Brian Rouse, who had replaced Brian Taylor, scored decisively on the opening day of the season. In the Lincolnshire Handicap Glasgow Central, who was well fancied, faded after showing prominently to halfway.

One new acquisition arrived in time for the flat-racing season – Ryan's first aeroplane. Ryan had often envied the jockeys' style of travel by light aircraft which, at the height of the season, enabled them to ride work at home then fly to an afternoon meeting and fly on again to take in an evening race. For twenty years Ryan had always driven his own Mercedes with dash and verve. He began to resent the hours spent on the roads getting home after race meetings and missing the vital evening stables.

Now, through the agency of Peter Clifford, an aviation broker and ex-test pilot, Ryan purchased a second-hand Piper 235 Dakota which had a six-cylinder single engine, fixed undercarriage and four seats. Peter Clifford and I flew down to Findon and found that there was plenty of room to land the plane. We promptly demonstrated the Dakota's fine short take-off and landing capabilities.

The deal was struck and Peter Clifford even found Ryan a pilot to go with the plane.

Ryan soon exploited his new freedom of the air and the sheer joy of being able to fly to Newbury in twenty minutes, and to Newmarket in forty minutes, made the summer of 1981 easier. When not in use, the Piper was parked on the gallops, but when the weather deteriorated in November Ryan was able to obtain hangarage at nearby Shoreham Airport, and the pilot, Malcolm Frost, went to his winter job.

20
The Finish

Ryan looks back at his active life with gratitude. Apart from the war, he would not have wished to change anything. 'Firstly, I must be grateful for my excellent health which has seen me through all these years of early morning exercise on the Sussex Downs.' In all weathers Ryan has rarely missed riding out with the string and even at the tender age of seventy, and against Dorothy's wishes, he himself schooled her chaser Broadleas over fences before the gelding won at Kempton in March 1982.

What was his most satisfying moment as a trainer? Surprisingly the answer was not his two Classic winners or when Kilmore won the Grand National, but when Persian Lancer won the Cesarewitch in 1966 at the then record age of eight.

As a three-year-old five years earlier, when trained by Sir Gordon Richards, Persian Lancer had been beaten into third place after leading almost up to the post. Subsequently he had broken down and had been given by his owner Mr Stavros Niarchos to his racing manager Lord Belper. Lord Belper had Persian Lancer gelded and then sent him to Ryan. Persian Lancer proved to be the most difficult horse that Ryan had ever had to train. It had become a standing joke with Lord Belper's sister, the Duchess of Norfolk. At the races she would continually ask Ryan when Persian Lancer would be running. 'Any day now, your Grace,' would be Ryan's reply.

Every time that he began to get Persian Lancer nearly fit, something always went wrong. Once, when the horse was turned out in a field in Gloucestershire, he escaped onto the road and was run over by a bus. The bus had to be jacked up before they could get the unfortunate horse from under it. After each setback Ryan merely postponed his attack on the Cesarewitch for another year. In 1966, five years to the day after his defeat in the race, Persian Lancer, ridden by Doug Smith, won the Cesarewitch by threequarters of a length. 'That,' said Ryan, 'was my greatest achievement as a trainer.' What incredible patience Lord Belper had shown for Persian Lancer had not won any race between 1961 and 1966. Ryan developed a tremendous affection for Persian Lancer who had a great deal of character. Now, at the age of twenty-four, his old friend has the freedom of the downs above Findon.

Lord Belper's faith in Ryan's ability is typical of many owners. 'I look back with intense gratitude to the owners who helped me along the way by their trust in me. Especially Gerry Judd, who got me started and put me on the jumping map. In recent years my luckiest owner has been Charles St George whose three great horses, Giacometti, Ginevra and Bruni cost only twelve thousand pounds the lot.

'I have been very fortunate with the staff that I have had, beginning with Sid Dale, who came on the same day that I got married. With Dorothy as a wife and Sid as head lad, how could anyone go wrong?

'When Sid Dale went to train at Epsom his place was taken by Ron James, then I had Giles Beeson, who now trains at Lewes, and then, when I switched to the flat, I brought Geoffrey Potts from The Downs to be head lad at Soldiers Field. He must share the credit for the £1.4 million in prize money we have won here.'

Another long-serving and loyal member of the staff is Tommy Winters, who joined Ryan as a lad from the East End and was responsible for Clair Soleil during his racing days. 'No horse ever had more care or attention lavished on him. Later Tommy became my travelling head lad and travelled all my big race winners.'

At The Downs the horses were travelled by Snowy Davis. However, when Ryan moved to Soldiers Field and switched to the flat, both Snowy and Ron James elected to stay with the jumpers and remain with Josh Gifford.

Though he would probably never admit it to their faces, Ryan takes a great pride in the success of his old jockeys now that they are training themselves, Fred Winter and Josh Gifford exclusively for jumping, Paul Kelleway for the flat.

Many of Ryan's assistants did well in racing after leaving him. Tim Neligan is now managing director of United Racecourses. Bob McCreery had a most fruitful term as president of the Thoroughbred

Breeders' Association and is a most successful commercial breeder. Guy Harwood, whose father helped Ryan on his return from the war by presenting him with a car, saying, 'Pay for it when you can,' is now one of the leading trainers in the land. Guy runs a training stable at Coombelands, near Pulborough in Sussex, with a skill and flair that has Ryan's total admiration.

Ryan is most certainly a survivor. During the war he had endured considerable personal danger in battle and witnessed at close quarters the death of many of his friends. Twice he had nearly ended his training career, but somehow he had survived. From a slow beginning he had finally made a great success of training racehorses, ending up by owning the entire Findon training complex.

What was the secret of his success? Like so many in his position, Ryan has no ready answer. His flair was a thorough knowledge of the horse in and out of the stable. He has the capacity through example, willpower and sheer force of character to get things done the way he wants them done, even if this means driving his staff to the point of exhaustion.

The horses that have passed through his hands have been fortunate in living in an environment that was geared to their every need. They have been well cared for, well fed and properly exercised. But, one can argue, so are most of the other racehorses in training. Here one can only attribute Ryan's success to his uncanny instinct for doing the right thing with every horse and somehow being able to discover the key to handling the difficult ones. His eye missed nothing. He practically lived with his horses, watching them sometimes when they were resting.

One side of Ryan's character which has not always received widespread approval is his enormous self-confidence. Let Ryan as usual have the last word: 'I have never done anything that I am ashamed of. I have been accused of many things but you don't help to make champion jockeys like Fred Winter four times and Josh Gifford four times by stopping horses from winning. No jockey ever employed by me has ever received instructions not to win. I wanted to train winners not losers.

'Every owner is entitled to a fair crack of the whip and I have never trained one horse for the benefit of another.

'I have enjoyed a wonderful life, getting a living from something that I have really enjoyed doing.

'It has been a hell of a lot of fun!'

D-Day Bibliography

Brigadier J. Durnford-Slater, *Commando*, Williams & Kimber, 1953.
Hilary St George Saunders, *The Green Beret*, Michael Joseph, 1949.
Chester Wilmot, *The Struggle for Europe*, Collins, 1952.
The Memoirs of Field Marshal The Viscount Montgomery of Alamein KG, Collins, 1958.
Bernard Fergusson, *The Watery Maze*, Collins, 1961.
Field Marshal B. L. Montgomery, *Normandy to the Baltic*, Hutchinson, 1946.
Warren Tute, John Costello and Terry Hughes, *D-Day*, Sidgewick & Jackson, 1974.
R. W. Thompson, *D-Day — Spearhead of Invasion*, Macdonald & Co., 1968.
Lord Lovat, *March Past,* Weidenfeld & Nicolson, 1978.

Index

Abergwaun, 175
Admiral's Walk, 98
Airlie Stud, 174
Alberquerque, Duc d', 92
Albinella, 133, 142
Alexander, Dr F. A., 143
Alexandra Park, 120
Alfarasio, 78, 81, 93
Al-Khalifa, Sheik Essa Bin Mubarak, 178, 181–2, 195
Allen, Albert, 159, 182
Aller, River, 53, 54
Allez France, 180
Altesse Royale, 162
Alto, 79
Alverton, 188
Anderson, Robert, 133–4, 135
Andy Capp Handicap, 196
Anglo, 118, 119
Anne's Pretender, 187–8
Annihilate 'em, 194
Another Flash, 103
Antiar, 100
Antwerp, 52
Apalachee, 178, 179
April Day II, 35, 36
Archibald, George, 66
Ardennes, 52
Arkle, 116
Armstrong, Sam, 88, 158
Arthingworth Manor, 32
Arun, River, 45
Arun Lad, 27, 30–31
Arundel, 91, 179
Ascot, 89, 101, 186, 188
Ascot Stakes, 158
Ash, Jack, 34

Ashton, Michael, 101, 105, 107–8, 109–10, 112, 143
Assad, 159
Asten, 52
Aston Tirrold, 68
Atlantic Wall, 40
Australia, 139
Auteuil Champion Hurdle, 157
Ayala, 96
Ayr, 138, 155, 161

Baerlein, Richard, 148
Bahrain Paddy, 181
Baillie, John, 85, 86, 105, 108, 113
Baker, Jane, 192, 193
Baker, Robert, 192–3
Balding, Gerald, 72
Balding, Toby, 169
Balliol, 174
Ballydoyle, 93
Baltic, 55
Bambi, 69
Banks, John, 155
Barracks Stud, 183
Barrott, Doug, 120
Barrow Boy, 178, 181
Bartholomew, James, 66, 98
Bastogne, 52
Bates, Bobby, 70, 71
Bath, 170
BBC, 87, 95–6, 132, 133, 136, 141, 152
Beard, Frank O., 131–2
Beasley, Bobby, 133
Beau Caprice, 142
Beaver II, 89–91, 119, 181

Becher Chase, 94
Beeby, George, 61
Beechener, Cliff, 88
Beeson, Giles, 199
Belper, Lord, 33, 198–9
Bennett's Hill, 61
Berkshire Hurdle, 101–2
Berkshire Stakes, 172
Bibury Club, 32
Biddlecombe, Terry, 126
Biegel, Peter, 86
Binet, Madame J., 195
Birmingham, 90
Bishop's Move, 32–3
Bishops Waltham, 43
Blackwell, George, 194
Blair, Colonel, 109, 112, 128
Blanks, Joe, 195, 196
Blue Steel, 56–7
Bobinski, Colonel, 74
Boismoss, 157
Bombazine, 184
Bora's Cottage, 62, 65
Bowsher, H. Gordon, 68
Bozovici, 195–6
Breasley, Scobie, 81, 170
Brennans Glen, 193
Bréville, 47, 48
Briar Patch, 181
Brighton, 56, 81, 119
Broadleas, 198
Brocade Slipper, 100, 101
Broken Tackle, 58
Bromley, Peter, 152
Brookshaw, Tim, 86
Brown, Mick, 93
Bruni, 184–7, 199
Buckfastleigh, 59

Buckley, James, 133–9, 142–3, 147, 148, 150, 155n.
Budgett, Arthur, 73, 83
Bulge, Battle of the, 52–5
Burlington II, 120, 125, 126, 128, 129
Burns, T. P., 80
Bustino, 180

Cabourg, 48
Cadogan, Lord, 105–8, 110–12
Caen, 50
Caen Canal, 43
Caernarvon, Lord, 194, 195
Cagnes-sur-Mer, 186, 192–3
Calais, 193
Cambridgeshire Hurdle, 123
Cameron, Tony, 95
Camp Hill Prison, Isle of Wight, 130
Campari, 73
Canardeau, 67–8, 81
Cantab, 88, 89, 99
Capelin, 'Ginger', 74
Carr, Frank, 155
Carrickbay, 73
Carver, Dick, Junior, 89
Catapult II, 90, 101, 103–4, 105, 108
Cauthen, Steve, 194
Cazalet, Peter, 61
Cecil, Henry, 164
Celtic Gold, 142
Cent Francs, 77
Cesarewitch, 99, 157, 160, 190, 198–9
Chamossaire, 98
Champagne Stakes, 178, 179
Champion Hurdle (Cheltenham), 67, 79–80, 85, 87, 89, 103, 122–3
Champion Stakes (Newmarket), 163, 180, 188
Chanelle, Enid, 89, 90
Chantilly, 63
Charles Brandon, 85
Charlie Worcester, 96, 100, 156
Chaseform, 56
Chaseform Notebook, 123, 124
Chaseform Private Handicap, 131

Cheltenham, 57, 62–5, 76, 79–81, 85, 87–9, 91, 94, 103, 116, 123–4, 128, 142, 156, 195
Cheltenham Gold Cup, 62, 63, 76, 79, 85, 88, 116, 156, 187
Chepstow, 88
Cherbourg, 50
Cherry Hinton Stakes, 164
Chester Cup, 157
Chester Vase, 162
Cheveley Park Stakes, 161
Chichester, 57
Chiddingfold point-to-point, 29
Chief Barker, 83–5, 117
Childrey, 78
Chissel, PC, 19
Christian, Lieutenant-Colonel John, 103, 125, 152
Churchill, Sir Winston, 50
Clair Soleil, 67, 74–6, 77, 79–80, 85, 199
Clapton, Captain Johnnie, 51, 54
Clark, Bob, 62
Clark, Dr E. C. G., 137, 141–5, 147–9, 153
Clark, Percy, 62
Clifford, Peter, 197
Clive, Mr, 64
Clontarf, 81
Clore, Sir Charles, 187–8
Cohen, Nat, 78, 83–5, 89, 93–4, 96, 109, 112, 117–19
Cole, Paul, 192
Coleman, David, 95
Coles, Andy, 176
Coles, George, 27–30
Colling, R. J., 131
Collins, Christopher, 119
Colonel Wood, 126
Commandos, 38–9, 40–55
Connaught, 188
Cook, Paul, 165
Cooke, Sir William, 73
'Cookie', 17, 26
Coombelands, 200
Cornuto, 161, 163
Coronach, 24
Coronation Hurdle, 81, 87
Cortego, 82
Cottage Rake, 62, 63
Cottenham, Lord, 105

County Down Hunt, 38
County Handicap (Cheltenham), 142
Coup de Feu, 179
Coventry Stakes, 194
Covertcoat, 70, 71
Coville, Len, 121–4, 126–7, 134–6, 138, 147, 149–53, 155
Coville, Mrs Len, 121
Cowley Brothers, 156
Cox, Don, 113
Craven Stakes, 162
Crawley and Horsham point-to-point, 29
Creek, 73, 99
Crimborne Stud, 86
Cronin, Rev., 131
Cruden, Captain Peter, 46, 53, 54
Crump, Neville, 82
Cumberland Lodge Stakes, 187
Cyclamen, 34

Daily Express, 114, 126, 132, 150, 195
Daily Express Triumph Hurdle, 195
Daily Herald, 113
Daily Mail, 93, 125, 131, 154–5, 189
Daily Mirror, 132, 196
Daily Mirror Punters Club, 196
Daily Sketch, 148
Daily Telegraph, 112, 114, 130
Dale, Dorothy, *see* Price, Dorothy
Dale, Sid, 13, 61, 68, 69, 71, 78, 96, 114, 116, 199
d'Alessio, Carlo, 182
Dandy Scot, 87, 93
Dante Stakes, 177
Darling, Fred, 23–4, 160
Davies, Owen, 135
Davis, Snowy, 159, 199
Davison, Harry, 70, 117
Davy Crockett, 87
Daykin, P., 143, 145–6
Deauville, 188
Demetriou, Harry, 190, 194, 195
Dempsey, General Sir Miles, 127, 128
Dempster, Nigel, 189

INDEX

Denaneer, 181
Derby, 24, 71, 92, 107,
    162–3, 177, 178–9,
    184–5, 186, 190, 194,
    195
Derby Trials, 179, 190
Dick the Gee, 67
Dinant, 52
Dives, 51, 53
Dixon, Oliver, 29, 30
Doctor Zhivago, 170
Dolly's Mate, 170
Doncaster, 65, 92, 98, 107,
    155, 170, 171, 173–4,
    178, 181, 195, 196
Doncaster Cup, 187
Done Up, 85, 86
Downpatrick, 38
Downs House, Findon,
    70–72, 81–2, 116, 117,
    156, 158–9
Doyle, Jack, 177, 181
Dozulé, 51
Drabbel, Cecil, 63
Dreaper, Tom, 160
Duncan's Bay, 32
Duneed, 142
Dutch Bells, 157

Early Mist, 76
East Hendred, 32
East Yorkshire Regiment, 46
Eastern Harvest, 97
Ebor Handicap, 188–9
Eborneezer, 89, 99, 189
Eclipse Stakes, 179–80, 187
Eddery, Pat, 161, 165, 186
Edinburgh, 85
Eisenhower, General, 42–3,
    52
Elan, 115, 123
Elbe, River, 54
Elbe–Trave Canal, 55
Emery, Réné, 73–4, 77, 78,
    79, 89
Enfield, Mr and Mrs Sonny,
    188–9
Epsom, 35, 72, 87, 114
    see also Derby
Equine Research Station,
    108, 137–8, 147,
    148–9, 151, 152–3
Errol Stakes, 172
Evening Standard, 114–15,
    126

Fabergé II, 177

Fala, 77
Falaise Gap, 51
Far East, 52
Fare Time, 85, 87
Fatum, 78
Fawley Stud, 88
Feakes, Matt, 36–7
Feerique, 78
Feilden, General Sir Randle,
    103–6, 108, 113, 118,
    126–9, 135–6, 152, 157
Fergusson, Bernard, 42
Final Straw, 195
Findon, 34, 60, 116–17
    R.P. moves to, 70–72
    R.P. buys Downs House,
    81–2
    lads' strike, 91
    after the Rosyth inquiry,
    113–15
Firestone, Bertram, 162
First World War, 18–19
Fitzgeorge-Parker, Tim, 93,
    125, 126, 131
Fitzpatrick, R.J., 143, 144,
    147
Flame Gun, 85
Flying Wind, 59
Folkestone, 60, 73, 78, 94
Fontwell Park, 34, 56, 59,
    60, 62, 73, 79, 108,
    109, 112, 126, 158
Ford Motor Company, 171
Foxhunters' Chase, 34
France, 63, 92, 192–3
    Normandy campaign,
    41–52
    R.P. buys horses in, 73
Franceville-Plage, 48
Francis, Dick, 121, 148, 149
Fredith's Son, 95
Free French Commandos, 46
Freeman, Keith, 190
Freeman, Norman, 159
French St Leger, 168
Friends of the Variety Club
    Stakes, 185
Frog, 157
Frost, Malcolm, 197

Gainesway Farm Stud,
    Kentucky, 180
Galaxy Gemini, 191
Galaxy Leo, 191
Galaxy Libra, 191–2
Galiani, 191
Garratt, Dr D. C., 143, 146

Gates, Tom, 74
Gatwick, 37
Gay Navaree, 95
Germany, Second World
    War, 40–55
Germon, Mick ('Jerry'), 184
Get Stepping, 127, 130, 142
Giacometti, 178–80, 199
Gibson, Major David, 105,
    110, 141, 152
Gifford, Josh
    rides for R.P., 88–9, 90,
    96, 160
    champion jockey, 98, 200
    Rosyth inquiry, 11–13,
    98–101, 103–5, 107,
    110–11, 114
    breaks leg, 119–20
    and Hill House, 123–30,
    149–51, 153
    buys Downs House,
    158–9, 199
Gilbert, Johnny, 79
Gilbey Champion Racehorse
    Futurity, 195
Gilpin, P. P., 70
Gilpin, Victor, 34
Gimcrack Stakes, 178
Ginevra, 163–8, 177, 199
Gladness, 189
Glasgow Central, 196
Glendenning, Raymond, 84
Glenhawk, 193, 195, 196
Go-Between, 174
Goater, William, 70
Gold Wire, 83, 84, 91–2, 93
Golden Dolly, 172
Golden Horus, 171
Goldfish III, 27–8, 29–30
Goldsmith, John, 58, 68, 73
Gone-Away Hunters Chase,
    29, 30
Good Bond, 161, 162, 163,
    182
Goodwood, 72, 188
Goodwood Cup, 77, 187
Gore, Bob, 34, 70, 71, 72,
    116
Gosling, Captain H. M., 141,
    149–50
Graham, Clive, 114, 126,
    132–3
Grand Course de Haies, 91
Grand National, 22, 30, 67,
    92–4
    1912, 71
    1948, 62

1949, 65
1953, 76
1955, 81
1957, 82–3
1960, 87–8, 97
1961, 94, 97
1962, 94–6, 198
1963, 96, 100
1964, 96, 116, 118
1965, 119
1969, 62
1970, 159
Grand Prix de Paris, 71, 190–91
Grand Prix de St Cloud, 177
Grand Steeplechase de Paris, 91
Grantham, Tom, 60
Grantham, Tony, 56–7, 58, 60
Granville, 92
Gratwick Blagrave Memorial Chase, 63–4
Great Voltigeur Stakes, 191
Greenhills Lad, 119
Gresson, Colonel, 64
Grey Baron, 187
Grosser Preis Von Baden, 195
Grundy, 184
Guildford, 56
Gus Demmy Stakes, 192

Hall, Charlie, 107
Halloween, 79
Hamble River, 43
Hambleton, 30, 32, 33
Hamlyn, Geoffrey, 128
Hard Tack, 160
Hardham Gate, 27
Hardwicke Stakes, 185, 186, 194
Hardy Annual, 34
Hardy Annual II, 34, 35
Hardy-Roberts, Brigadier, 119, 129
Harkaway I, 27–8
Harland, 160
Harland and Wolff, 29
Harter, J. F. A., 142, 152
Hartigan, Hubert, 32–3
Harwood, Guy, 74, 200
Hatvany, Baron, 68, 73, 74, 78, 99
Hawkhurst Court, 56, 57, 86
Haydock Park, 83, 170, 192, 196
Hedges, David, 189

Henley-in-Arden, 82
Hennessy Gold Cup, 94
Henry II Stakes, 187
Henry VII Chase, 92
Hermit, 71
Hern, Dick, 168, 196
Heron Bloodstock Agency, 168
Hill House, 96, 98, 104–5, 121–55
Hills, Barry, 191–2
Hislop, John, 33, 111–12
Hitler, Adolf, 40, 52
Hobart, 42
Hobbs, Reg, 61
Holman Cup, 64–5
Hook Money, 163
Horgan, Cornelius, 178, 179, 180
Hornung, Colonel, 120
Horris Hill Stakes, 161
Horse of the Year Show, 122
Horses in Training, 61
Horsham, 62
Houghton Stakes, 161
Hove, 40, 52
Howard, Stanley, 64
Hudson, Frank, 82
Hudson, G. A. 148
Hudson, Peter, 166, 167
Hughes-Onslow, Andrew, 97
Hungerford Stakes, 182
Hurst Park, 36, 74–6, 83, 85, 88, 90, 92
Hypernod, 64

The Igloo, 72
Imperial Cup (Sandown Park), 100, 101, 102, 106, 108, 110, 142
Inglis, Lieutenant-Colonel R. T., 152
Ingram, Mrs E.A., 183
Inverlochy, 64–5
Ireland, 59, 62, 92, 93
Irish St Leger, 182
Irvine, 164
Isaac, Tom, 148
Isle of Wight, 43
ITA, 133, 136
ITV, 141
Ivanjica, 187
Ivy Green, 85

Jaazeiro, 192
Jacinth, 172

Jack Tatters, 64–5
James, Sir Archibald, 88
James, Ron, 159, 199
James, Dr V. H., 137, 143, 145–7, 148, 153
Jarvis, Ryan, 98, 101, 105, 107
Jellaby, 181–2
Jerry M, 70, 71
Jockey Club, 11–14, 109, 133–4, 154, 170
John O'Groats, 94
John Porter Stakes, 77
Johnson, Ernie, 164
Johnson, Rolf, 169
Jones, Buck, 99, 120
Jones, Davy, 120
Jones, Harry Thompson, 79
Judd, Gerry, 59, 62, 81, 199
and Priorit, 63–4, 65, 66
helps R. P. buy Downs House, 70, 82, 116, 117
buys Clair Soleil, 74–5, 76, 85
and Nid d'Abeilles, 78–9
owns Vermillon, 80
Juliana Canal, 52
Julio Mariner, 191

Kantaka, 68
Kelleway, Paul, 89, 91, 120, 170, 199
Kelly, Paddy, 62
Kempton Park, 63, 72, 87, 91, 123–4, 129, 141–2, 160, 191, 198
Kempton Park Hurdle, 102, 106
Kentucky Derby, 183
Kilmore, 92–6, 100, 109, 114, 116, 117, 118, 198
Kim Muir Challenge Cup, 94
Kindersley, Guy, 94
King, Rex, 131
King George and Queen Elizabeth Stakes, 173, 174, 180, 185, 186
King George VI Chase, 63
King Pellinore, 185
King's Stand Stakes, 173
Kingsley, Maurice, 75, 76
Kipling, Rudyard, 65–6
Knock Hard, 76
Knox, Teddy, 91, 92
Kyle, George, 175–6

INDEX

Lake City, 194
Lambourn, 118, 192
Lancashire Hurdle, 82, 87, 100
Lancashire Oaks, 168
Lavant, 59, 60–69, 72
Lavington Park Stud, 160
Law, Alex, 34
Lawrence, John (Lord Oaksey), 104, 112, 114, 130
Leafy, 56
Leconfield, 35
Leconfield, Lord, 20–21
Leconfield Hunt, 35
Leconfield point-to-point, 31
Leese, 53
Leicester, 85, 99–100
Leicestershire, 31–2
Leigh, Sir John, 27–8, 29–30
Leonard, Chris, 176
Le Plein, 46, 47
Levanter, 161, 162–3
Leventis, 188
Leverhulme, Lord, 141, 149–50
Levy, Morry, 68
Levy, Stuart, 84, 93, 109, 112, 117–18, 119
Lewes, 115, 119
Lewis, Mrs E. J., 62, 72
Lewis, Geoff, 81
Lewis, Lieutenant-Colonel Tony, 48
Lexamine, 59
Lexicon, 158
Limekiln Stakes, 183
Lincolnshire Handicap, 118, 193, 196
Lindley, Jimmy, 119, 163
Lindsay, Lady, 34
Lingfield, 29, 30, 63, 64, 77, 81, 83, 94, 95, 166, 178–9, 183, 188, 190, 196
Links Stables, Newmarket, 180
Linwell, 85
Littlehampton, 41, 45
Liverpool, 67, 110
  see also Grand National
Liverpool Handicap Hurdle, 101
Lock, John, 72
Lockinge Stakes, 182
Logan, Jack, 150–51

London, 38
Longchamps, 174–5, 190–91
Lonsdale Hurdle, 123–4, 141
Lorenzaccio, 163
Lovat, Lord, 38, 40, 43, 46–7, 48
Lovely Cottage, 30
Lower Slaughter, Glos., 121
Lucky Dog, 68
Luneburg, 54, 55
Lynch, 'Kipper', 83
Lyons, 193
Lyphards Wish, 194

M-Lolshan, 182, 190, 191, 195
Maas, River, 52, 53
Maastricht, 52
McCarthy, George, 54
McClory, Kevin, 180
McCreery, Bob, 82, 91–2, 93, 121, 134, 199–200
McCreery, General Sir Richard, 92, 127, 128
Mackeson Gold Cup, 156
Mackeson Hurdle, 91, 123, 124, 128
McLean, James, 83, 91
Madrid, 'The Championship of the World', 91–2
Magic Court, 103
Magner, Eddie, 84
Major Rose, 96, 98, 157, 190
Malton, 155
Manchester, 80, 83–5
Mandarin, 86, 91
Mann-Thompson, Irene, 34
Manna, 24
Manning, J. L., 154–5
Manor Farm, Lavant, 59, 60–69, 72
March Brown IV, 30
Market Harborough, 31
Marriam, Dr G. F., 139–40
Marshall, Bryan, 33, 63, 64, 66, 130
Masson, Tom, 13, 115, 119
Mathews, Victor, 195
Mecca Dante Stakes, 194
Mellor, Stan, 88, 97–8, 100, 170
Meredith, Mr, 142
Merville, 47
Michel Grove, 34, 70
Middleton-on-Sea, 41

Midhurst, 57
Mildmay, Lord, 66
Mildmay Memorial, 94, 120
Mildmay of Flete Challenge Cup, 69
Mill Reef, 185
Millbank, Charles, 186
Mills-Roberts, Lieutenant-Colonel Derek, 40, 47–8
Mirror Boy, 196
Mr What, 95
Mitchell, Cyril, 62
Molony, Martin, 63, 64, 65
Molony, Tim, 75, 76, 81
Money Glass, 56
Montgomerie Stakes, 161
Montgomery, Field Marshal, 42, 50–51, 52, 55
Mooney, Vince, 63
Moonlight Bay, 98
Moraville, John de, 78
Moreton Paddox Stud, 92
Morgan, General, 42
Morrissey, Jimmy, 155
Morston, 190
Mort, David, 194
Le Moss, 191
Moss, Michael, 137, 143–8, 153
Mountgreenan, 109, 118
Moussac, Paul de, 189
Muir, Ian, 88
Muldoon, Ian, 88
Muldoon, John, 191
Mullins, Ken, 79
Murless, Noel, 30, 32, 33, 148, 162, 188
Murray, Mrs E. A. S., 27–8
Murray, Tony, 160, 161, 164–9, 172, 173, 175, 179–80, 184–6
Murray-Wilson, Peter, 122, 135
My Rajah, 196
Mylerstown Stud, 173

National Hunt Committee, Rosyth inquiry, 11–13, 104–13, 114–15, 117, 118
  Hill House affair, 125, 129, 131–48, 150–55
National Hunt Steeplechase, 57
National Stakes (Sandown Park), 158

Neal, Archie, 34
Neapolitan Lou, 102, 106
Neligan, Tim, 71–2, 199
Nell Gwynn Stakes, 162
Nelson, Campbell, 133
Nepcote Green, 116–17, 156–7
Netfor Lodge, 34
Neustadt, 55
New Jersey Racing Commission, 139
Newbury, 37, 73, 77, 87, 94, 101–15, 120–55, 161, 163, 172, 182, 188, 192
Newcastle, 165, 195
Newmarket, 98, 101, 161, 164, 177, 190, 192
Newport, 62
News of the World, 111–12
Newton Abbot, 77, 78, 81, 87, 122
Niarchos, Stavros, 198
Nicholls, Jack, 118
Nicholson, 'Frenchy', 165
Nicolaus Silver, 94, 95
Nid d'Abeilles, 79
Nijinsky, 163
No Alimony, 184
No Worry, 107–8
Nobby's Pet, 61–2
Noble, D., 184
Nonoalco, 179
Norfolk, Duchess of, 198
Norfolk Stakes, 194
Normandy campaign, 41–52, 53
North Staffordshire Regiment, 38–9
Northern Goldsmiths Handicap, 163
Northern Ireland, 38
Nottingham, 119
November Handicap Hurdle, 83–5, 106
Nuage Dore, 77, 99
Nunburnholme, Lord, 32–3
Nunthorpe Stakes, 174

Oaks, 164, 166–8
Oaks Trial, 166
Oberon, 142
Obratzovy, 190, 191, 194, 195
O'Brien, Elizabeth, 180
O'Brien, Vincent, 62, 63, 76, 81, 93, 168, 178, 180
Observer, 148

O'Dell, 34
Offaly Prince, 62, 65
Oliver Twist, 63
Olley, Charles, 170–75
Olley, Robin, 170–74
1000 Guineas, 162
Opening Bars, 96
Orange Bay, 186
Organon Ltd, 143
Orne, River, 43–5, 46, 48, 50
O'Sullevan, Peter, 130, 132–3, 150, 151, 170
Ostrer, Maurice, 77
Otari, 75–6, 80
Oteley Hurdle, 85, 87
Ouistreham, 43, 46
Overlord, Operation, 41

Padwick, Henry, 70
Paget, Dorothy, 63
Pajgar, Dr, 196
Pallissy, 82
Parker, 'Tubby', 62
Pavot, 100
Peacock, Dick, 73
Peacock, Dobson, 159
Persian Lancer, 96, 198–9
Persian War, 98, 157
Petre, Bobby, 30, 34
Petworth, 57, 60
Petworth Park, 20–21, 52
Piggott, Lester, 81, 157, 161, 162, 164, 177, 179–80, 184–6
Piggott-Brown, Sir William, 100
Pilgrim Stakes, 161, 172
Pirrie, Lord, 28, 29
Pitfold Farm, Hindhead, 16
Plumpton, 34, 58, 60, 66–7, 73, 88, 99
Polar Lodge, *see* Chief Barker
Porter, John, 70–71
Portslade, 40
Potts, Geoffrey, 159, 199
Pounds Farm, Kingsnorth, 114
Pratt, Charlie, 118
Predominate Stakes, 162, 184
Prendergast, Paddy, 131
Press Association, 84, 113, 125, 150
Price, Catherine (R.P.'s mother), 16–18, 20, 26

Price, Catherine Anne, 82
Price, Dorothy (R.P.'s wife), 59, 87, 182, 189, 198, 199
  marriage, 57–8
  at Lavant, 60, 61
  and Fred Winter, 66
  moves to Findon, 72
  buys Downs House, 82
  children, 85
  Rosyth inquiry, 12, 116, 117
  Hill House inquiry, 134, 155
  house at Nepcote Green, 156–7
  dislike of flat racing, 158
Price, George Penry (R.P.'s father), 15–19, 22–4, 25–7, 31
Price, George Percy, 16–17
Price, John Rhys Lymington, 16–17
Price, Mary Catherine Irene (Kitty), 15, 16–18, 22–3, 27
Price, Lynkie, 20, 57
Price, Penry Williams, 14, 16–17, 18
Price, Ryan, childhood, 15, 17–23
  point-to-point races, 23–4, 25–6, 27–31
  works for Arthur Thompson, 31–2
  trains steeplechasers for Lord Nunburnholme, 32–3
  turns professional, 35
  joins Army, 35, 36–9
  in the Commandos, 38–9, 40–55
  Montgomery's bodyguard, 50–51
  returns to training, 56–9
  marriage, 57–8
  at Lavant, 60–69, 72
  Priorit inquiry, 64–5
  buys Downs House, 70–72, 81–2
  interest in flat racing, 81, 83–5
  leading National Hunt trainer, 81, 85
  children, 81–2
  Rosyth inquiry, 11–14, 98–115

INDEX

suspension, 111–15, 116–17
licence restored, 117, 118–19
Hill House inquiry, 104–5, 121–55
turns to flat racing, 157–61, 162
and Ginevra, 163–8
and Sandford Lad, 170–75
and Giacometti, 178–80
buys aeroplane, 196–7
Price, Ryan George Victor (Joe), 82
Price, Sheila, 20, 21, 26, 27, 57
Primera, 189
Prince Charlemagne, 80
Prince of Wales Stakes, 187
Princess Elizabeth Stakes, 162
Prior-Palmer, Lucinda, 34
Prior-Palmer, Major, 34
Priorit, 63–4, 65–6, 99
Prix de l'Abbaye, 174–5
Prix de l'Arc de Triomphe, 168, 180, 185, 187
Prix de la Salamandre, 90
Prix Edmund Blanc, 192–3
Prix Royal Oak, 189
Prix Vermeille, 168
P T P Plant Hire, 194
Puttick, Jack, 60
Pycombe, 56
Pyman, Alan, 47
Pytchley Hunt, 31–2

Quare Times, 81
Quarryknowe, 158, 161
Queen Mary Stakes, 168
Queen's Hussar, 195

The Raceform Notebook, 184
The Racing Calendar, 111, 114–15, 150, 151
The Ranger, 71
Rapid River, 174
Rattler, 82
Reavey, Eddie, 62
Redcar, 196
Rees, Fred, 76
Regimental, 129
Remainder Man, 192
Reverando, 119
Rheingold, 177
Rhine, River, 53

Rhymney Breweries Chase, 120
Ribblesdale Stakes, 168
Richards, Sir Gordon, 77, 198
Richards, Peter, 163, 164, 168, 177–80
The Ridge, Fittleworth, 19–20
Rimell, Fred, 78
Rimell, Tom, 61
Ripley Handicap Hurdle, 102–6
Roberto, 177
Robinson, Peter, 84
Roger-Smith, Althea, 158, 159
Rogers, Mick, 163
Rogers, Tim, 174, 175
Roi de Mai, 191
Roman Flight, 59
Romeo Romani, 194
Rooney, Willie, 38
Rose Charter, 195
Rose of Lancaster Hurdle, 80
Rosenfeld, Ben, 84, 93, 117, 119
Rosyth, 11–14, 90, 98–115, 117–18, 119, 126
Rous Memorial Nursery, 183
Rouse, Brian, 192, 196
Rowlands, Bob, 191, 192
Royal Air Force, 50, 53, 54
Royal Artillery, 35, 36–7
Royal Lodge Stakes, 157
Royal Mount, 62
Royal Veterinary College, 137, 143, 146
Rufus III, 27–8
Ruisselet, 155

Sadler, George, 30
Sagaro, 187
St Alphage, 170, 171, 173
St Cloud, 192–3
St George, Charles, 183, 196
buys Ginevra, 163, 164, 167–8, 199
buys Sandford Lad, 174, 175
and Giacometti, 177–80, 199
and Bruni, 184–6, 199
St James Handicap Hurdle, 142
St James's Palace Stakes, 192

St Leger, 168, 180, 182, 185, 190, 191
St Mary's Hospital, 137, 143, 148
Salisbury, 32, 33, 184, 188, 194
Salmon Spray, 101–2, 103, 104, 106
Salute, 81
San San, 168
Sandford Lad, 168, 170–75, 193
Sandown Park, 64–5, 72, 79–80, 85, 92, 94, 100–106, 124, 127–31, 140–42, 158, 184–5, 190
Sandwich Stakes, 195
Sangster, Robert, 180
Sankey, John, 98–9, 101, 107, 108–10, 114
Santac, 58
Sant Elia, Contessa di, 79
Saulingo, 174
Saunders, Hilary St George, 47, 51
Scarab, 87
Scarborough, 33
Scarlet Cloak, 119, 129
Schweppes, 90, 97–8, 102–3
Schweppes Gold Trophy, 11, 97–8, 100–115, 117, 120, 121, 123, 124–55, 157
Scotland, 92
Scott, Brough, 92
Scott, Gerry, 155
Scottish Champion Hurdle, 138
Scottish Derby, 194
Scrimgeour, Bill, 67, 169
meets Dorothy Price, 57–8
at Lavant, 61
buys Priorit, 63–4
and the Rosyth inquiry, 12–13, 113, 118
and the Hill House affair, 125, 130, 132, 133–4
moves into Soldiers Field, 156
Sea Hawk, 184
Seaton Delaval, 195
Sebastian, 122
Second World War, 35, 36–55
Seine, River, 51
Selsey, 57–8

Selsey Bill, 99
Semley Stud, 163
Serge Lifar, 194
Serpentine, 62
Seven Barrows, Lambourn, 188
Shaftesbury, 163
Shangamuzo, 188
Shangarry, 196
Shantung, 163, 184
Sharp, A. E., 131
Sheppard, Don, 64, 142
Shetland Isles, 38
Shirley Heights, 190
Shoreham, 41
Shoreham Airport, 197
Shorncliffe, 37–8
Shottsford, 79
Shuwaiman, 181
Side Hill Stud, 191
Silly Abdul, 195
Silver Steel, 183
Simpson, Stephen, 109, 112
Sir d'Orient, 73–4, 99
Sir Ken, 75, 123
Sir Montagu, 188–9
Sister Rose, 168
Skrine, Lieutenant-Colonel Walter, 130–31
Sky Pink, 88
Skyliner, 192
Slapton Sands, 41
Slender, 60, 65, 69
Slip the Ferret, 192
Smirke, Charlie, 77, 130
Smith, Doug, 73, 81, 157, 160, 165, 199
Smith, Harvey, 155
Smith, Pat, 73
Smoke Piece, 66
Smyth, Vic, 61
Smyth, Willie, 91
Smythe, Andrew, 193
Snow Knight, 178, 179
Soldiers Field, Nepcote Green, 156–7, 158, 159–60, 181
Le Soleil, 194
Solomon, Philip, 191–2
South Downs, 33–4, 52, 56, 60, 70, 198
Southfleet, 66, 78
Southwell, 88
Southwick House, 42, 43
Spa Hurdle, 80, 85
Spaceman, 84
Spain, 91–2

Spartae, 124
Special Service Units (Commandos), 39, 40–55
Speed Bonny Boat, 193
Spithead, 43
Sporting Life, 128, 150–51, 154, 189
Sprague, Harry, 86
Spring Hurdle (Sandown Park), 128–9, 130, 131, 140–42
Stacey, Don, 192
Staghound, 87
Stanislavsky, 196
Star Appeal, 185
Star Ice, 139
Star Ship, 168, 177
Steel Heart, 191
Stephenson, Willy, 75, 76, 92
Stewart, Martyn, 169–70
Strassburger, 89
Stratford, 81, 88, 117
Stroller, 80
Strutt, Ronnie (Lord Belper), 33, 198–9
Suffolk, Lord, 163
Sullivan, Joe, 89–90, 181
Sunday Express, 121, 148, 149
Sunday Telegraph, 104
Sundew, 67, 82–3
Sunley, Bernard, 91, 119
Super Honey, 161, 162
Surrey Union point-to-point, 29
Sutcliffe, John, Senior, 87, 130, 133
Sutcliffe, John, Junior, 87
Sutton Bank, 33
Swan River, 27
Sy Oui, 68, 69, 74, 99
Sylvan's Boy, 119

Tap on Wood, 194
Tankerville Nursery, 163, 164, 165
Tasman, 61, 62, 67
Tattersalls, 163, 168
Taunton, 66, 91
Taylor, Brian, 182, 186–8, 191, 193, 194, 196
Taylor, Pinky, 84, 117, 119
Thistle Blue, 28, 29–30
Thompson, Arthur, 31–2
Thompson, John, 48
Thrale, Peter, 35, 36

Thrown In, 22
Thynne, Colonel, 70
Tiberetta, 83
Tipperary, 93
Todd, George, 73, 133, 157
Toller, Captain Charles, 102, 105, 106, 128, 141–2, 152
Tonbridge Selling Race (Wye), 58
Topham Trophy, 120
Tote Free Handicap, 192
Tovaritch, 88
Towcester, 34
Treasury Bond, 182–3
Trepan, 187
Trigg, Roy, 159
Triple A, 78
Tripp, Miss, 96
Triumph Hurdle, 74–5, 89, 90
Truly Thankful, 157, 168
Turnell, Bob, 130, 133
2000 Guineas, 178–9, 182, 192, 194
2000 Guineas Trial, 162

Unconditional Surrender, 63
United Racecourses, 72
United States of America, Battle of the Bulge, 52
Ur, 72
Utrillo II, 99–100

Van Cutsem, Bernard, 122, 123, 131, 133, 152
Van der Ploeg, G., 157, 169
Variety Club, 83, 84
Varingo, 194, 195
Varnavas, George, 67–8
Vermillon, 80–81, 99
Le Vermontois, 96, 120, 123, 126, 127
Vickerman, F. L., 63
Vickerman, Mrs F. L., 62
Vinall, Ted, 62
Vultrix, 100

WAAF, 57
Wahed, 182
Walcheren, 52
Wales, 92
Walker, Dennis, 84–5
Walpole, 120
Walworth, 100
Walwyn, Fulke, 61
Walwyn, Peter, 92, 188, 196

INDEX

Wantage, 88
Warsash, 43
Warwick, 184
Warwickshire Oaks, 167
Washington International, 192
Watson, Tommy, 131, 133
Weatherby's, 135, 138–9, 143
Weir, Lady, 88, 129, 134, 139, 156–7
Weir, Lord, 139, 160, 161
Welcome News, 99, 109, 117–18
Welsh Grand National, 62
Wernher, Derek (Lord Wernher), 37
Wesel, 53
Weser, River, 53
West Wittering, 60
Weth Nan, 182, 192–3
Wetherall, Bernard, 27
What a Myth, 88, 96, 120, 156
Whelan, 'Boggy', 84
Whitbread Gold Cup, 82, 85, 86
Whitcombe, Noel, 196
Whitstead, 190–91
Wigan, Major Derek, 13, 113, 114, 117, 120, 125, 126, 129, 154
Wigan, Mrs, 129
Wilhemina Henrietta, 102

Williams, Michael, 28, 30, 149–50
Williamson, Bill, 161
Willoughby de Broke, Lord, 134, 141, 143–4, 146–8, 149–50
Wilson, Gerry, 61
Wincanton, 62, 65, 90
Winders, George, 78
Windsor, 36–7, 56, 89, 100, 101, 108, 110, 120
Winter, Diana, 87
Winter, Fred, Senior, 66, 67, 79
Winter, Fred, Junior, 13, 85, 99–100, 199
 rides for Price, 66–7, 72
 rides Clair Soleil, 74–6, 79–80
 accident at Newton Abbot, 77, 78
 rides Nid d'Abeilles, 78–9
 champion jockey, 81, 200
 wins Grand National, 82–3
 fractures skull, 85–6
 falls off Dandy Scot in Grand National, 87–8
 rides Beaver II, 89–90
 wins Grand National on Kilmore, 92–6
 rides Catapult II, 103–4, 107

 and the Rosyth inquiry, 113
 becomes trainer, 118
 Anglo wins Grand National, 118, 119
 retirement, 160
Winters, Tommy, 159, 166, 180, 199
Wisborough Green, 19, 56
Withers, Mrs, 61
Withington, Fred, 64
Witley Park, 27, 28–30
Wolver Hollow, 191
Woodman, Syd, 61
Woodroffe, Harry, 84
Woods, Peter, 62
Woodside Terrace, 189
Workboy, 174
Worthing, 78, 116
Wragg, Harry, 120
Wrexham, 40
Wright, Whitaker, 28–9
Wye, 34, 60, 66, 68, 73, 81, 87, 96, 99
Wyndburgh, 83, 95

XYZ Handicap, 165

Yeatman, Jack, 26
York, 164, 172, 195, 196
Yorkshire, 32–3
Yorkshire Cup, 186
Yorkshire Oaks, 168

Zahia, 62